TOWARD AN ARCHITECTURE

Published by the Getty Research Institute

LE CORBUSIER
TOWARD AN ARCHITECTURE

INTRODUCTION BY JEAN-LOUIS COHEN
TRANSLATION BY JOHN GOODMAN

Texts & Documents

Translation of the 1928 printing of Le Corbusier, *Vers une architecture*, 2nd ed. (Paris: G. Crès, 1924)
Published by permission of the Société des Auteurs dans les Arts Graphiques et Plastiques (A.D.A.G.P.) and the Fondation Le Corbusier, Paris

© 2007 J. Paul Getty Trust
Published by the Getty Research Institute, Los Angeles
Getty Publications
1200 Getty Center Drive, Suite 500
Los Angeles, California 90049-1682
www.getty.edu

11 10 09 08 07   5 4 3 2 1

First published in the United Kingdom in 2008 by Frances Lincoln Ltd

Cover: Parthenon, Athens, fifth century B.C.; Delage Grand-Sport, 1921. See p. 181.
Frontispiece: Le Corbusier, Moscow, 1928 (detail). Photo: Fondation Le Corbusier, Paris
Title page: Civilian version of the Farman Goliath (detail). See p. 175.

Library of Congress Cataloging-in-Publication Data
Le Corbusier, 1887–1965.
   [Vers une architecture. English]
   Toward an architecture / Le Corbusier ; introduction by Jean-Louis Cohen ; translation by John Goodman.
      p. cm.
   Includes bibliographical references and index.
   ISBN 978-0-89236-822-8 (pbk.) — ISBN 978-0-89236-899-0 (hardcover)
   1. Architecture. 2. Functionalism (Architecture) I. Cohen, Jean-Louis. II. Goodman, John, 1952 Sept. 19– III. Title.
   NA2520.J413 2007
   720 — dc22
                    2006101591

Contents

Acknowledgments

The idea of publishing a new translation of *Vers une architecture* goes back to the late 1980s and the initial steps in the shaping of the Texts & Documents series. The perseverance of Julia Bloomfield—editor of the series with Kurt W. Forster, Harry F. Mallgrave, and Thomas F. Reese but also, long ago, the editor of two special issues of *Oppositions* that remain milestones of Corbusian studies—and my own determination finally led to this volume after many years of discussion and research.

The making of this edition has been made possible by the generosity of the Fondation Le Corbusier in Paris, the thorough, yet gracious, keeper of the architect's memory and above all of his inexhaustible archive. My gratitude goes to its director since 2004, Michel Richard; to its secretary-general, Claude Prelorenzo; to its librarian, Arnaud Dercelles; and to all the staff who assisted me in the research and production of the illustrations for this book.

The documentary research for the introduction was developed by Florence Allorent. In looking for materials on the reception of *Vers une architecture*, I benefited from the help of many friends and colleagues: Marida Talamona shared her knowledge of Le Corbusier's ventures in Italy, Ken Tadashi Oshima alerted me to the Japanese response to his work, Panayotis Tournikiotis told of the book's reverberations in Greece, and Benoit Jacquet provided me with his research on Tange Kenzô's debt toward it. Caroline Gautier located materials relative to its Dutch echoes, and Anthony Vidler led me to overlooked English responses, while Joseph Rykwert clarified for me the tricky issue of *modénature*.

The analysis of Frederick Etchells's role owes much to Dinah Adams, who gave me access to her master's thesis. My research on Jeanneret's early readings was furthered by Catherine Corthésy at the school of art in La Chaux-de-Fonds. I also thank Malka Schwartz for her insights on Brooklyn, Kai Gutschow for his information on Adolf Behne, Naïma Jornod for her help in collecting illustrations, and Paolo Scrivano and Tara Bissett, at the University of Toronto, for gathering precious materials on the grain silos.

The completion of this project would have been impossible without the input of all my esteemed Corbusianist colleagues, who criticized in a most constructive way my drafts and made many useful remarks. Warmest thanks to Tim Benton, Mary McLeod, Guillemette Morel Journel, Carlo Olmo, and Francesco Passanti, who called my attention to Geoffrey Simmins's thesis.

But most of the credit for this long-awaited reissue of Le Corbusier's first major book should go to the rigorous translator John Goodman, to the meticulous series editor Harry Mallgrave, to the imaginative yet attentive designer Chris Rowat, and to the excellent staff of the Getty Research Institute's Publications Program, headed by Julia Bloomfield, who deserves my highest appreciation for having carried through this project with which the remarkable Texts & Documents series might come to a premature end after having set new standards in historical scholarship in architecture.

— Jean-Louis Cohen

From the Translator

T he first English translation of *Vers une architecture* was published in 1927 as *Towards a New Architecture*. It did its work well, making Le Corbusier a crucial reference point in the battle for modernism in the anglophone world. Prepared by the British artist and architect Frederick Etchells (1886–1973), it aggressively naturalized Le Corbusier's French into English. *Vers une architecture* has since become a classic of the literature of architecture, however, which makes this naturalization a problem. Etchells captured the book's peremptory tone but homogenized its diction, obscuring its willfulness, its incantatory rhythms, and its readiness to sacrifice common usage, even clarity of sense, for euphony. The book is far more difficult—more rhetorically sophisticated and allusive—than is apparent from Etchells's work. He also excised a few passages and committed the occasional outright blunder, notably his consistent rendering of *volume* as "mass."

During the preparation of this new translation, Etchells proved an invaluable aid, and I have gratefully retained some of his solutions to vexing problems. But I have tried to produce a text that retains more of the imagery, abstraction, and cussed idiosyncrasy of the French than Etchells did, on the premise that the book is as much prose poem as polemic and that its vital analogies with modernist French literature—notably Mallarmé, greatly admired by Le Corbusier—should not be played down.

To give some idea of my thought processes, I offer three examples:

Les tracés régulateurs. The only alternative renderings I could come up with—"regulative schema," "regulating schema"—are stiffer than Etchells's "regulating lines," which in any event has now entered English studio usage. So I retained it.

Ordonnance. This word is primarily a term of jurisprudence meaning "ordinance," a statute carrying the force of law. Le Corbusier was alert to the overtones determined by this usage (still current in French), which he made to harmonize with other legal and military locutions that are integral to his rhetorical machinery. All this is lost in Etchells's rendering of it as "arrangement"—a word that has no prescriptive force and one that strikes precisely the wrong note insofar as it is often used to designate a mode of ethical laxity, a way of finessing rules without paying the penalty. Given the importance of moralizing, "return to order" language in postwar French discourse, it seemed important, even at the cost of some awkwardness, to retain at least an echo of the word's juridical associations. Noting the near homophony of *ordonnance* and "ordinance" (and the manifest relation of both to "order"), I opted to take the French term directly into English. For what it may be worth, I found a precedent in the important early dictionary of technical terms by John Harris, who wrote, "Ordonance, in Architecture, is the giving to all the Parts of an Edifice that just Quantity and Dimensions which they ought to have, according to the Model."[1]

Modénature. This term figures in one chapter only ("Architecture: Pure Creation of the Mind"), but it is key. It comes from the Italian *modenatura* or *modanatura* (molding), which derives from the Latin *modulus*, a diminutive of *modus* (measure, but also model, form, *disegno*). Although there are occasional earlier instances, it entered the mainstream of French architectural discourse in Antoine-Chrysostome Quatremère de Quincy's *Dictionnaire d'architecture* (vol. 2, part 2 of Charles-Joseph Panckoucke's *Encyclopédie méthodique,* fascicle 1820, full volume 1832), where it is defined as "the assembly and distribution of the components, profiles, and moldings of an order [*ordonnance*]." Quatremère recommended that it be taken into the *Dictionnaire de l'Académie française,* advice that was duly followed in its sixth edition (1832–35): "Architectural term. Proportion and curve of the moldings of a cornice. 'La *modénature* determines the character of the various architectural orders. Corinthian *modénature* is elegant.'" Le Corbusier probably picked up the word from Auguste Choisy's *Histoire de l'architecture* (1899), where it is said to be "essentially Greek" — in terms very like those used in *Vers une architecture* to assert its centrality to the Greek architectural achievement. Choisy defined it as "the abstract art of accentuating masses," a formulation much more consistent with the aesthetic and rhetoric of Le Corbusier than was the traditional, more classically oriented one of Quatremère.[2] But Le Corbusier imparted to the term an almost mystical quality that was new. For him, it referenced a governing "plastic system" that, in classical architecture, finds visual articulation in moldings. It was also related to the concept of ordonnance developed in *Vers une architecture,* as well as to his subsequently elaborated notion of the "modulor" (which has the same Latin roots).[3]

There is no analogous term in English. My first translation was "modeling," but this proved unsatisfactory. In the second of his "Three Reminders to Architects" ("Surface"), Le Corbusier uses *modeler* to designate the addition of smaller shapes to primary geometric forms to produce more complex ones, a practice taken to extremes by the Beaux-Arts architects of his day in ways he thought antithetical to architectural harmony ("contradictory intentions — boulevard Raspail"). This passage — along with the French verb's inapposite contemporary association with Auguste Rodin — militated against the use of "modeling." Nonetheless, it seemed important to find a solution that would similarly reflect the Latin root of *modénature,* and thus activate a lexical network that is operative throughout the text (*module / moduler / modulaire /*

modulation). Etchells's rendering is "contour and profile," which is apt but obscures this etymology. It also undoes the singular economy of the French word and mitigates the mystery with which Le Corbusier infused it. In the end, I opted for "contour modulation," which has several advantages: it is relatively concise, it is a bit mysterious, and, in its musical reference, it evokes Le Corbusier's "harmonic-sounding-board" and the symphonic formal integration that was so important to him.

Given its many odd locutions and unexpected word choices, the translation published here may disconcert readers familiar with the Etchells version. I can only beg their indulgence and suggest that, if possible, they consult the French before condemning my work. They may be surprised by the strangeness of what they find there.

In closing, I offer my sincere thanks to Jean-Louis Cohen, Harry Francis Mallgrave, Mary McLeod, and Robin Middleton for their help in refining the translation. Ultimately, however, all missteps and errors of judgment are mine.

— John Goodman

Notes

1. *Lexicon Technicum; or, An Universal English Dictionary of Arts and Sciences,* vol. 1 (London: Printed for Dan. Brown et al., 1704; facsimile, New York, Johnson Reprint, 1966), s.v. "ordonnance."

2. As noted by Jean-Louis Cohen in his introduction to the present volume (p. 22).

3. We are grateful to Cesare Birignani, who generously made his unpublished research on the history of the French term available to us during the preparation of this volume.

Introduction

Jean-Louis Cohen

Few books have had an effect comparable to that of *Vers une architecture*. In this volume — both a transcription of his youthful experiences and his first program — Le Corbusier presented himself simultaneously as historian, critic, discoverer, and prophet. The book's peremptory tone and visual provocations have elicited strong reactions and contradictory interpretations. Reyner Banham, one of its perspicacious readers, saw in it "one of the most influential, widely read, and least understood of all the architectural writings of the twentieth century."[1] Its effect is implied by Vincent Scully in 1966 in his preface to Robert Venturi's *Complexity and Contradiction in Architecture*, where he wrote that the latter book was "probably the most important writing on the making of architecture since Le Corbusier's *Vers une architecture* of 1923."[2] At the very least, this statement points to the canonical status the book was accorded for several decades and the success it met with in schools and offices worldwide.

The L'Esprit nouveau *Test Bed*

Vers une architecture is composed of articles that had appeared previously in the periodical *L'Esprit nouveau*, along with some new elements. It is the character of this review that makes *Vers une architecture* provocative from its very first page. Created in 1920 by the architect Charles-Édouard Jeanneret (who on this occasion adopted the pen name Le Corbusier), the painter Amédée Ozenfant, and the publicist and poet Paul Dermée, *L'Esprit nouveau* takes its title from that of a lecture given by the poet Guillaume Apollinaire, one of the figures with whom its founders identified.[3]

Dermée had passed from lyricism to Dadaism and also had the commercial know-how required to create and distribute a publication. The closeness of Jeanneret and Ozenfant is apparent in how they signed their articles in the periodical, using fictive identities suggested by Ozenfant.[4] Only essays on architecture and the initial edition of 1923 of the present book bore the signature "Le Corbusier-Saugnier," which indicates that the text was largely written by Jeanneret but may contain additions by Ozenfant, whose mother's name was Saugnier.

These last contributions have the most refined visual structure of all those published in the twenty-eight issues of the periodical, issued between 1920 and 1925.[5] The fashionable gathering of essays covered a vast field — from literature to psychoanalysis, from painting to cinematography — and took a

Fig. 1. Publicity flyer for *Vers une architecture* proclaiming:
"This book is implacable. It is unlike any other," 1923
Paris, Fondation Le Corbusier

marked interest in international matters, most notably the recent artistic developments in Russia. All of the articles employed a deliberate strategy of seduction-by-image. Jeanneret had doubtless seen the almanac *Der Blaue Reiter,* published in 1912 in Munich by the painters Franz Marc and Wassily Kandinsky. Its intriguing juxtapositions of modern paintings and "primitive" works called into question the clichés of official art history. He had also read the *Kulturarbeiten* (Culture works) of architect Paul Schultze-Naumburg, which use contrasting images in a critical way.[6] The layout of these publications anticipated the visual approach taken in *L'Esprit nouveau.* The contemporary French reviews that Jeanneret knew—for example, the critic George Besson's *Cahiers d'aujourd'hui,* which published "Ornament und Verbrechen" (Ornament and crime) by Adolf Loos in 1913—lacked this radical character, as did *L'Élan,* which Ozenfant published during the war.

It was in the midst of World War I that the very form of the review was turned upside down by a new generation of titles. *De Stijl,* published by Theo van Doesburg from October 1917, limited itself to art and architecture, but *391,* founded by Francis Picabia in Barcelona a few months earlier, interspersed photographs of industrial objects—ship propellers and electric lightbulbs—among its columns and calligrams. *L'Esprit nouveau* paid homage to Picabia, probably on the initiative of Dermée, but, since the magazine aimed to seduce a "serious" audience, it instituted a more conservative graphic design.[7]

In the pages that follow, I will first perform an autopsy of the "machine for persuading" that is the book-extension of the review, then analyze its rhetorical and visual structure and discuss its first English and German translations, and conclude with a study of its reception (fig. 1).[8]

From Jeanneret to Le Corbusier

The first article in *L'Esprit nouveau* devoted to architecture, "Trois rappels à MM. les architectes; premier rappel: le volume" (Three reminders to architects; first reminder: volume), is found in the initial issue, dated October 1920; "Architecture III; pure création de l'esprit" would be published in the sixteenth issue in May 1922. Between these two dates, twelve essays appear in succession, all of which would be reprinted, in 1923, in slightly altered form, in the first edition of *Vers une architecture.* The segmentation introduced in the first article—a "reminder" announcing sequels but also alluding to Jean Cocteau's *rappel à l'ordre* (return to order) and thereby suggesting sympathy for conservative positions—revealed Le Corbusier's intent from the outset: to finally publish a real book.[9] At the time, all he had to his credit were the articles on his trip to the Balkans, Turkey, and Greece published in *La feuille d'avis de La Chaux-de-Fonds* and the thin volume *Étude sur le mouvement d'art décoratif en Allemagne,* published in 1912 after an investigation, extending from Berlin to Munich, and from Dresden to the Ruhr region, into the genesis and achievements of the Second Reich in the field of architecture and the applied arts.[10]

He had already abandoned a projected book on "the construction of cities," however, which would have brought together his observations on

European urbanism, notes on the history of cities taken at the Bibliothèque nationale de Paris, and his proposals for La Chaux-de-Fonds, where he was born.[11] Entitled *France ou Allemagne?* and undertaken in 1915, it would be set aside after the Armistice of 1918.[12]

Since Le Corbusier's early education has already been examined in minute detail, only those episodes pertinent to the genesis of *Vers une architecture* will be mentioned here.[13] The first reminder was published at a critical moment in a career begun in 1906 with the construction of the Fallet House on the outskirts of his native city. Over a period of fourteen years, Jeanneret had traversed Europe from France to Turkey, from Germany to Italy. He had worked with Auguste Perret in Paris and Peter Behrens in Berlin, two figures committed to imagining the architecture of the industrial age. He had tried to reinvigorate the art school in La Chaux-de-Fonds, where he received his early training. He had reflected on contemporary architecture, as his correspondence with Perret testifies.[14] Finally, his dreams carried him toward the conquest of both Paris and America.

Recording his impressions in notes and sketches in his travel journals, photographing the urban landscapes, and tirelessly providing accounts of his feelings in his correspondence, Jeanneret constructed a personal interpretation of the contemporary world, its culture, and its cities. In his search for a self, he devoured the *Vie de Jésus* by Joseph-Ernest Renan, *Les grands initiés* (*The Great Initiates*) by Édouard Schuré, and especially *Also sprach Zarathustra* (*Thus Spake Zarathustra*) by Friedrich Nietzsche.[15] At the end of these "zig-zag travels," as Stanislaus von Moos has dubbed them, alluding to the comic strip drawn by the Genevan Rodolphe Toepffer, Jeanneret was ready to make public the ideas that he had been pondering ever since his Grand Tour.[16]

His professional status was quite incongruous when the first issue of *L'Esprit nouveau* appeared. With the exhibition of his drawings and works by Ozenfant at Galerie Thomas in 1918 and the concomitant publication of the manifesto *Après le cubisme,* he was beginning to be known on the artistic scene. But the painful financial failure of the Société des applications du béton armé (SABA) (Company for the implementation of reinforced concrete) created in 1917 in Alfortville, in the suburbs of Paris, burdened him with debts he struggled to meet, despite the support of his family, which he had left penniless.[17] His articles were part of a campaign to win recognition as an intellectual and architectural reformer.

Literary and Graphic Strategies

In *Vers une architecture,* the twelve articles published in *L'Esprit nouveau* are gathered into three blocks, to which three isolated articles were added. In the order of their publication, they are "Trois rappels à MM. les architectes" ("Three Reminders to Architects"), "Des yeux qui ne voient pas" ("Eyes That Do Not See"), and "Architecture." The isolated articles are "Les tracés régulateurs" ("Regulating Lines"), "Esthétique de l'ingénieur, Architecture" ("Aesthetic of the Engineer, Architecture"), and "Maisons en série" ("Mass-Production

Housing"). An unpublished text, "Architecture ou révolution" ("Architecture or Revolution"), was added.[18] The book is introduced by a summary of the "argument," thereby framing the reader's understanding of the rest of the work. Over five pages, Le Corbusier presents résumés of the chapters that are reiterated at the head of each. He made a point of justifying his inversion of the sequence of blocks as published in the review, asserting that the "three reminders"—now placed at the start of the book, after an opening entitled "Aesthetic of the Engineer"—were written for architects, while "Eyes That Do Not See," having been written for clients, now preceded the section "Architecture." The opposition of an "academic" block ("Three Reminders to Architects," "Regulating Lines," "The Lesson of Rome," "The Illusion of the Plan," and "Pure Creation of the Mind") and a "mechanical" block ("Aesthetic of the Engineer," "Eyes That Do Not See," and "Architecture or Revolution") reflects the dual focus on aesthetic and machinist concerns, constituting the base of Jeanneret's and Ozenfant's post-cubist doctrine defined by them as Purism, correctly underscored by Banham.[19] The contrast between chapters dealing with the spirit of the time ("a spirit of construction") and the ones that explore timeless architectural issues is obvious from these very first pages of the book.

In accordance with a scheme that would continue to be refined into the 1950s, quadripartite layouts combining title headings, text, images, and captions—arranged so as to surprise and shock the reader—construct the book's argument step by step. This allowed for the formulation of striking aphorisms and slogans and the elaboration of sequences that advance the argument or play on opposition and comparison.

Although he can cut the figure of a traveler or a reporter, Le Corbusier is often quite simply an archivist bringing together images and documents, including those pertaining to his own activities. His book is also an extension of the reflections he sketched out in the intense correspondence of his youth. The places visited during his "useful journey"—sites related to industry, culture, and folklore—provided a great deal of visual evidence for points made in the text.[20] Like *Urbanisme* and *L'art décoratif d'aujourd'hui,* published two years later, *Vers une architecture* exploited the collection of photographs and newspaper clippings that Le Corbusier would augment as long as he lived and that continued to serve him well into the 1960s. These materials documented engineering projects such as Gustave Eiffel's Garabit viaduct and ancient sites such as the Parthenon—with short circuits creating electric sparks between objects in the two series.

The Engineer Exalted

The mode of argument changes as the book unfolds, moving from technological models to unchanging concerns of architectural theory. The opening section, "Aesthetic of the Engineer," is also the title of a rubric in *L'Esprit nouveau.* Le Corbusier radicalized the opposition between architects and engineers that appeared in the nineteenth century and that Sigfried Giedion would later make a touchstone of his historical account.[21] In 1930, Le Corbusier would note in *Précisions:* "I carried the engineer shoulder high. *Vers une architecture*...was largely dedicated to him. I was looking ahead a bit. I would soon have a premonition of 'the constructor,' the new man for a new age."[22]

Apart from writings by Eugène-Emmanuel Viollet-le-Duc, it was probably in several German analyses, notably those published in 1902 by Hermann Muthesius in *Stilarchitektur und Baukunst* (*Style-Architecture and Building-Art*) and in 1910 by Joseph August Lux in *Ingenieurästhetik* (Engineer aesthetic),[23] and in some French texts such as the ones of Robert de la Sizeranne that Le Corbusier found direct precedents for his panegyric.[24] Praising the "healthy project" of the engineer, in 1913 he wrote his mentor, the Swiss essayist William Ritter, that, while "architects are puppets," he had "unreserved admiration for engineers, who throw their phenomenal bridges, who work for what is useful, strong, and healthy."[25] Already in 1914, he had published in Switzerland the article "Renouveau dans l'architecture" (Renewal in architecture), where he announced the postwar reminders and declared: "Our Romans, our Gothics, our Louis XIV, those are now the engineers."[26]

The first illustration in the book, the Garabit viaduct, engineered by Eiffel, is linked to Perret (fig. 2). As early as 1914, Jeanneret remembered that he had "showed him in 1909 or 1910, in [his] album of photographs, a famous and immense iron bridge that must be in the Cévennes," making a sketch of it from memory.[27] After reading Loos, he asserted:

> When the architect has put into the house the honest expression of the constructor of ocean liners, it seems that all the make-up and filth that soils us will fall away like scales....
>
> So I would dream of being a builder of bridges or a driller of tunnels, or someone who fights against an immense river to block it and form a lake, or someone who throws railroad tracks across our Alps or through the steppes. Then I would be on the way toward liberation.[28]

He wrote his friend and engineer-partner Max Du Bois at the time that he was preparing an article for *L'Oeuvre* entitled "Le renouveau en architecture" (The renewal in architecture): "Engineers will have the better part in it and architects, that of the cretins...which they often are."[29] After the failure of his entrepreneurial adventure at SABA, Le Corbusier would again celebrate the model of concrete engineering with which he had identified in his youthful dreams and that was fundamental to the modernization of postwar France.

Factories as Cathedrals
"Aesthetic of the Engineer" exposes the decrepitude and sterility of architects. Le Corbusier confronts them with three consecutive reminders grounded in the psychological reality that "blind" eyes are nonetheless "made for seeing." To evoke the first two reminders, "volume" and "surface," he presents images of industrial buildings, often American ones. As early as 1917, Le Corbusier said he was studying abattoirs made of reinforced concrete.[30] The article published

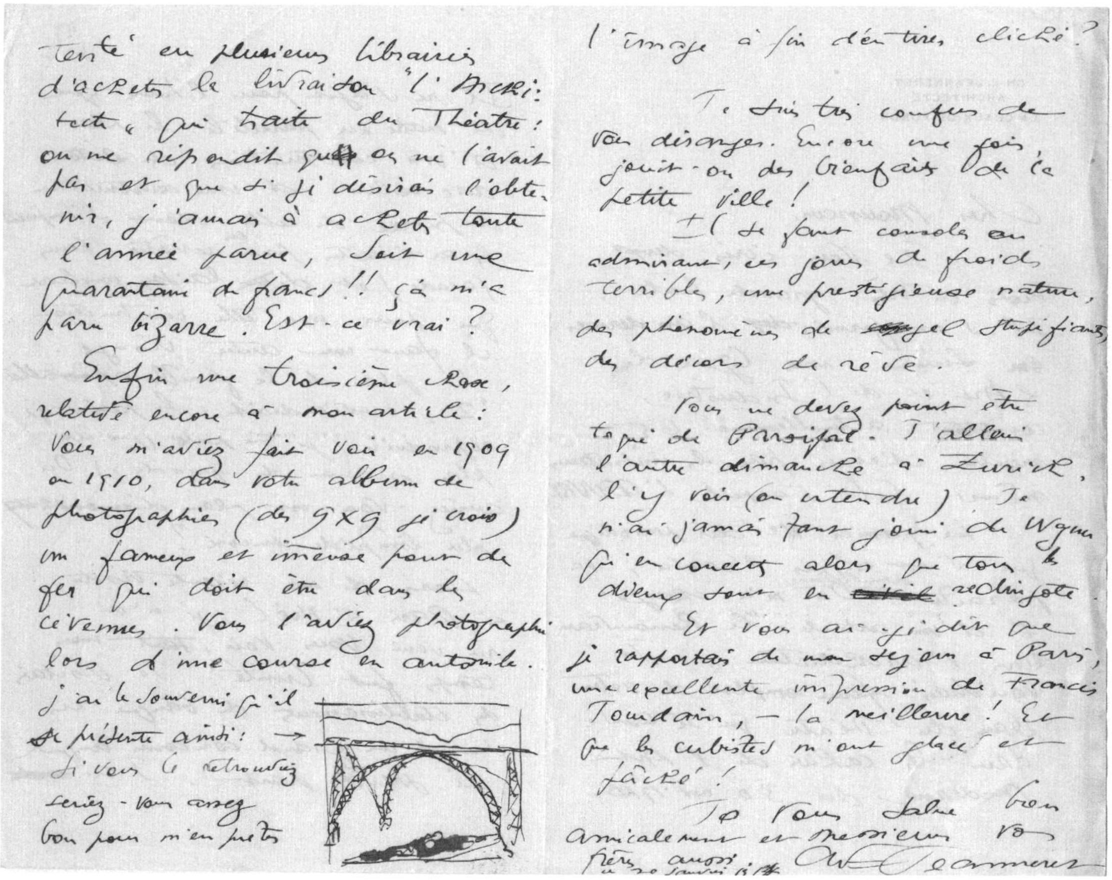
tenté en plusieurs librairies d'acheter la livraison "l'Architecte" qui traite du Théâtre: on me répondit qu'on ne l'avait pas et que si je désirais l'obtenir, j'aurais à acheter toute l'année parue, soit une quarantaine de francs!! ça m'a paru bizarre. Est-ce vrai?

Enfin une troisième chose, relative encore à mon article: Vous m'aviez fait voir en 1909 ou 1910, dans votre album de photographies (des 9x9 je crois) un fameux et immense pont de fer qui doit être dans les Cévennes. Vous l'aviez photographié lors d'une course en automobile. j'ai le souvenir qu'il se présente ainsi: → si vous le retrouviez seriez-vous assez bon pour m'en prêter l'image à fin d'en tirer cliché?

Je suis très confus de vous déranger. Encore une fois, jouit-on des bienfaits de la petite ville!

Il se faut consoler en admirant, ces jours de froids terribles, une prestigieuse nature, des phénomènes de gel stupéfiants, des décors de rêve.

Vous ne devez point être toqué de Parsifal. J'allai l'autre dimanche à Zurich, l'y voir (ou entendre). Je n'ai jamais tant joui de Wagner qu'en concerts alors que tout devenait ridicule.

Et vous ai-je dit que je rapportais de mon séjour à Paris, une excellente impression de Francis Jourdain, — la meilleure! Et que les cubistes m'ont glacé et fâché!

Je vous salue bien amicalement et messieurs vos frères aussi

Ch E Jeanneret

Fig. 2. Charles-Édouard Jeanneret
Letter to Auguste Perret, 20 January 1914, with sketch of the Garabit viaduct later reproduced as the first illustration in *Vers une architecture*
Paris, Archives nationales, Institut français d'architecture, Fonds Auguste Perret

in 1913 by Walter Gropius about American factories had not escaped his notice.[31] He had acquired the *Jahrbücher* of the Deutscher Werkbund in 1915 for Perret, judging the one containing Gropius's article "very significant."[32]

His interest in industrial America was not unusual for his generation, even if its knowledge of such remained secondhand.[33] Jeanneret's desire for America was intense. In a letter of 1910 to the Perret brothers, he said that he had not lost sight of the "perspective toward a sojourn in Chicago that Monsieur Auguste opened up" for him.[34] Four years later he wrote of his wish to see "the immense concrete works of Panama, the crazy houses of the new world, the depths of this wholly modern life" that so "fascinate" him.[35]

The buildings by means of which "American engineers crush with their calculations an architecture in its death throes," as he puts it in *Vers une architecture,* actually are located in quite a variety of places—the United States, the location of Cass Gilbert's Army Supply Base and William Higginson's Gair Building in Brooklyn, reproduced on page 111, but also Canada and Argentina—something that the absence of captions obscures. In one of the most notorious falsifications in the history of modern architecture, Le Corbusier retouched the photograph of the silos in Montreal, hiding the dome of the Bonsecours market. The grain silos in Buenos Aires, previously published by Gropius, were retouched so as to eliminate their culminating triangular pediments, making their crowning elements perfectly horizontal.[36] The graphic manipulation would be claimed by Ozenfant:

> There were indeed, here and there, atop of these powerful batteries of monumental cylinders resembling donjons, some pediments in the Greek manner. The engineer, or some architect hanging around the calculating tables, wanted to "embellish" the pure work of the technician, as if one could embellish an egg! . . . I removed these excrescences with gouache and everything became pure, or rather was restored to purity.[37]

Ozenfant said he obtained these images from Henri-Pierre Roché, the author of *Jules et Jim* and *Deux Anglaises et le continent.* Curious about the scene on the other side of the Atlantic, Roché had spent three years in New York in the company of Marcel Duchamp.[38] A handwritten note by Le Corbusier confirms the role of Roché in conveying the images.[39]

The second reminder is also supported by images of American industrial buildings, with one exception: the Fagus factory in Alfeld-an-der-Leine by Gropius and Adolf Meyer, which would be replaced in the 1928 edition by an image of a Ford factory, a substitution that Le Corbusier already had in mind in 1924.[40] The Renaissance appears by way of overture, in the guise of the courtyard of San Damaso in the Vatican, succinctly captioned "Bramante and Raphael," and also as conclusion, in an image mocking the overdecorated concrete dome of the Spreckels Building by James and Merritt Reid in San Francisco, an unidentified sign of architectural depravation. The point is driven home by a handwritten note on the typed manuscript: "Let us fear American architects. Proof:. . ." (fig. 3).[41] Le Corbusier was probably unaware

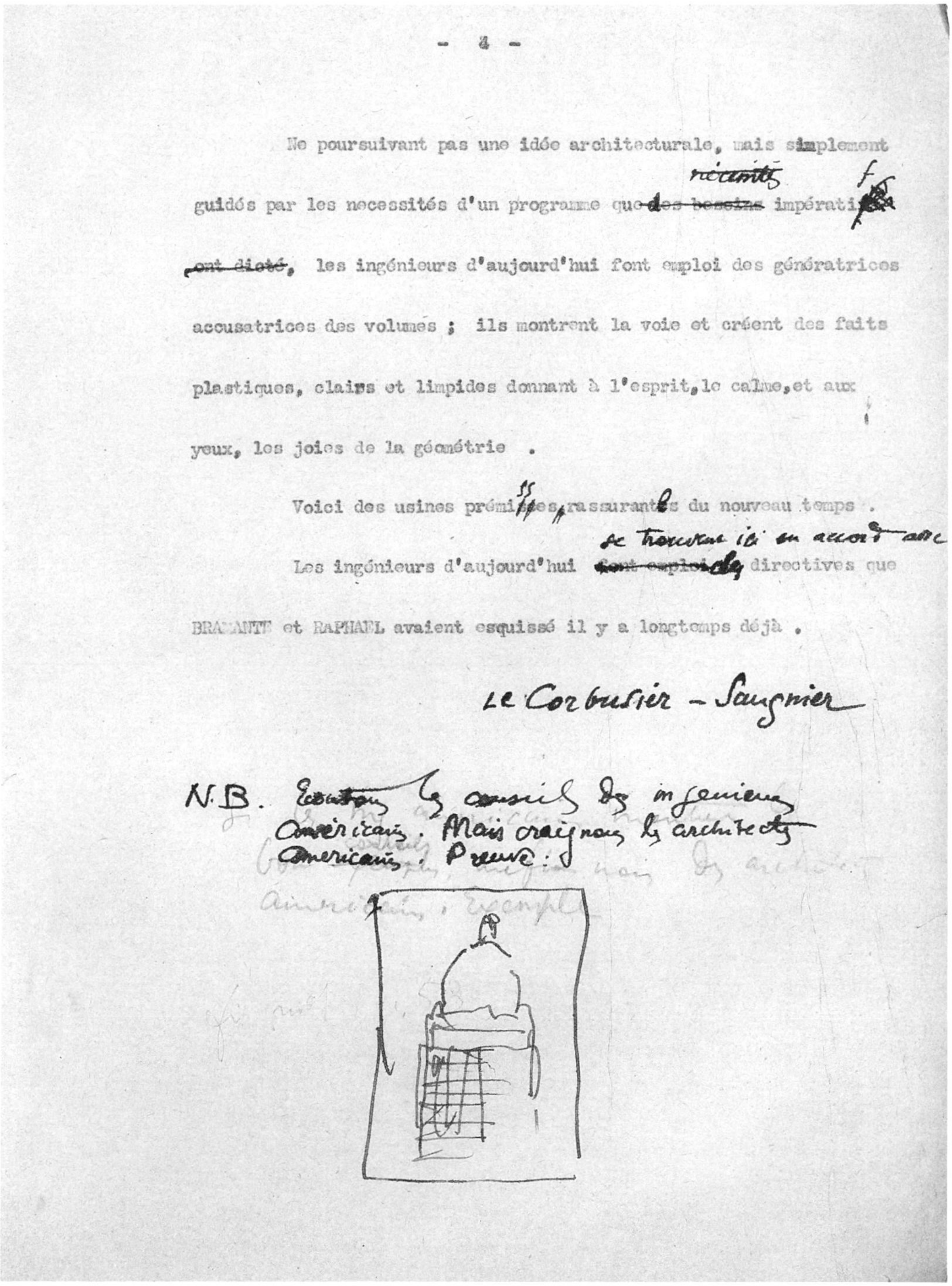

- 4 -

Ne poursuivant pas une idée architecturale, mais simplement guidés par les necessités d'un programme que ~~des besoins~~ récentes impératifs ~~ont dicté~~, les ingénieurs d'aujourd'hui font emploi des génératrices accusatrices des volumes ; ils montrent la voie et créent des faits plastiques, clairs et limpides donnant à l'esprit, le calme, et aux yeux, les joies de la géométrie .

Voici des usines prémisses, rassurantes du nouveau temps .

Les ingénieurs d'aujourd'hui ~~sont explicit~~ se trouvent ici en accord avec les directives que BRAMANTE et RAPHAEL avaient esquissé il y a longtemps déjà .

Le Corbusier - Saugnier

N.B. Écoutons les conseils des ingénieurs américains. Mais craignons les architectes américains. Preuve :

Fig. 3. Le Corbusier
"Esthétique de l'ingénieur" (Aesthetic of the engineer), typescript of article published in *L'Esprit nouveau*, with handwritten addition by Le Corbusier: "Let us heed the advice of American engineers. But let us fear American architects. Proof: . . ."; and sketch of the Spreckels Building, [1921]
Paris, Fondation Le Corbusier

that the Brooklyn base was designed by Gilbert, the architect of the Wool-
worth Building, in short, one of these "American architects" he was trashing.

The Plan, or Rationalist Order

The argument of the reminder devoted to the plan is of a different order. It
plays on the term's two meanings: on the one hand, in the field of representation, it signifies the horizontal projection of a building or an urban ensemble;
on the other hand, in the field of organization, it implies a concerted strategy
of modernization. At the start of a decade that would see the launching of a
plan to industrialize Russia, Le Corbusier sensed the potential of a notion that
had gained currency during the war and that would inspire the title of the
periodical *Plans,* which he founded in 1931.

Le Corbusier considered the plan as a "generator." Such an attitude was
not unprecedented—it was found in the instruction at the École des Beaux-
Arts, as codified by Julien-Azaïs Guadet and, earlier, in the teaching of
Jacques-François Blondel in the eighteenth century.[42] Le Corbusier relied on
engineer Auguste Choisy, architect Tony Garnier, and Perret in presenting his
argument. The axonometric projections taken from the history of architecture
published in 1899 by Choisy—one of the main sources of *Vers une architecture*—represent the illustrated buildings simultaneously in plan, section, and
elevation, thereby making it possible to connect the "generator" with the volumes.[43] But the graphic analysis of the layout and processional route of the
Acropolis in Athens, borrowed from Choisy, underscores the "skills of a great
stage director," despite the "apparent disorder."[44]

The illustrations taken from Garnier's book of 1917, *Une cité industrielle,*
are likened to grand compositions such as the Saint Louis des Invalides and
Versailles. Le Corbusier had been corresponding with Garnier since 1914 and
met with him in 1915 to discuss his abattoir designs and solicit his aid as an
intermediary with the mayor of Lyon, Édouard Herriot. He recalled his ambiva-
lence toward the "excessively Greek tendency" of the houses in *Cité* but maintained that Garnier was "the first to have *realized* an entente between art and
our magnificent era."[45]

Le Corbusier's reminder about the plan positioned his own ideas as a critique of Perret's concept of "tower-cities," which he dismissed as "dangerous
futurism." He also constructed his argument around the principle of the
"pilotis-city," borrowing Perret's theory of an artificial ground level, initially
a proposal of Eugène Hénard, who also invented the indents (*redents*) mentioned later in the book as early as 1903.[46] As Le Corbusier acknowledged in
a note added to the text published in January 1921 in *L'Esprit nouveau,* the
idea of the "tower-city" had just been presented to a general readership in an
article in *L'Intransigeant.*[47] If the plan is a "generator," as the beginning of the
chapter claims, then that of a single edifice—the tower—would generate the
entire city.

Regulating the Facade

The principle of order enabled by the plan is in a sense reshuffled onto the vertical plane in Le Corbusier's discussion of "regulating lines." He was quite familiar, in all likelihood, by way of Theodor Fischer in Munich, with *Die Proportionen in der Architektur* and *Die architektonische Komposition* by August von Thiersch.[48] In 1932, he would thank Fischer for welcoming him in 1910, when he was in Germany looking for "healthy and constructive architectural elements."[49] This suggests that, at the time, he was pondering the question of proportions in recent work by Munich architects and their predecessors and of proportion grids used by Behrens for the Oldenburg Pavilion of 1905. These grids were published in a monograph by Fritz Hoeber that Jeanneret bought for Perret in 1915.[50] On this point, Ozenfant's contribution on grids in painting seems to have been significant.

Le Corbusier sets forth the "sensory mathematics" of the regulating line with more illustrations taken from Choisy (e.g., the facade of the Arsenal of Philon at Peiraeus), although these are not credited, as well as some from Marcel Dieulafoy, whose analysis relying on circles and right angles had been used by Jeanneret for an interpretation of Notre-Dame de Paris sketched on a postcard in 1921 (fig. 4).[51] To interpret Blondel's Porte Saint-Denis, the Capitol in Rome, and the Petit Trianon, Le Corbusier made use of diagonal lines. Their appearance dates back to an article he cosigned with Ozenfant in the first issue of *L'Esprit nouveau*, "Sur la plastique" (On plastic qualities), where the linear analysis of the Capitol was juxtaposed with another one by the authors applied to a landscape by Paul Cézanne.[52]

Le Corbusier made an important change in this chapter when he revised the 1923 edition. He removed two of the four illustrations of Villa Schwob (his last building in La Chaux-de-Fonds), including the one with a linear analysis of the elevation, and introduced photographs, with triangular patterns, of the Ozenfant atelier and the La Roche–Jeanneret House, which had just been completed. In the meantime, Hendrik Petrus Berlage had objected to the absence of any mention of his writings in the first edition, as well as to Le Corbusier's claim that he had "not yet had the pleasure of encountering contemporary architects who had concerned themselves with this question":

> I hasten to inform you that, since as early as 1890, this question was studied in Holland (initiator: the architect de Groot) and with such success that many architects then began to design their plans and facades in accordance with regulatory lines.
>
> And, as an example, I inform you that the new bourse in Amsterdam, 1897–1904, was built in accordance with a 3-4-5 triangle.[53]

Le Corbusier responded politely, confirming that he had "known the bourse in Amsterdam for quite some time" and had "always admired" it.[54] In all probability, Berlage's reflections in his *Grundlagen und Entwicklung der Architektur* ("The Foundations and Development of Architecture") had not

Fig. 4. Notre-Dame and the Seine, postcard with regulating lines drawn by Le Corbusier, 1921
Paris, Fondation Le Corbusier

escaped his attention. His assertion that "the regulatory line is a guarantee against arbitrariness" can also be related to a remark by Gottfried Semper relayed by Berlage: "Nothing is arbitrary."[55] This did not, however, prevent Le Corbusier from maintaining in 1926 that he had "taken a stand" against Berlage's regulating lines, which he reduced to "diagonal lines," a "framework": "By this account," he claimed, "all cross-stitch embroidery would be made with regulating lines."[56] Nevertheless, Le Corbusier's interest in proportions never flagged, and from 1928 regulatory lines would be one of his apples of discord with radical figures in European architecture such as El Lissitzky and Karel Teige. These reflections would eventually lead, after World War II, to his elaboration of his "Modulor" proportional system.

In his defense of regulating lines, Le Corbusier condemned Paris's turn-of-the-century boulevard Raspail—the creation of "modern man," who "uses nothing at all"—in terms of geometric construction, and he also disparages it in his reminder about surface.[57] The reminder about volume moreover included a list of contemporary buildings from which Le Corbusier explicitly excluded the Gare d'Orsay and the Grand Palais on the grounds that they "are not architecture."[58] He no longer deigned to mention the buildings by Anatole de Baudot, Georges Chédanne, Charles Plumet, and Henri Sauvage that he had listed in 1915.[59] Paris was becoming an architectural wasteland; the liners of the Compagnie générale transatlantique evinced a "more technical beauty" than that of the Gare d'Orsay.

Rekindling "Deadened Eyes"

Le Corbusier's ferocity toward the work of French architects and decorators is unleashed in the book's central triad, where the modern world is revealed to "eyes that do not see." This phrase derives from a prose poem by Stéphane Mallarmé, "Le phénomène futur," the first sentence of which Jeanneret quoted in a letter of 1915 to Perret.[60] In this text, reprinted in a volume Jeanneret had bought in 1914, Mallarmé relates the discovery of a "woman from another time" in the house of an "exhibitor of things past" and ends thusly:

> When everyone will have contemplated the noble creature, a vestige of some already cursed era, some of them indifferent, since they will not have had the strength to understand, whereas others, devastated, their eyelids wet with resigned tears, will gaze at one another; while the poets of that time, feeling their deadened eyes rekindle, will wend their way toward their lamps, brains briefly drunk with a confused glory, haunted by Rhythm and oblivious of existing in an era that had outlived beauty.[61]

Another source might be found in the Paris press of the times—Jeanneret may have read Georges Rozet's article "Les yeux qui ne voient plus" (Eyes that no longer see), published in 1919.[62] But the question of vision, discussed in the field of experimental psychology since the end of the nineteenth century, is implicit in a number of earlier texts about industrial culture, and *L'Esprit nouveau* did not fail to discuss the point of view of experimental psychology. In 1924, Ozenfant and Jeanneret would publish a text on "the formation of the modern optic."[63]

Le Corbusier's assertions cannot be considered apart from their German precedents, even if his adventures beyond the Rhine go unmentioned in *Vers une architecture*. In his *Ingenieurästhetik*, Lux introduced the slogan of a "new eye" observing industrial buildings and machines.[64] The German Werkbund evidenced this outlook in its publications, notably in the almanac of 1914 devoted to modes of transport. Jeanneret surely had seen its images of ships, locomotives, automobiles, and airplanes, since he had purchased a copy for Perret.[65] The French sources are more theoretical. Paul Souriau had published not only *La beauté rationnelle* (1914)—a book known to Jeanneret (it was in the library of the La Chaux-de-Fonds school) that formulated the programmatic alliance between art and technology of the school of Nancy— but also *L'esthétique du mouvement* (1889), a work in which he discussed ground and air locomotion.[66] Souriau's son Etienne, and the philosopher Charles Lalo, both of whom contributed to *L'Esprit nouveau*, were also significant sources.[67]

Le Corbusier's fascination with ocean liners, the first class of objects taken up in his ocular triad, long predated his writing of *Vers une architecture*. The travel notebooks from his journey to the East contain drawings of the ship that took him from Patras to Brindisi. As we saw, texts by Loos also led him to praise "the honest expression of the constructor of ocean liners," and his school owned a book in which critic Camille Mauclair compared houses and liners.[68] Furthermore, in 1922 he indicated to Ritter: "You will see here my ideas about architecture recalling that at school, when I was twenty years old, they nicknamed me 'ocean liner.' That hasn't changed."[69] This celebration of the virtues of ships was not merely praise for an isolated technical object. The ocean liner is what inspired Le Corbusier to create the provocative aphorism: "La maison est une machine à demeurer" (The house is a machine for residing). This formulation of 1923 is even more vigorous than the 1924 version, in which *demeurer,* with its static and bourgeois connotations, is replaced by *habiter,* "to live in" or "to inhabit."

Le Corbusier's relation to the airplane was shared by an entire generation of poets, artists, and architects.[70] Impressed by Louis Blériot's crossing of the English Channel in 1909, when "the chimera was captured by men and driven over the city," he again took the stance of an engineer when he declared that he looked at things "from the point of view of architecture, in the state of mind of the inventor of airplanes."[71] The planes presented in this chapter, beginning with the Farman Goliath, were of military origin (fig. 5). Airplanes had been purposefully designed to serve in a "useful war," whereas the questions pertaining to housing had not been posed with any clarity during the same time. The problem, having been "badly posed" by "eyes that ha[d] not seen," resulted in projects whose frivolous lines were at odds with the tension

Fig. 5. The "Goliath"
From an Avions Farman brochure, ca. 1920, owned by Le Corbusier
Paris, Fondation Le Corbusier

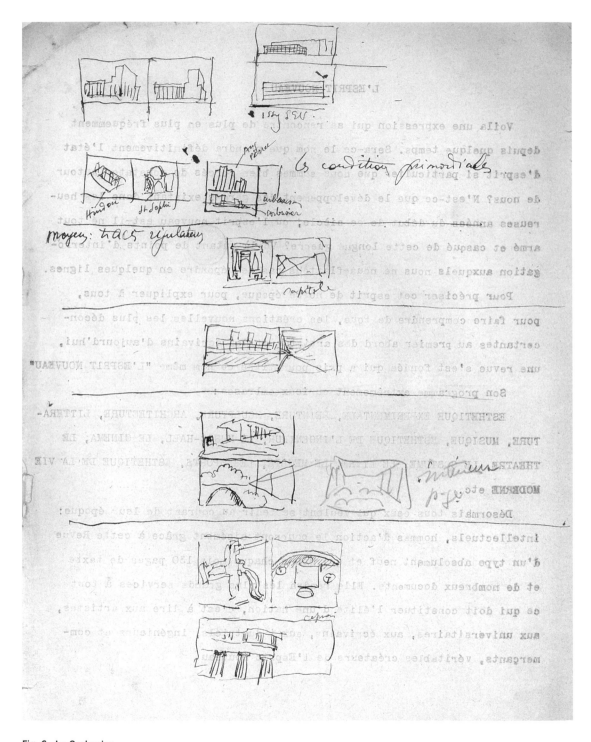

Fig. 6. Le Corbusier
Sketches for illustrations in *Vers une architecture,* including the Parthenon and a Delage
brake, [ca. 1920]
Paris, Fondation Le Corbusier

and sleekness of the French bombers, even if the latter were by no means the most technologically advanced.

Finally, locked onto autos, the eyes of the era were invited to accept a literally iconoclastic rapprochement between Greek temples and automobiles (fig. 6). Françoise Ducros has noted Le Corbusier's clear debt to Ozenfant in this regard. The two friends liked to take motorcar excursions together, but it was the painter who would drive a rather idiosyncratic English Morgan car and publish articles devoted to automobiles in *L'Esprit nouveau*. He himself even designed, with his brother, a Hispano-Suiza coachwork that was published in the review.[72] Ozenfant would note in 1924: "You liked ocean liners, myself, automobiles.... My greater familiarity with mechanical things and your taste for construction soon led to a mutual understanding."[73]

The concordance of temple and automobile, probably conceived when Jeanneret attended the Werkbund conference in Cologne in 1914, led to a third term.[74] Yet again, it was housing that was called into question by machines. Like the Parthenon, the Delage Grand-Sport established a *standart*. (Le Corbusier used an idiosyncratic spelling here, replacing the final *d* with a *t*, as in the German term denoting a flag) This *standart* was the object of a process of refinement or selection, as much for the temple as for the automobile. Le Corbusier considered it a necessary evolution if "Greek" perfection were to be recovered and a modern Pheidias were to appear. It was less a matter of reproducing the automobile than of going "toward" new Parthenons by assimilating the lesson of the automobile. Mallarmé's motif of "outliving beauty" reappears, minus its nostalgia for this unexpected return to currency of Greek architecture.

But looking with new eyes at antiquity and machines, the images of which often came from advertising brochures for automobiles and airplanes, was not meant only as a rejection of academic architecture.[75] The progressive French political and social scene emerged gradually with the rise of Louis Loucheur's program for low-cost housing.[76] The revelation of relationships between these seemingly distant universes introduces Le Corbusier's reflections on applying the laws of economy to housing—something that mass production, discussed later in the book, could make possible.

Return to the Antique

To reassure readers put off by these parallels, Le Corbusier returns in the book's third triad to the idea that architecture transcends the utilitarian. After his 1921 trip to Rome, in the company of Ozenfant and his friend Germaine Bongard, sister of the couturier Paul Poiret, he opposed Roman "bad taste" to that of the Greeks in an architectural anthology proceeding from ancient to modern Rome (fig. 7). The jumble of Rome is likened to both Hadrian's Villa and the projects undertaken in the "conquered" regions, which Le Corbusier compares in passing to regions "devastated" by war and in course of reconstruction (fig. 8). The metaphor of the automobile is here reversed: the "superb chassis" of the buildings are hidden by "dreadful coachwork." He

Fig. 7. Amédée Ozenfant
Le Corbusier at Saint Peter's, Rome, 1921
Paris, Fondation Le Corbusier

Fig. 8. Le Corbusier
Sketches for illustrations in "Rome antique" (Ancient Rome), [1921]
Paris, Fondation Le Corbusier

even proposes getting rid of the marble, about which the Romans "knew nothing,"[77] so as to retain only the brick and cement and thereby enable the development of the primary volumes that, in a drawing, he juxtaposed with a view of the city.[78]

The "lesson of Rome" was never taken more literally than when he declared his design for a bridge at Geneva to be "in the manner of Caracalla."[79] The alternatives to Roman ambiguities will be the "spiritual mechanics" of Byzantine architecture and the "drama" of the Basilica of Saint Peter by Michelangelo, two discoveries he made during the 1921 tour and illustrated with doctored images. But he deplores the transformation of the latter building by "barbaric hands"—pronouncing the changes mere "empty verbosity, misplaced words" —and he holds the baroque period and historical eclecticism in like contempt, not sparing along the way institutions located in Rome like the Académie française. This trip also occasioned a tiff with Ozenfant:

> You know that ten years ago Michelangelo, for me, showed Raphael the door. It would have given me great joy to verify with you this implacable law of the world, in an intimacy that I would have done anything to reestablish. For the time being let's see Rome on our own. There will have been no lesson of Rome for us.[80]

Beaux-Arts plans are subsequently identified as the enemy by Le Corbusier, who on this point uses martial language. The military plan leads to "battle," to the "clash of volumes in space." To establish the (proper) sequence of the operation, from inside to outside, he mobilizes his sketches of Greece and Istanbul against the "axis of the École" or the peacock's tail symbolized by the plan of Karlsruhe, a "lamentable failure" reproduced at the head of the chapter. For this opening spot, his first thought had been to use a plan of the Place de l'Étoile in Paris or a view of the Villa Schwob's upper floor.[81]

Once again, Choisy, whose analysis indicates that the buildings are placed off the "driving axis" of the Acropolis, is mobilized. And the horizons toward which the plans lead are not just built landscapes: distant views of Attica, of Campania, and of Latium appear beyond the Propylaea, the Poikile wall at Hadrian's Villa, and the temple in Pompeii. But when these panoramas are visually cut into fragments at Saint Peter's or at Versailles, it is attributed to vanity. One must return to Athens to rediscover the "pure creation of the mind" that is architecture. Here, the analogy used is that of the "beautiful face," employed by the nineteenth-century French art critic Charles Blanc in his *Grammaire des arts du dessin*, or that of the axial body.[82] It is the consistency between the axis of a machine or building and the axis "that lies within man" and gives birth to harmony.

Le Corbusier did not make do with his sketches of Athens. He also bought and read the *Prière sur l'Acropole* (Prayer on the Acropolis) by Renan, for whom this site where "perfection exists" was the "ideal crystallized in Pentelic marble."[83] He corresponded with Ritter in 1920, citing "the Parthenon, that drama" as a "model" for the paintings with which he struggled (fig. 9).[84]

Fig. 9. West side of the Parthenon
Detail from *L'Acropole d'Athènes, le Parthénon*, intro. Gustave Fougères (Paris: Albert Morancé, 1910), pl. 10
Le Corbusier extracted two illustrations from this plate, on pp. 184 and 185 of the present edition.

He reproduced photographs by the Genevan Frédéric Boissonnas, used as illustrations in *Le Parthénon* by the archaeologist Maxime Collignon and in the portfolio *L'Acropole d'Athènes, le Parthénon,* published by Albert Morancé.[85] One might also advance the hypothesis that Jeanneret had read Charles Maurras's book of 1918, *Athènes antique.* Maurras deplored that "this force" that was the Parthenon had gone "unappreciated" and refuted the interpretations in Renan's *Prière sur l'Acropole,* which he found verbose.[86]

The effects of the Parthenon, a "machine for stirring emotion," are produced by the use of a modular composition whose "plastic mechanics" create an impression of "cut and polished steel."[87] The unusual term *modénature* (rendered in the present translation as "contour modulation")[88] surprised readers, beginning with Louis Bonnier, city architect of Paris, who asked him to specify its origins, which he thought were Helvetian:

> I have culled my memories. The word is not used in Switzerland. At least, I never heard it there. But having spent some weeks on the Acropolis in Athens, the sense of *modénature* struck me, and it must have been at that moment that I searched for a word corresponding to the thing.
>
> ...The word is worth introducing into the practical language of architecture, signifying [as it does] something of capital importance in the architectural art.[89]

Le Corbusier took this apparently mysterious concept from Choisy's *Histoire de l'architecture* of 1899, where it is defined as "the abstract art of accentuating masses" (fig. 10).[90] It had first appeared as a term translated from the Italian *modanatura* in the 1752 edition of the Trévoux dictionary; then Quatremère de Quincy in 1832 included it in his *Dictionnaire historique d'architecture,* defining *modinature* or *modénature*—a word he considered to still not be accepted in French—as the architectural expression of the "assembly and the distribution of the components, profiles, and mouldings of an order."[91]

If architecture is the "masterful, correct, and magnificent play of volumes brought together in light," modeling strictly adheres, "still and exclusively," to the same definition. To illustrate its effects, Le Corbusier isolated details from the plates in Collignon's album to underscore their "passion" and "rigor." Reverting to the initial emphasis of the book, Le Corbusier compared the profile of the cornice of the pediment to "the line of an engineer." Had not Maurras already seen the Parthenon as an "immense hangar made of marble"?[92] And Nietzsche's remarks on the Greeks would not have escaped him:

> Oh, those Greeks! They knew how to *live:* what is needed for that is to stop bravely at the surface, the fold, the skin; to worship appearance, to believe in shapes, tones, words—in the whole Olympus of appearance! Those Greeks were superficial—out of profundity![93]

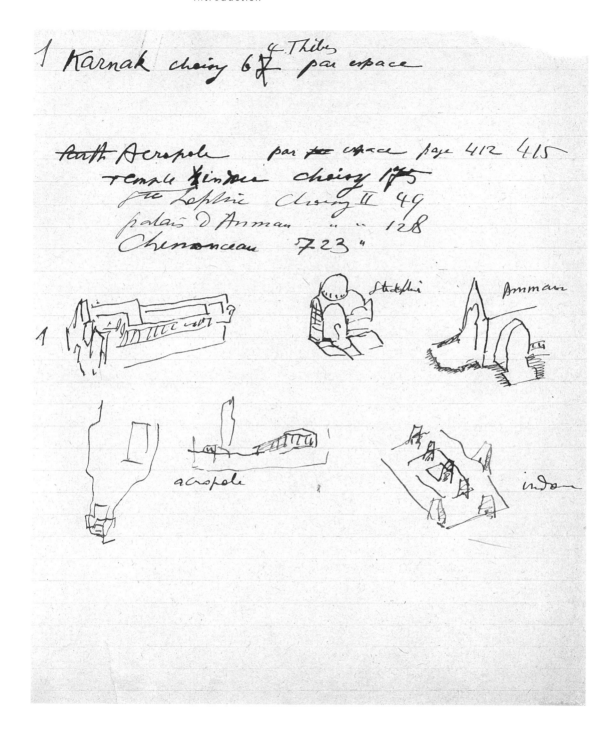

Fig. 10. Le Corbusier
Sketches of the Karnak Temple and the Acropolis, after Auguste Choisy, *Histoire de l'architecture* (Paris: Gauthier-Villars, 1899), 1:64, 412
Paris, Fondation Le Corbusier

Mass-Production Housing

To focus his readers on a pressing issue of the moment, Le Corbusier inserted after the third element of his triad—"Architecture"—a revised version of the text on "mass-production housing" published in the December 1921 issue of *L'Esprit nouveau*. It effectively functions as personal propaganda; this chapter is among the ones that were the most heavily revised for publication in *Vers une architecture*. He kept the title page and the photograph of an automobile with its door open, but he removed the three images of houses by Perret that had appeared at the beginning of the December 1921 version.[94] The pages showing the variations on the theme of the Domino House, the earliest designs for worker housing, and the Monol houses, based on Perret's shell vaults, are again brought together. Le Corbusier added a view of his "villa by the sea" project of 1921 and, most importantly, the villa apartments (*immeuble-villas*) that he had just presented at the 1922 Salon d'automne. He unhesitatingly maintains that it is "under construction in Paris," although despite his efforts, and some promising contacts, he had been unable to find a patron determined to realize it.[95]

Jeanneret vigorously denounced the standing preference for vernacular architecture in the reconstruction of areas "devastated" by the war because he had intended to sell the Domino House project to the French authorities for precisely this purpose. And Le Corbusier mocked the unusual logistical problems involved in the use of traditional masonry because, thanks to his experience trying to negotiate construction materials for SABA, he understood the practical difficulties of transport. Finally, he objected to the notion that a house is a "poem," the culmination of its owner's life, and promoted the idea of "having a house as practical as our typewriter." Here he endorsed—in an effort to exclude housing from the field of art—Loos's position identifying architecture with the monumental in his article "Architektur," which he knew from its 1912 translation.[96] Just as much a "tool" as the little Ford that Le Corbusier owned at the time, the house was a model of residential design not only because of its livability and its degree of finish but also because it could be produced on an assembly line. It is at this point in *Vers une architecture* that Le Corbusier's long-sustained passion for Taylorism and Fordism becomes apparent.[97]

The syncretism of this chapter is quite stunning. Le Corbusier moves among his readings (from Loos to the Jesuit priest Marc-Antoine Laugier, discovered while he was preparing *La construction des villes*), his own projects, the problems of domestic life in apartment buildings, his observations about the politics of reconstruction, and his critique of the Parisian suburban landscape. He also sets forth his idealistic vision of America, where a "new state of mind" had made possible the elimination of fences between subdivision lots. On this point, he had asked a picture researcher to find him material "about American skyscrapers, about American garden cities (Los Angeles, Chicago, or elsewhere) as well as about factories with gardens."[98]

An Ambiguous Political Position

The political undertones become more emphatic in the chapter "Architecture or Revolution," the book's only previously unpublished text; although slated to appear in issue number 19 of *L'Esprit nouveau,* it never did because the review's publication was suspended between June 1922 and November 1923.[99] Le Corbusier's political positions are rather elusive, but they are of a piece with the industrialist credo of Saint-Simonism.[100] In the preceding years, his correspondence with Ritter clearly expressed his wariness of Socialists from Chaux-de-Fonniers; he told him, in 1915, that he had stopped being *socio* (socialist) and become *national* (nationalist).[101] But in postwar Europe, *L'Esprit nouveau* took a stand against French nationalist forces, opening its pages to echoes from Germany and Bolshevik Russia. Socially, the review espoused conservative positions. Le Corbusier identified with the industrialists affiliated with the modernization of capitalism, adhering to their paternalist strategies, and showed no inclination to support the workers' movement. He maintained that "things have changed," referring to the new factory equipment to which the "human beast" (*la bête humaine,* after the eponymous novel by Émile Zola) was enslaved and, above all, to the regulation of working hours. Le Corbusier certainly had in mind that a law limiting the workday to eight hours had been passed by the French Chambre des députés (Chamber of deputies) in 1920, which made the question of leisure time as pressing as that of production.

Jeanneret uses an animal metaphor to call into question the "dwellings," what's more hideous, of the said "beast." These "snail shells" full of tuberculosis are contrasted with new objects, with factories, and with offices. In his preparatory notes, he mentioned his work on the transformation of land property laws and drafted an assessment even more critical than the one that appears in the final text: "There are too many wretched, disgraceful, scandalous neighborhoods in old cities, which are worm-eaten and impossible to disinfect."[102]

Le Corbusier seems to rule out any autonomous initiatives on the part of the producers and place his confidence in a "special class of intellectuals so large that it constitutes the active social stratum." These wage earners, whose numbers were on the rise, were in revolt and called the existing social framework into question. It was not by chance that Le Corbusier, indignant about a possible "destruction of the family," introduced a paragraph challenging the "current principle of ownership" and calling for initiatives that would make people "enthusiastic about building." His position was quite clearly reformist, which permitted him to end his book with the calm assertion that "we can avoid revolution," a phrase added in pen during the revision of the first typescript.[103]

Another reading is possible, however, one in which "architecture" would signify the lessons of history and "revolution" would signify modernity. Given the disillusionment that the amateur industrialist Jeanneret experienced in the postwar context, he may have felt that social conflict could be settled only by reconciling the modern world with a carefully vetted past. His reading of *Also sprach Zarathustra* cannot be ignored, nor the way this encouraged both his iconoclasm and his resolve to construct a modern cult.

Rhetorical Tactics

So it was by going "toward" an architecture that the social threat would be avoided. This kinetic image (which recalls the title of an article written in 1910 by the Czech architect Pavel Janák) raises the question of Le Corbusier's rhetorical strategies in the text, illustrations, and page layouts.[104] Thus the cover chosen for the 1923 edition, with its view down the promenade of the *Aquitania,* intimates motion "toward" the bow of the ship. The window opened in the rectangle of the cover designates a horizon at which the hopes expressed in the book would converge.

Initially, when the book was provisionally titled *Architecture ou révolution,* Le Corbusier had sketched a cover with the same image placed above the title (fig. 11). The final version is imbued with a certain mystery. It was a question not of going toward a "new" or "modern" architecture but of dismissing the possibility of any sort of architecture.

In 1924, reacting to the first reviews, Le Corbusier would claim to have written the book "in bold strokes," but examination of the successive manuscript versions of the articles for *L'Esprit nouveau* and analysis of the changes made between their initial publication and the book of 1923 reveals a sedimentation of revisions and refinements.[105] Le Corbusier's manner of writing has been analyzed more than once.[106] He read and assimilated Nietzsche, the French poet Lautréamont, and Charles Baudelaire, from whom his borrowings are more structural than literal. Jean-Claude Garcias has discerned something of John Ruskin's prophetic tone in the writing for *L'Esprit nouveau,* as well as formulations worthy of a "mid-level bureaucrat Barrès or a department-store countess of Noailles," noting as evidence the many "paradoxes and oxymorons" that recur throughout the argument.[107]

Each chapter, heralded by a summary repeated from the beginning of the book, shares the same structure—title page, reiteration of the initial synopsis, body of the argument—a fact that belies Le Corbusier's claim to spontaneity. Taking advantage of the hiatus in the production of the review between issues 17 and 18 (dated June 1922 and November 1923), he loosened up the *Esprit nouveau* page layouts, notably to accommodate the résumé headings at the start of the chapters. A principle of oratorical amplification was brought to bear on each. The title serves as a kind of textual concentrate; its words are scattered rhythmically throughout the text proper, akin to the well-known title of Mallarmé's poem "Un coup de dés jamais n'abolira le hasard" (A throw of the dice will never abolish chance). Beginning with the title page, a parallel progression of text and image leads through a network of oppositions, affirmations, and syllogisms to a final deduction, as Guillemette Morel Journel has shown in a penetrating analysis of the chapter on automobiles.[108]

The text itself constitutes a veritable anthology of rhetoric. Le Corbusier's

Fig. 11. Le Corbusier
Sketch for book cover with the working title *Architecture ou révolution*, [1923]
Paris, Fondation Le Corbusier

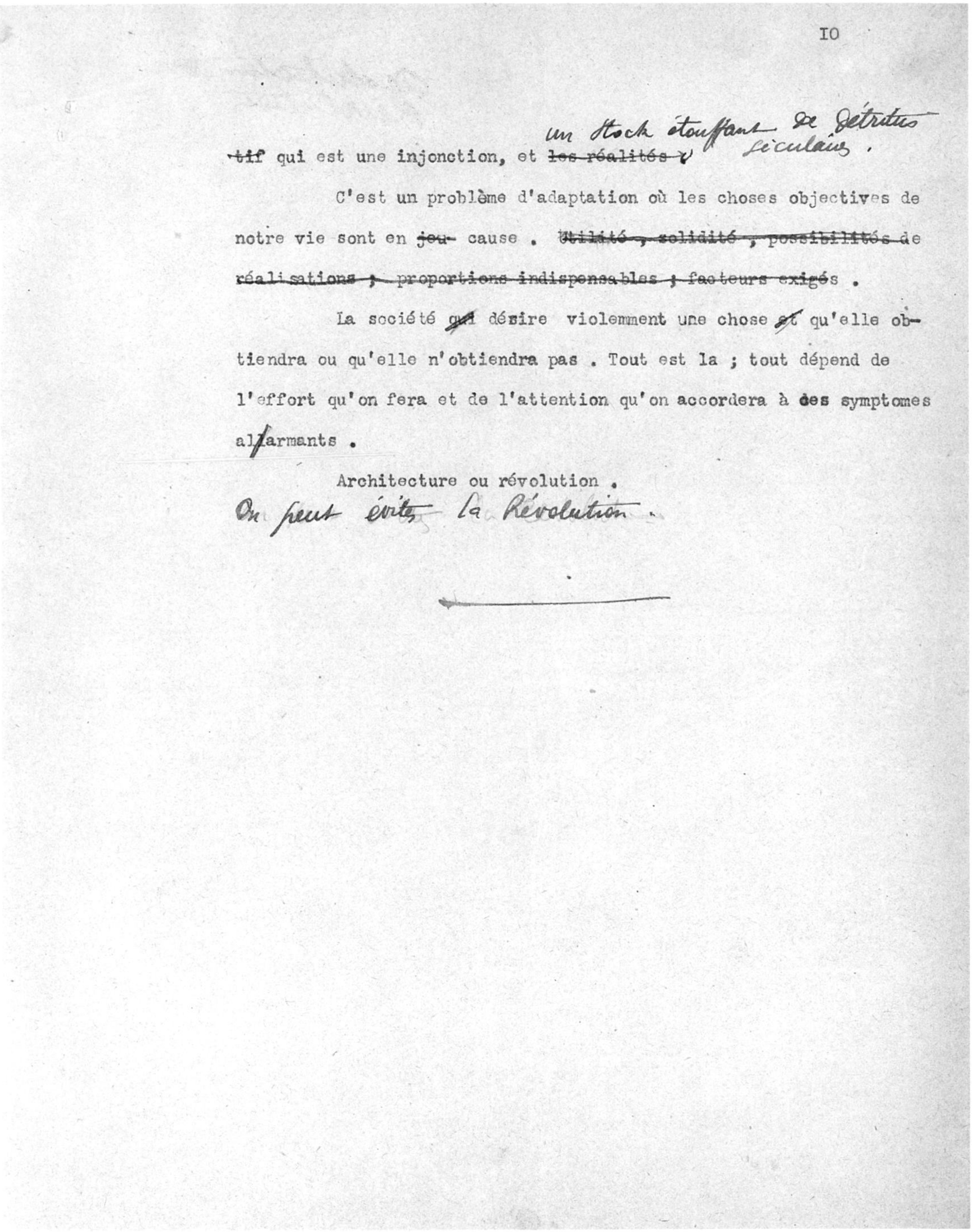

un Stock étouffant de détritus séculaires.

~~tif~~ qui est une injonction, et ~~les réalités ;~~

C'est un problème d'adaptation où les choses objectives de notre vie sont en ~~jeu~~ cause . ~~Utilité , solidité ; possibilités de réalisations ; proportions indispensables ; facteurs exigés~~ .

La société ~~qui~~ désire violemment une chose ~~et~~ qu'elle obtiendra ou qu'elle n'obtiendra pas . Tout est la ; tout dépend de l'effort qu'on fera et de l'attention qu'on accordera à ~~des~~ symptomes alarmants .

Architecture ou révolution .

On peut éviter la Révolution .

Fig. 12. Le Corbusier
"Architecture ou révolution," typescript with handwritten addition by Le Corbusier: "On peut éviter la Révolution" (Revolution can be avoided), [1923]
Paris, Fondation Le Corbusier

reminders give the text the character of a public address to architects. The recourse to anaphora, or repetition of the same word at the beginning of several sentences, is part of this stance, as is the use of a mode of punctuation inspired by newspaper headlines and publicity brochures. In the body of the book, he brings together a long series of affirmations in the present indicative, extending from banal observations to revelation, even paradox. The likening of the engineer's work to "great art" is one of the recurrent paradoxes, while "eyes that do not see" is another. The assertions are supported by "proofs" taken from current developments in Paris and from journalistic accounts of, for example, life in the United States. But Le Corbusier also draws on personal experience: his travels, his industrial failures at SABA, his first construction sites. He even goes as far as addressing himself to the reader in a feigned first person, when he imagines owning a Citroën because he is "a dandy."[109]

This inventory leads to prescriptive statements such as, "We must see to the establishment of standards," and "We must create a mass-production state of mind." Le Corbusier seems to divide society into a "coalition" of the backward-looking ("architects and aesthetes") and those collaborators, either already "committed" ("major industry, specialized factories") or "desirable," to whom the orders are directed. This dialectic of statement and prescription or injunction henceforth became a staple of Corbusian argumentation. The recourse to verbs heuristic ("to study," "to seek"), didactic ("to recognize," "to show"), and prescriptive ("to remind," "to demand") is, according to Morel Journal, one expression of his "rhetorical violence."[110] Furthermore, adjacent terms in the chapter titles generate contradictory expectations on which the book plays.[111] Thus the meaning of the comma separating "aesthetic of the engineer" and "architecture" in the first chapter becomes apparent only gradually, and the question "Architecture or revolution?" finds an affirmative response ("We can avoid revolution") only in extremis (fig. 12).

The book constructs a world consisting of admirable professions (engineering), contemptible institutions (the Beaux-Arts), and oppressive territories (slum neighborhoods). The great building projects of the day, such as the reconstruction of "devastated" regions, appear only as background. Analogies lead to eminently memorable slogans that sometimes obscure the book's subtler arguments. Characterizing the house or the Parthenon as machines "for living in" or "for stirring emotion," Le Corbusier revives the organicist analogy of the nineteenth century, but buildings are no longer made of bone, flesh, and skin, although he still invokes the "shell" of the slums. In the age of the automobile, the latter is said to have simultaneously a "chassis" (*châssis*) and "coachwork" (*carrosserie*).

The Book's "Physique"

The ambitions of the text are reinforced by many visual effects first used in *L'Esprit nouveau*. The raw material is the space on the page, an extension of Mallarmé's explorations with scattered "blanks" and Apollinaire's with calligrams. Utterly experimental in semantic and aesthetic terms, the book plays on all the typographic registers but relies on a proportional grid using the golden section. The running text is set in Elzevir and the titles in sans serif capitals that are either wide or narrow.[112] The discourse is modulated by the use of boldface type and a variety of font sizes and by recourse to dashes and italics but remains tame in comparison with contemporary Dutch, German, or Russian ventures.

The images are not straightforward illustrations of the title statements or "extrinsic evidence for the discourse," as has been noted by Morel Journel, but enter into an ironic or distanced relationship with it in accordance with techniques tried out by Picabia and Giorgio de Chirico, whose paintings Ozenfant and Jeanneret had published.[113] Farther upstream, there are precedents for the word-image relationship established by Le Corbusier in illustrated French periodicals published since the mid-nineteenth century, from *Le Magasin pittoresque* to *L'Illustration* and the dailies.[114] In 1915, while developing his *France ou Allemagne?* Jeanneret had proposed an imitation of an Austrian Werkbund publication featuring "images taken from old publications, reduced and grouped on a page."[115]

The provenance of the images, especially the photographs, is quite diverse and is documented in the "Editor's and Translator's Notes" in the present volume (fig. 13 and see fig. 10).[116] Le Corbusier uses books like Choisy's *Histoire de l'architecture* and newspaper clippings and advertising materials from automobile and aircraft makers but also pictures purchased in Paris and while traveling, duly cropped and retouched, if he felt it necessary, as in the case of the silos mentioned above. The manipulations made to the illustrations for "The Lesson of Rome" are perhaps the most striking. He uses prints by Alinari or Anderson, bought during his 1921 trip (see fig. 7, fig. 14). Besides the multiplication of images achieved by using two frames of the same photograph, he performs a subtraction, for instance by getting rid of half of an illustration of Saint Peter's, which is furthermore flipped (figs. 15, 16, and p. 204).[117] He also proceeds by addition when grouping Beaux-Arts architecture images to produce an effect of saturation, repeated with "The Rome of Horrors" (see fig. 14 and p. 215).[118] Finally, his severe visual editing modernizes buildings such as the silos in Buenos Aires, as well as, most strikingly, the Roman church Santa Maria in Cosmedin, whose columns are carefully inked out (figs. 17, 18, and pp. 200–206).[119]

The rhythm of the page assemblages suggests cinematographic montage, with slow sequences and rapid sequences, close-ups of details (the Delage brake mechanism), and distance shots of industrial landscapes. Despite their modest audacity, when compared to *De Stijl* or *G*, Le Corbusier's page layouts shocked the printers, as Le Corbusier recounts in his preface to the 1958 reprint:

> The galleys of my articles (then brought together) provoked astonishment and indignation at the imprimerie Arrault in Tours (our printer); they said, speaking of me: "He's a madman!" Already! And this, with regard to typography and (typographic) craft. *Vers une architecture* (1920–21) testifies to a spirit of its own.[120]

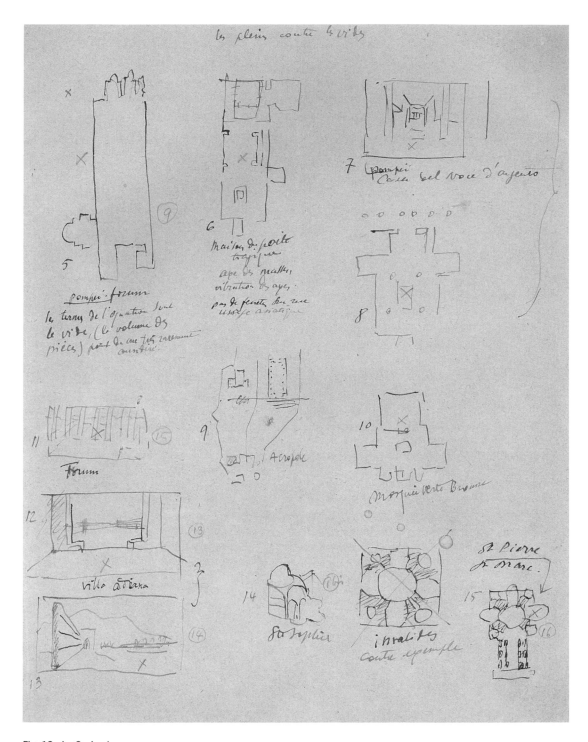

Fig. 13. Le Corbusier
Sketches for illustrations in "Les pleins contre les vides" (Solids against voids), [1921]
Paris, Fondation Le Corbusier

Fig. 14. Le Corbusier
Sketches for illustrations in "Rome et nous" (Rome and us), [1921], elements for the
assembly on p. 211
Paris, Fondation Le Corbusier

Fig. 15. Le Corbusier
Sketches for illustrations in "Michel-Ange" (Michelangelo), [1921]
Paris, Fondation Le Corbusier

Fig. 16. Apse and sacristy of Saint Peter's, Rome
Le Corbusier's cropped and inverted version of this Alinari photograph is on p. 204 of the present edition. See also the corresponding sketch in fig. 15.

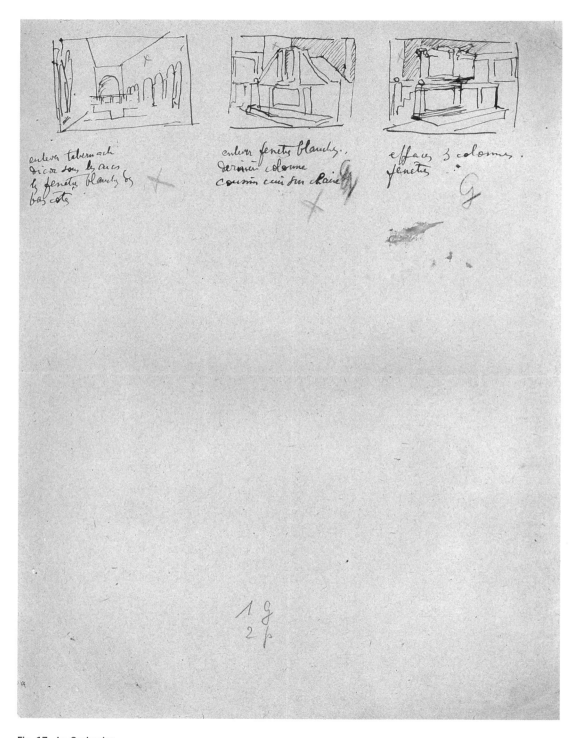

Fig. 17. Le Corbusier
Sketches for illustrations in "Rome byzantine" (Byzantine Rome) with marks for
retouching the photographs of Santa Maria in Cosmedin, [1921]
Paris, Fondation Le Corbusier

Fig. 18. Interior of Santa Maria in Cosmedin, Rome
Le Corbusier's retouched version of this Alinari photograph is on p. 203 of the present edition.

Doubtless it makes more sense to assess the book's page designs in terms of dissonance than of harmony. They do not reflect an unapproachable *Gesamtkunstwerk,* in which different expressive modes are smoothly integrated, so much as a *Merzbild* of juxtaposed fragments. What's more, the conditions under which *L'Esprit nouveau* was pulled together led to comic discrepancies that were preserved in *Vers une architecture.* Received too late to be included in the June 1921 issue on airplanes, the photographs of the Caproni cockpit were used in July to illustrate the article on automobiles! Le Corbusier maintained that "their signification holds," a comment that confirms the commutativity of the technical objects: a plane replaces a car, and the discourse goes on.[121] Readers who have not paid close attention to the chapter sequencing will often be surprised by the choice of illustrations, including the initial image of "Mass-Production Housing": a photograph of an automobile that, to reinforce the domestic analogy, has its door open, as if onto the interior of a house.

Elsewhere the connection with technical objects such as turbines is more mysterious (fig. 19). And the book's final illustration, a tobacco pipe from the Saint-Claude cooperative in the Jura, remains puzzling (fig. 20). This object might derive from Mallarmé's nostalgic prose poem "La Pipe."[122] Its inclusion was a last-minute idea; the object was photographed as the result of an exchange with Besson, born in Oyonnax, also a pipe-manufacturing center. Le Corbusier had communicated to him "his furious desire to know the works of art that you fabricate at Saint-Claude."[123] This "precious instrument" with its streamlined form is perhaps also a signature of Le Corbusier, who was not averse to using a pipe, as can be seen in the famous photograph of his meeting with Mies van der Rohe in Stuttgart in 1926. Oddly, it was with regard to this "exquisitely anonymous" instrument that Lewis Mumford remarked how Le Corbusier was "very ingenious in picking out manifold objects, buried from observation by their very ubiquity, in which this mechanical excellence of form has manifested itself without pretence or fumbling."[124] Nothing is further from this observation than the "infidelity of images" evoked by René Magritte in 1928, when he painted his picture *Ceci n'est pas une pipe* (This is not a pipe), which is sometimes linked to this illustration.

The "physique" of *Vers une architecture* greatly charmed French intellectuals. In 1935, the art historian Élie Faure, who was published by Crès before Le Corbusier was, subscribed to *L'Esprit nouveau* in 1921, and informed the editors of his interest in "the beginning of [their] effort" and of his "full" approval of its "essential tendencies," recalled his initial reaction as follows:

> Remember those singular layouts, chaotic at first glance, but arranged with so much mischief. Remember the use of surprising photographs as illustrations, sometimes beautiful, sometimes comical, aerial views, images of wheels and motors, of outdated tableware, of "style" furniture, of pipes, of telephone receivers; or even of pen and ink sketches, sometimes charming and carefully finished, other times dashed off with verve, but always tied to urging the rigor of an argument that fixed

Fig. 19. Low-pressure ventilator
From "Société Rateau, ventilateurs à haute pression" (Société Rateau, high-pressure ventilators),
Société Rateau brochure, n.d., owned by Le Corbusier
Paris, Fondation Le Corbusier

Fig. 20. Le Corbusier
Sketches for illustrations in "Architecture ou révolution" (Architecture or revolution), [1923]
Paris, Fondation Le Corbusier
The pipe is not yet conceived of as the concluding illustration but is left in the middle of the chapter.

the thinking of the reader as if with a makeshift nail. It shook him up, tickled him, knowing him to be apathetic and dense. With its deadpan humor, it incensed him after having terrified him.[125]

Le Corbusier's project was also appreciated by the poet Paul Valéry, who was sensitive to architecture. In 1921 he had published his dialogue *Eupalinos ou l'architecte* in response to the work of Perret. In 1925, Valéry congratulated Le Corbusier on the publication of *L'art décoratif d'aujourd'hui*, saluting its preoccupation with "links" to the past, assuring him that "purity cannot even begin if you don't introduce it through the scattered examples of it that one finds in the past."[126] Valéry was interested in the book's "physique," using one of the most interesting metaphors in *Vers une architecture* to call it, in 1926, "a perfect *machine for reading*."[127]

Relations with the Publishers

The book's genesis was by no means straightforward. Five years passed between the mention, in 1918, of a work "in press" and its distribution to bookstores in 1923. In a full-page advertisement published in *Après le cubisme*, Ozenfant and Jeanneret announced, as early as 1918, a series of volumes that included *Vers une architecture*, which is mentioned again in the November 1921 issue of *L'Esprit nouveau*.[128] In the interim, Jeanneret told his parents in January 1919 that he had "a new book commission that will be called *Vers une architecture* [and] that will be an avant-garde thing."[129] He had always expected to publish his *L'Esprit nouveau* articles as a book. Preparing them first for the journal substantially reduced the cost of the book's initial text composition and printing, but publication was delayed by unexpected difficulties.

The first edition of *Vers une architecture*, like the articles in *L'Esprit nouveau*, was signed Le Corbusier-Saugnier, the joint pen name of Jeanneret and Ozenfant. However, Le Corbusier implicitly acknowledged his responsibility with the dedication "to Amédée Ozenfant" on the false title page of the book, which, by elimination, designates him as its sole author, a status he claimed openly for himself beginning in 1924.

In February 1922, Le Corbusier took stock of his project in a letter to Paul Laffitte, director of Éditions de la Sirène, the publishing house founded by Jean Cocteau and Blaise Cendrars.[130] Then in April he announced to Ritter the pending publication of a book entitled *Architecture et révolution*, "a set of articles from *L'E[sprit] N[ouveau]*."[131] Forty years later, he still maintained to Jean Petit that he had brought together his articles at the suggestion of Laffitte, who seems to have proposed the new title.[132]

From the end of 1921, Le Corbusier was in contact with the publisher Georges Crès, with whom Faure had just published the sequel to his *Histoire de l'art*, to request review copies of his books.[133] Besson, the head of publications at the house who had published *Cahiers d'aujourd'hui* before the war, would be Le Corbusier's interlocutor regarding all questions pertaining to content. Le Corbusier delivered his "final manuscript" to Besson on 4 January 1922, even as he continued to negotiate with Laffitte, playing the one against the other for reasons that remain obscure.[134] Besson reread the book over the summer, in his room at the hospital in Lariboisière.

Still called *Architecture et révolution* and already in press, the book as yet lacked a proper contract. Doubtless spurred by the *succès de scandale* of the presentation of the "Ville contemporaine" at the Salon d'automne, an agreement was reached with Crès in December 1922 for a printing of three thousand copies of a book now entitled *L'architecture nouvelle*.[135] But in January 1923, *L'Esprit nouveau* invoiced Crès for an advertisement for *Vers une architecture* to appear in issue number 18 of the review.[136] In the end, the title announced five years earlier was retained.

In Le Corbusier's view, the book seemed "well printed"; he had no qualms about production issues.[137] Financial questions seem to have been more delicate, however, and he asked Crès repeatedly when he would be receiving royalties, even as he sought to recover costs for *L'Esprit nouveau* by selling the printing plates used by the publisher. Overall, the experiment was such a commercial success that a second edition, augmented by a new preface, was issued in 1924. This was so completely unexpected that the plates of the first edition had already been dismantled.

Toward a Series

The series of books debated by Ozenfant and Jeanneret in 1918 would be started in 1924. On April 7, Crès agreed to issue new titles, and Le Corbusier, in his preface to the new edition of *Vers une architecture*, employed a military metaphor to explain the meaning of the phrase *"collection de l'Esprit nouveau"* on the cover.[138] It was, he wrote, a matter of "expanding the terrain around the breakthroughs that had been made" with *Urbanisme* and *L'art décoratif d'aujourd'hui,* described as the "right and left flanks" of this army on the march. The central element would be "flanked by two far-flung supports — on the one hand, the urban architectural phenomenon, through which architecture is located; on the other hand, what has come to be called by the sad phrase 'decorative art.'"[139]

Other volumes would appear in the series, such as *La peinture moderne* by Ozenfant and Le Corbusier and the *Almanach d'architecture moderne*, a transformation of the unpublished last issue of the review (no. 29), followed by the last three titles: *Une maison, un palais* (A house, a palace) (1928), *Précisions sur un état présent de l'architecture et de l'urbanisme* (*Precisions on the Present State of Architecture and City Planning*) (1930), and *Croisade, ou le crépuscule des académies* (Crusade, or the twilight of the academies) (1932). Moreover, Le Corbusier adamantly defended the trademark of his series. In 1928, partly to thank Giedion for supporting his design for the League of Nations competition, he recommended to Crès that he publish a translation of *Bauen in Frankreich* (Building in France) — but on the condition that it not appear in his collection![140] Beyond the Crès collection, the publication of the first volume of his *Oeuvre complète*, compiled in 1930 by Willi Boesiger and Oscar Storonov under his guidance, can also be considered as an extension of the chapters featuring his works in *Vers une architecture*.[141]

Publicity and Initial Reception

A virtuoso since 1920 at attracting advertisements for *L'Esprit nouveau*, Le Corbusier did a remarkable job of orchestrating the release of his book. Before it was issued, he wrote a prospectus that, in late July 1923, was handed out at the congress of the Société française des urbanistes in Strasbourg. He publicized the book in the pages of *L'Esprit nouveau* by insisting that it would be possible to avoid revolution through housing. Another vigorously worded pamphlet was distributed by his friend Jean Budry, who was responsible for marketing the book. Its opening lines snapped in the wind: "This book is implacable. There is none like it" (see fig. 1). The text clarified the title, which still carried a certain aura of mystery: "Modern tools and the modern spirit are at the limit point of fusion; a great architectural period begins. We are heading *toward an architecture*."[142] He tried to increase the book's readership by asserting that it "is not intended only for professionals" but "was made instead for the general public." The prospectus, like the book, has a tone of imperative necessity. The masses were "obliged, in their own interest, to reguire" another architecture, a formulation that Le Corbusier would take up again, twenty years later, in *La charte d'Athènes* (Athens charter).[143]

Subscribers to *L'Esprit nouveau* would constitute the book's first echo chamber. Two reviews were devoted to it in the December 1923 issue. The writer Paul Budry, who founded *Cahiers vaudois* with Edmond Gilliard, Ernest Ansermet, and Charles Ferdinand Ramuz, took malicious pleasure in refuting Le Corbusier's examples, emphasizing that the "pure hulls of ocean liners ... harbor countless salons copied after the gare d'Orsay," that "in Goliath dining- and sleeping-cars, the copper fittings are shaped like poppies," and that "Americans with their silos acquire ... Romanesque basilicas to set down in their English gardens."[144] He recalled that the Greeks had "their Tanagra figurines and their shacks at the foot of the Parthenon" without dismissing the intentions of a book that was "constructive and steely."[145] Budry could envision a day when "this line of argument about the automobile will outclass the Prayer on the Acropolis."[146]

The review by Ozenfant was more effusive. The painter was full of praise for this "architecture course like none other." In his view, the "luminous demonstration" of this "realist but winged" book came at just the right moment. While "old, melancholy, back-breakingly thick walls" distressed Le Corbusier, he sketched "new shells worthy of beings who are really new, which is to say lucid and poetic: in a word, complete." Ozenfant paid particular attention to his "organic" houses, evidence that "his art is worthy of Purist intentions."[147]

The Break with Ozenfant

On the copy that Le Corbusier gave to Ozenfant, he inscribed the words, "This book is dedicated to you in testimony to our friendship and in virtue of our work together."[148] But the printed dedication to Ozenfant disappeared from the 1924 reprint, the one translated in the present edition. Le Corbusier maintained that an error had occurred when the printer reset the text and claimed he was distraught about "not being able to fix things except in the future, if by some miracle there should be a new edition." Ozenfant said he had seen "proofs with the dedication crossed out."[149]

In 1924, Le Corbusier reproached him for being jealous of his "success" and took umbrage at his having "claimed that the book Architecture was also by [him]."[150] For his part, Ozenfant still judged *Vers une architecture* "capital."[151] But by 1925 their friendship was "fissured,"[152] as Le Corbusier himself admitted, and thereafter the split continued to widen. In 1926, Ozenfant went so far as to offer this genealogy of the book's driving ideas:

> Of course I did not write it, but what you say in it is a translation of what you and I, you as much as I, in other words we, said and thought during the long years of our collaboration: I having never maintained anything else. Moreover I have no author's vanity about ideas that are neither yours nor mine, but Loos' and Perret's, as a reading of Ornament and crime...proves; and as regards machines, long before knowing you we talked about them almost daily with our old master Auguste Perret, and if I got on so well with you, that's because Perret (it was Perret who introduced you to me)—Perret, you, and I had ideas in common.[153]

In an ironic drawing of 1932, Le Corbusier would represent Ozenfant in the guise of a male but quite busty wet nurse holding in his arms a chubby black baby (himself) shown devouring his teat, adding as sole commentary a quote from a letter sent to him by the painter: "Corbu, having had his fill, bit the breast of his wet nurse" (fig. 21).[154] Having clearly reclaimed a portion of the paternity (or rather maternity) of the book, Ozenfant noted in 1928 that "it is not customary for one of a book's signatories to dedicate that book to the other one."[155] The wounds caused by this controversy, which largely remained secret, continued to fester. As late as 1936, the *Cahiers d'art* published a rumor attributing *Vers une architecture* to both Le Corbusier and Ozenfant.[156] And in his *Mémoires*, Ozenfant would write, "He wanted to be alone; I withdrew," adding that his former friend had "many gifts, but not [one] for gratitude."[157]

Work on new versions of the book continued to occupy Le Corbusier as he dealt with various struggles throughout the decade. In 1928, when Le Corbusier was pondering his defeat in the League of Nations competition, there was a third edition with a new introduction, "Température." This text, illustrated by his project and those of the winners, closed with a mocking reproduction of a fragment of the facade of the Cercle Militaire, built on the place Saint-Augustin by Charles Lemaresquier, a professor at the Beaux-Arts and influential as a jury member who favored the conservative architect Paul-

Fig. 21. Le Corbusier
Caricature of Amédée Ozenfant as a nurse and Le Corbusier as a suckling baby, sent by
Le Corbusier to Ozenfant, 8 July 1932
Private collection

Henri Nénot, whom Le Corbusier had denounced ceaselessly.[158] This image is a pendant of sorts to that of the Spreckels Building in the first chapter. In an understated and rather cynical turn of phrase, Le Corbusier claims to have thought that the book "had accomplished [its] task" and that, "being a manifesto, it had had its moment, and this was past." But since the war with the Académie had resumed, "*Vers une architecture* remains mobilized. After the German, English, and American translations, this book-manifesto goes to harness again and continues its work."[159]

Toward Translations

The successive French editions of the book were accompanied by some instances of quasi-plagiarism, and the demand for translations was growing. In October 1923, the writer Ilya Ehrenburg, in Berlin at the time, contacted Le Corbusier on behalf of Gosizdat. The Soviet state publishing house was looking for "a book on architecture" and wondered if he would agree to a Russian translation of his book.[160] A year earlier, Ehrenburg had already mentioned "the proposal from a Russian publisher to write a book on the machine aesthetic," transmitted by Ozenfant.[161] The project came to nothing and only *Urbanisme* would be translated into Russian in 1933. Another early project was initiated by the Prague critic Karel Teige, who kept close track of developments in *L'Esprit nouveau*. In 1922, Teige had republished parts of the book as they appeared in *L'Esprit nouveau* in the almanac *Život II* (Life II), and in 1923 he discussed the positions taken in *Vers une architecture* in the new periodical *Stavba* (Construction).[162] In 1925, Teige alludes to an inquiry from Otokar Storch-Marien, head of the publishing house Aventinum.[163]

A Japanese version by Miyazaki Kanemitsu was published in Tokyo in 1929. It was preceded by a long series of partial translations published in Japanese periodicals beginning in 1924.[164] Kanemitsu's translation was complete—based on both the original French edition (provided him by the architect Fujushima Gaijiro) and the German translation—but the layout was entirely different, and the volume was given a variant title that translates as "Toward artistic architecture."[165] Finally, a Spanish translation, accurately titled *Hacia una arquitectura* but in a smaller format than the French edition, appeared in Buenos Aires in 1939. The layouts were tightened, the captions were simplified, and some illustrations (e.g., the Fagus factory) were omitted. Curiously, the silos in Buenos Aires, although visible from the center of the city, were said to be situated "in the United States."[166]

But it was in Germany that the enterprise was carried out most quickly. Unauthorized translations of individual chapters were published here and there, and parts of "Mass-Production Housing" were translated by the assistants of Karl Moser at the Eidgenössische Technische Hochschule in Zurich before 1925.[167] Early in 1924, the book also attracted the interest of Gropius, Alexander Dorner, the curator at the museum in Hanover, and Roger Ginsburger, a young architect from Alsace.[168] The latter proposed to the Munich publisher Hugo Bruckmann that he translate *Vers une architecture*, a book, he said,

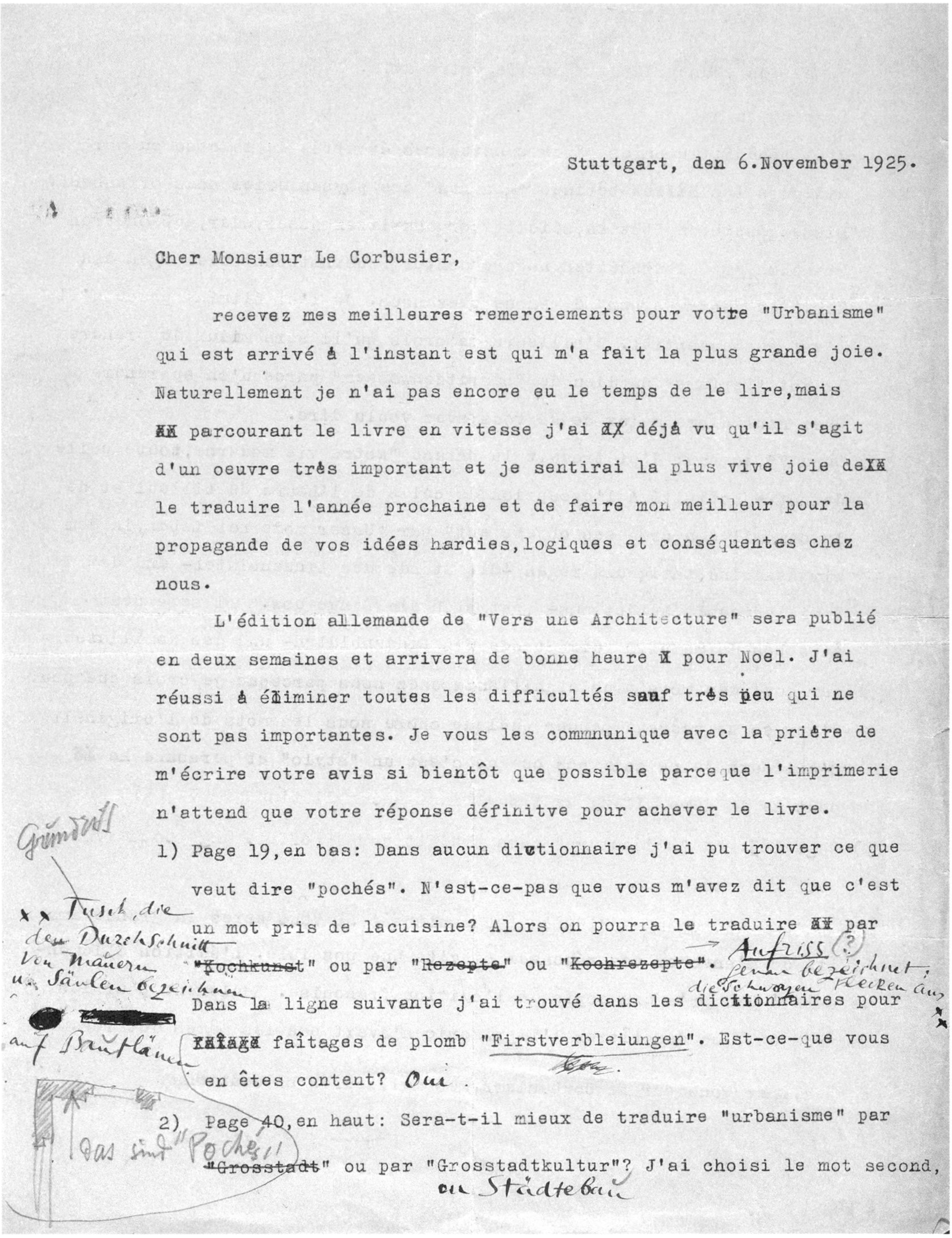

Stuttgart, den 6.November 1925.

Cher Monsieur Le Corbusier,

recevez mes meilleures remerciements pour votre "Urbanisme" qui est arrivé à l'instant est qui m'a fait la plus grande joie. Naturellement je n'ai pas encore eu le temps de le lire,mais en parcourant le livre en vitesse j'ai déjà vu qu'il s'agit d'un oeuvre très important et je sentirai la plus vive joie de le traduire l'année prochaine et de faire mon meilleur pour la propagande de vos idées hardies,logiques et conséquentes chez nous.

L'édition allemande de "Vers une Architecture" sera publié en deux semaines et arrivera de bonne heure pour Noel. J'ai réussi à éliminer toutes les difficultés sauf très peu qui ne sont pas importantes. Je vous les communique avec la prière de m'écrire votre avis si bientôt que possible parceque l'imprimerie n'attend que votre réponse définitve pour achever le livre.

1) Page 19,en bas: Dans aucun dictionnaire j'ai pu trouver ce que veut dire "pochés". N'est-ce-pas que vous m'avez dit que c'est un mot pris de lacuisine? Alors on pourra le traduire par "~~Kochkunst~~" ou par "~~Rezepte~~" ou "~~Kochrezepte~~". → Aufriss (?) genau bezeichnet; die schwarzen Flecken an

Dans la ligne suivante j'ai trouvé dans les dictionnaires pour faîtages de plomb "Firstverbleiungen". Est-ce-que vous en êtes content? Oui.

2) Page 40,en haut: Sera-t-il mieux de traduire "urbanisme" par "~~Grosstadt~~" ou par "Grosstadtkultur"? J'ai choisi le mot second, ou Städtebau

Grundriss
x x Tusch, die den Durchschnitt von Mauern u. Säulen bezeichnen auf Bauplänen
Das sind "Pochés"!!

Fig. 22. Hans Hildebrandt (German, 1879–1957)
Letter to Le Corbusier, 6 November 1925, with Le Corbusier's answer concerning the term *poché*
Los Angeles, Getty Research Institute

that "would be of the greatest interest in German-language countries and that would help to eliminate many tendencies toward the decorative and the artificial in the new architecture of these countries."[169]

The art historian Hans Hildebrandt would be more successful; in 1926 he published a translation of the second edition of the book under the title *Kommende Baukunst* (The emerging architecture), perhaps an intentional echo of the title of a book by Walther Rathenau.[170] The genesis of this version was rather tortuous. A professor at the Technische Hochschule in Stuttgart and a subscriber to *L'Esprit nouveau,* Hildebrandt and his wife, Lily, first contacted Le Corbusier in 1923, naming Ozenfant and Gropius as references.[171] In 1924, Hildebrandt offered to translate his "brilliant" book, saying he had shown it to a great many architects and predicting that it would be very successful on the level of "ideas," as well as in bookstores.[172] In his response, Le Corbusier offered his own analysis of the situation in Germany:

> Wasmuth…answered that the book would contribute nothing new in Germany, where these ideas have long been known and where they have been amply tested. Now such is not my idea: for forty years Germany has rebuilt its cities; which occasioned theories and a "search for the modern." But in my opinion they have not gotten to the bottom of architectural things and have worked on the surface: they have done modern styles (Olbrich, Behrens, Fischer, Paul, etc.). And they continue to do this today, according to formulas closer to construction, but here again, they are sentimental and do demonstrations of modern style, they do modern objects for show. Of course in France my book would have a more violent—and perhaps more brutal—impact on architectural professionals; but it also reached a stratum of people accustomed to the modern spirit through practice and their sense of construction. I am persuaded that modern architecture will be born in France. I do not want to seem exclusionary, but the career of a Behrens is typical, that of Poelzig is demonstrative, etc.[173]

Le Corbusier pressed Hildebrandt to publish the book "shortly before the international exposition of 1925."[174] Toward the end of the year, Crès and the Stuttgart-based Deutsche Verlags-Anstalt publishing house reached an agreement, while Le Corbusier asked Hildebrandt to begin the translation without delay, taking into account the "very slight modifications" in the second edition.[175] Once the contract was signed,[176] Le Corbusier was insistent about the book's form: "I find it indispensable that the typography of the book be exactly like that of the French edition and you will oblige me by asking your printer to submit to me a sample of the characters he means to use; it is very important that the typographic presentation of this book be consistent with the spirit of the text."[177]

Hildebrandt failed to understand certain terms. He asks Le Corbusier if *poché* is "a cooking term" (fig. 22). The latter returned his letter with annotations, recalling that in the lingo of the Beaux-Arts, this widely used word designates the representation in plan of a section through load-bearing masonry.

In answer to Hildebrandt's perplexity at the word *coco*, Le Corbusier specifies that he is alluding to a "high-society poison" (cocaine) and not the licorice-based French drink of that name. More importantly, Hildebrandt notes his willingness to translate *modénature* as *Profilierung*.[178] In his preface to the German edition, he compares the revolutionary use of concrete to two other breakthroughs: the transition from wood to stone in antiquity, and the invention of vaulting.

On examining *Kommende Baukunst*, Le Corbusier paid homage to the "devotion," "conscientiousness," "enthusiasm," and "generosity" of Hildebrandt's work. He thought it was something of a "miracle to have managed to get such fine images from negatives that had already served for three editions." Knowing that his translator and his former associate were friends, he deplored the absence of the dedication to Ozenfant and explained their quarrel: "Ozenfant becomes more convinced every day that he thought and said what I wrote, to the point that I was led to dedicate *V[ers] u[ne] a[rchitecture]* to him to remove all plausibility from this claim."[179] In 1936, he claimed to have found only one "erroneous" sentence in the translation, one that contained "studio argot" (i.e., *poché*) (see fig. 22), and to have no problems with it, contrary to what was being maintained by an "old friend...lying with such cold-bloodedness that it has been impossible to continue to share the concerns and pleasures of an undertaking with him."[180] The "friend" in question was, of course, Ozenfant.

The title itself is an indication of the semantic difficulties involved in creating the German edition. Hildebrandt opted to use not *Architektur* but *Baukunst*, a term less corrupted by eclecticism, echoing positions formulated at the start of the century by Hermann Muthesius, who also opposed the term *modern*, as being too close to *Mode* (fashion).[181] In 1963, when a revised edition of the book was published in Germany in the new collection *Bauwelt-fundamente* (Bauwelt's classics) the title was changed to *Ausblick auf eine Architektur* (View of an architecture), as if the earlier debate had become irrelevant.[182] The 1926 design was largely faithful to the original, with some typographical exceptions—the German printers did not have the capital "block letters" that were requested for the titles.[183] There are also some amusing changes in the illustrations. In the reminder about "surface," a caption attributes the Fagus factory in Alfeld—uncredited in the French version—to Gropius. And in a patriotic gesture, the pipe that was the original book's final image was replaced by a view of the interior of the Zeppelin ZR III, which, as Hildebrandt duly notes, had been seized as war reparations and now bore the name Los Angeles.

An English Version
In 1926, Le Corbusier informed Hildebrandt that "the Americans translate [my] books" and boasted that "the dollar permits them [to offer] terms that console me for those made by Deutsche Verlag [*sic*]."[184] However, it was from across the Channel that a happy ending would come. Early in 1924, Crès

informed Le Corbusier of a query from the English magazine *Country Life* before the London publisher John Rodker committed to publish an English edition of the book.[185] After the war, under the imprint of the Ovid Press and the Egoist Press, Rodker published T. S. Eliot, Ezra Pound, and James Joyce and would bring to completion the publication of Sigmund Freud's works in German. A subscriber and a contributor to *L'Esprit nouveau,* he would himself translate *Les chants de Maldoror* by Lautréamont, as well as Ozenfant's book *Art.*[186] On this occasion he entrusted the undertaking to the architect Frederick Etchells, whom he had met in Paris.

Etchells had studied at the Royal College of Art with William Richard Lethaby and Arthur Beresford Pite, who inspired an interest in the applied arts.[187] Close to Roger Fry, with whom he participated in the Omega Workshops, he produced some mural paintings before 1914 and assimilated cubism and futurism into his work. Etchells took part in the Vorticist exhibition of 1915 at the Doré Galleries in London. In 1929, he and Herbert A. Welch designed the remarkable offices of Crawford's Advertising Agency on High Holborn.[188] In 1932, while working for the Grosvenor Estate in a neo-Georgian vein, he would build two modern houses. Beginning in 1935, he devoted himself to religious architecture, about which he would publish a book in 1948, coauthored by the priest G. W. O. Addleshaw.[189]

Although interested in publishing matters, Etchells had none of Hildebrandt's academic rigor, and it was more as a propagandist than as a critic that he would tackle first *Vers une architecture,* then *Urbanisme.*[190] There is inaccuracy even in the title, which he recast as *Towards a New Architecture.* Etchells did not hesitate to replace the 1924 preface with his own twelve-page introduction illustrated by rather plain British structures and building components and an operating theater. He admitted to "some awkwardness in phrasing and the retention of a certain number of Gallicisms" in his translation and then took full responsibility for its literalism: "I have not felt it incumbent upon me to modify somewhat rhetorical passages such as the above."[191]

If the placement of the images conformed to the second French edition, the use of larger characters for the running text and the suppression of the contrast between the latter and the block lettering of the title headings made the design more traditional. The most emblematic of the many embarrassing textual inaccuracies is the transformation of the reminder about "volume" into a reminder about "mass," which would leave the book open to criticism from Frank Lloyd Wright.[192] This became especially worrisome in 1932, when Henry-Russell Hitchcock and Philip Johnson made "architecture as volume" the first principle of the "international style" that they were promoting, to which they added, again echoing *Vers une architecture,* "surfacing materials" and "plans."[193]

Etchells compounded his mere modifications and improprieties with outright mutilations. He dropped not only the preface but also a passage from "Maisons en série" in which Le Corbusier likens certain domestic practices to neurosis: "When I build my house . . . I'll put my statue in the foyer and my little dog Ketty will have his salon. When I have a roof over my head, etc. A subject for the neurological specialist."[194] Etchells's version of this key text misled the English-reading public in many ways.[195]

A Parisian Success

Le Corbusier used *Vers une architecture* as a kind of catalog, as an instrument for canvassing possible future clients. He asked them to "point out" to him the projects in the book that interested them.[196] Reading it convinced the Bordeaux industrialist Henry Frugès to commission him to design residential complexes in Lège and Pessac.[197] Le Corbusier also took pains to distribute it to people with whom he maintained or was trying to foster relations. He sent a copy not only to the historian Marcel Poëte but also to Eduard Beneš, the Czech minister of foreign affairs.[198]

The consequences of Le Corbusier's personal use of the book were nothing compared to the effect it had on architects, critics, and historians, whose reactions were sometimes solicited with copies sent in homage. Jacques-Émile Blanche, a former professor of Ozenfant's, said in 1925 that he was "giving it out" to "young engineers whose parents are industrialists."[199] It was brought by Oscar Nitzchké and Jacques Guilbert to the Laloux-Lemaresquier architectural atelier of the École des Beaux-Arts. The book stirred up a latent rebellion, and the students challenged their boss to appeal to Perret and to create the atelier of the Palais de bois, the first serious alternative to academic training.[200] But in *Paris-Journal* Perret asserted his differences of opinion with Loos and Le Corbusier, condemning their "volume effects."[201]

Sympathetic to the criticism of the "pitiful bad habits of contemporary architecture," the architect Pol Abraham drew attention in 1924 to the "very sure instinct for publicity" evidenced by Le Corbusier's "categorical aphorisms" and "judgments without appeal." He congratulated him for having used Choisy.[202]

Also praised by moderate modernists such as Michel Roux-Spitz, *Vers une architecture* became *the* canonical book-manifesto for at least a generation, in terms of both its rhetoric and its visual structure.[203] This became evident in 1929 with the publication of *Architecture* by André Lurçat, Le Corbusier's rival on the Parisian scene (fig. 23). It exalted the virtues of the "lesson of the engineer" and brazenly paraphrased the reminder about "volume." Lurçat also deplored the "loss" of modeling, "the subtlest and most difficult science of the architect"; the derivation of his aphorisms from those of Le Corbusier did not go unremarked.[204]

The Paris-based Serbian theorist Miloutine Borissavliévitch considered that "this curious book was not an 'Aesthetics.'"[205] His colleague Faure was more clearly engaged. In his preface to the 1923 edition of his *Histoire de l'art*, he reproduced an American factory from *L'Esprit nouveau* and asserted that "the machine, which is architecture … is universal" and that "the factory and the machine are going to give the face of the planet the unique form of the mind."[206] In *L'esprit des formes*, he would profess admiration for "the

Pont de Tanus.

Tout était à rejeter à priori, puis à reviser, ou à recréer.

La technique est l'ensemble des moyens matériels que nous trouvons à notre disposition, et qui nous permettent de réaliser toute œuvre constructive sur des bases logiques et durables.

La technique n'est qu'un « moyen » et non une « fin » à vrai dire, c'est uniquement la science permettant de résoudre au mieux les divers problèmes constructifs.

Pour l'architecte, la connaissance des meilleurs moyens techniques est le premier stade en même temps que le

85

Fig. 23. Pont de Tanus, Aveyron, France
Page from André Lurçat, *Architecture* (Paris: Au Sans Pareil, 1929), 85

benevolent necessity" of Le Corbusier's effort to investigate the capacity of reinforced concrete "to substitute an anthropocentric geometric abstraction for climactic and ethnic empiricism."[207] He would later note that Le Corbusier acts "much more like a metaphysician than like an architect, a practitioner" and recalled that he "opposed the (if I may say) Lecorbusian pastime of the regulating line" and "the excessive industrialization of architecture."[208]

In *L'architecture française,* Marie Dormoy maintained in 1938 that this "violent indictment against pastiche, against copying, against the unintelligent use of the technical means now at our disposal" revealed the name of Le Corbusier to the public and thereby "purified the air." But, faithful to Perret, she condemned the excessive emphasis on plasticity and "dissimulation of construction" heralded by the book's slogans, even while praising *Vers une architecture* for having reasserted the "preponderant place" occupied by the plan until the end of the eighteenth century.[209]

A Rallying Point for the Moderns

Vers une architecture was quickly taken up by the most engaged critics and modern architects, beginning with those in Germany. In early 1922, the left-wing critic Adolf Behne comments on the reminder dealing with the plan in *Frühlicht* (Dawn), a magazine led by Bruno Taut, and elsewhere gives a long appraisal of the other essays. In 1923, the Berlin critic Paul Westheim sees Le Corbusier as a "leader" without a movement.[210] He took account of the "resolute struggle" that Le Corbusier led with his "examples of striking illustrations" but related his "glorification of technical thought" to the painting of Robert Delaunay and Fernand Léger, considering this "unreserved fascination" outmoded in Germany. Happily, there was compensation for this "materialism of the engineer" insofar as architecture was seen as "plastic creation, spiritual speculation, superior mathematics."[211]

Gropius read the translations of articles from *L'Esprit nouveau* distributed by Lily Hildebrandt. When he had been in Paris in 1923, he wrote Le Corbusier that the book interested him "immensely" and asked him to trade a copy for an album of Bauhaus works.[212] Echoing Le Corbusier's negative comments about German architecture and architectural training, he asserted in March 1924 that "while with regard to many questions you have taken positions contrary to my intentions at the Bauhaus, I have never read a publication that, at its very core, comes as close to my own thoughts and writings as your book does."[213] He subscribed to Le Corbusier's positions regarding industrial production but remained skeptical about training artists at the school of the factory.

Some Dutch modernists were favorably disposed toward Le Corbusier's book. In 1932, looking back at the beginning of his career, Gerrit Thomas Rietveld noted that "during the world war a great deal of experimentation took place in Holland. At the same time, in France, the brilliant Le Corbusier has worked and produced writings with the aim of replacing a worn-out romanticism with new life."[214] For all that, the book's reverberations would

Аэроплан фабрики Ансальдо

Одной из основныхъ особенностей машины, какъ самостоя-
тельнаго организма, является ее до чрезвычайности четкая
и точная организованностЬ. Действительно, врядъ ли мы
можемъ встрѣтить въ природѣ или въ произведеніяхъ человѣческой
дѣятельности явленіе, столь опредѣленно организованное.
Нѣтъ такой части или элемента машины, который бы не за-
нималъ совершенно опредѣленнаго мѣста, положенія и роли
въ общей схемѣ и который бы не явился результатомъ безуслов-
ной необходимости. Въ машинѣ нѣтъ и не можетъ быть ничего
лишняго, ничего случайнаго, ничего «декоративнаго» съ той
точки зрѣнія, какъ это понимается въ общежитіи. Ничего не
можетъ быть въ машинѣ ни прибавлено, ни убавлено, безъ того,
чтобы не нарушить цѣлаго. Въ сущности мы сталкиваемся
въ машинѣ прежде всего съ наиболѣе четко выраженнымъ идеаломъ

93

Fig. 24. Airplane manufactured by the Ansaldo factory
Page from Moisei Ginzburg, *Stil' i epokha, problemy sovremennoi arkhitektury*
(Moscow: Gosudarstvennoi Izdatelstvo, 1924), 93

extend far beyond professional architectural circles. Opening a Le Corbusier retrospective exhibition in 1947, Willem Sandberg, director of the Stedelijk Museum, recalled the book's intellectual and visual impact on him twenty years before.[215] One of the most active Dutch supporters of Le Corbusier during this period, however, was the architect Alfred Boeken, who in 1930 pronounced *Vers une architecture, L'art décoratif d'aujourd'hui,* and *Urbanisme* the "three gospels of designers." In 1936, he would publish *Architectuur,* the diction and page layouts of which manifestly plagiarize *Vers une architecture.*[216]

In Moscow, Nina Yavorskaia, curator of the Museum of Contemporary Western Art, declared in September 1924 that "the great value of this book consists in the author's having transcended the romanticism of the machine…so distinctly perceptible among the Russian Constructivists."[217] Moisei Ginzburg, leader of the said Constructivists, then published *Stil' i epokha* (Style and epoch), which included carefully selected alternate views of the same objects (e.g., the Caproni triplane, the silos in Buffalo, and the Fiat factory in Lingotto), maintaining that he was looking for a new "style" (fig. 24).[218] With a Corbusian emphasis, he evoked the "organisms of industry and of engineers."[219]

Modern Irritations and Jealousies

Jealousy, however, animated some figures in the modernist camp. Van Doesburg's manifesto "Vers une construction collective," published in 1924 with Cor van Eesteren but ostensibly written in 1923 at the time of the De Stijl group exhibition at the Effort Moderne gallery, bore a similar title, as did the contemporary proclamation "Tot een beeldende Architectuur" (Toward a plastic architecture) of 1924.[220] These formulations indicate differences that would only grow more pronounced.[221] For his part, J. J. P. Oud published an article in 1924 that, while quite favorable, played false with Le Corbusier's visual argument, using as its sole illustrations picturesque ink-line drawings. Although deeming the book "really propaganda," Oud said it was a "pleasure" for him.[222] In response to this positive assessment, van Doesburg acrimoniously declared in *De Stijl* that Oud had ignored the textual precedents published in his review in 1917–18.[223]

Wright, always attentive to architectural developments in Europe, maintained the precedence of his pursuit of an architecture of "surface and mass" (a view that was shared by Sullivan). He noted that while Le Corbusier omitted the "third dimension" — depth — Wright approved of the enterprise:

> I should be content were France — our fashion-monger in this school of "surface and mass" — to again set a fashion among us for a generation or two — as seems likely. Lean, hard plainness, mistaken for simplicity, has the quality of simplicity to a refreshing extent, where all is fat or false. It is aristocratic, by contrast. I say this fashion would be good for what ails these United States in Architecture, this cowardly, superficial artificiality. Any transient influence in the right direction is welcome.[224]

Unpublished during his lifetime, this text was the basis for a more concise article by Wright in *World Unity,* where the claim of American precedence is more emphatic: "France the discoverer must 'discover' these plain truths anew," but the operation is just as salutary in America:

> We are, by nature of our opportunity, time, and place, the logical people to give highest expression to the "New."...We fail to see it in ourselves because we have been imitating an old world that now sees in us, neglected, a higher estate than it has even known in its own sense of itself.[225]

Wright never stopped making ironic comments about the slogan "A home is a machine to live in,"[226] and Lewis Mumford would criticize Le Corbusier's "conscious exaggeration."[227] By contrast, Richard Buckminster Fuller would find in it a justification for his Dymaxion industrialized house project.[228]

Skepticism and Hostility

The reception was by no means unanimously favorable. Writing in *Wasmuths Monatshefte* (Wasmuth's monthly) in 1926, the Danish architect Steen Eiler Rasmussen questioned the *Kommende Baukunst* of Le Corbusier, comparing his theoretical statements with his buildings: the hall of the La Roche House illustrates a project that is "not spatial and still less plastic," being all "line and surface." He concluded that Le Corbusier had created "a new architecture that corresponds to the abstract representations, stripped of spatial and plastic sense, of modern man."[229] The Russian conservative Alexei Shchusev refused to see a new style in the "silos in Buffalo."[230] By the end of the 1920s, the most adamant reactionaries, such as the Swiss Alexander von Senger, found that no words could be too harsh for the book.[231]

Reactions to the publication of the Italian edition of *Vers une architecture* were among the liveliest. Giuseppe Giovannoni judged it so dangerous that he forbade its inclusion in the collection of the library of architecture faculty in Rome.[232] However, his colleague Marcello Piacentini praised several chapters from it in 1923, lauding "the perfect knowledge of the material" and the "brilliant images sparkling with conviction" but above all the search for an architecture that was "neither new nor old" but simply "truthful."[233]

In the United States, Paul-Philippe Cret, an adherent of the Beaux-Arts doctrine at the University of Pennsylvania, reacted to the "aesthetic of the engineer" and stressed in 1928 that the architect must take into account the limits imposed on him by "mechanical conditions": "He must control these limitations and with them, rather than in spite of them, express an organic harmony between the mechanical and architectural factors of the structure." Cret concluded his analysis with language taken directly from Le Corbusier: "The architect, by establishing a relationship of forms, realizes a pervasive order that is the pure creation of his mind."[234]

In London, the *RIBA Journal* judged the book to be as "annoying" as it was "stimulating" and expressed regret over the "confusion of thought" that reigned "below the entertaining flutter of its sentences."[235] But the most extraordinary response was one by Edwin Lutyens, published in 1928 under the title "The Robotism of Architecture." The builder of New Delhi declared himself to be "amused, sometimes excited, sometimes angry at the boil of M. Le Corbusier's emotions." He did not impugn the "delightful photographs of grain elevators," but he took umbrage at drawing a connection between the Parthenon, "a pure creation of mind, of fair and fine minds," and the airplane, "which one faulty stay or bolt may crash to the ground." Fortunately, the "lesson of Rome" "comes as a relief." The book takes the reader "down a channel of architectural adventure," but its axioms ring false to Lutyens, who opines that, if it is "to be a home, a house cannot be a machine." Above all, "emotion will never be controlled by sparking plugs" and "the logic of a French mind may make a Corbusier house, or even a Versailles, but never a Hampton Court." The houses promised in the book can thus be only for robots, and blind ones at that: "robots without eyes—for eyes that have no vision cannot be educated to see."[236]

An Eye-Opener for the Young

Widely debated throughout the world, *Vers une architecture* functioned as a kind of photographic developer for the youngest architects and critics. The Berlin architect Julius Posener, a student of Hans Poelzig, underlined in his memoirs that, far more than Le Corbusier's buildings, it was the book and the principles it articulated that rallied his generation.[237] For contemporary Italians, it was a trigger. This is evident in the letter sent to Le Corbusier in 1927 by Carlo Enrico Rava, founder of Gruppo 7, who affirmed that he and his friends, among them Giuseppe Terragni, "were enlightened and spurred on by two books, *Le rappel à l'ordre* and *Vers une architecture*: two men, also young, Jean Cocteau and you, sir, showed them the path to follow, the true one."[238] Moreover, the group's first manifesto used slogans from Le Corbusier's book.[239] *Vers une architecture* would also be fundamental reading for the young Carlo Scarpa, who discovered the book during the Milan Triennale of 1933.[240]

In Great Britain, of course, young architects could read the Etchells translation relatively soon after the French edition was published. Recalling his studies at the Architectural Association, J. M. Richards wrote: "We read the magazines and the latest books (the first English version of Le Corbusier's *Vers une architecture* came out in 1927, when I was in my third year)."[241] As for Maxwell Fry, he claimed to have read the book "concurrently" with Ozenfant's *Arts*.[242] The architectural historian John Summerson would not hesitate to note the book's "explosive emphasis" in his texts from the early 1930s, observing that "everybody has heard of Le Corbusier. *Vers une architecture* was a very witty book, which brilliantly overstated the case for functionalism." Elsewhere, he would write that "very few people are interested in architectural mouldings, but everybody is susceptible to the charms of an aeroplane, a fine modern car, an express locomotive or even less spectacular works of the age such as a finely made gold club or tobacco pipe."[243]

The reading of Le Corbusier in Japan was facilitated by the translation of 1929: ten years later, in his article "Michelangelo shô — Le Corbusier ron he no josetu toschite" (Homage to Michelangelo: introduction to the study of Le Corbusier), Tange Kenzô leaned directly on chapters from *Vers une architecture*. He borrowed a few phrases from "The Lesson of Rome" and, above all, compared the creative stance of the two men, stating, "Le Corbusier inhabits now the same temporal space as Michelangelo once did and bears the same historical mission."[244]

The London translation soon occasioned comment in the United States. Early in 1928, the architectural historian Henry-Russell Hitchcock praised this "immensely stimulating" volume, lauding Etchells for having "succeeded admirably," pardoning his omissions but reproaching him for the inaccuracy of the English title. He moreover rejected the "staccato and aphoristic" style of the original, too often "broken," and its "method of arrangement" based on repetition. In a somewhat forced rapprochement, he compared Le Corbusier's analyses to those of Rhys Carpenter on Greek art: "Against this cool, abstract presentation, the vigorous heat, the constructive positiveness and the intellectual and emotional contemporaneity of *Vers une architecture* stand in the highest possible relief. For all its faults it is the one great statement of the potentialities of an architecture of the future and a document of vital historical significance."[245] Henceforth, the book was part of the "cultural bath" of American architecture and shaped the destiny of young architects such as Max Abramovitz, who would recall that he "took [it] seriously" and "decided it backed up [his] life."[246]

The book was also a discovery for the generation of Josep Lluis Sert in Catalonia: he returned from Paris in 1926 with *Vers une architecture* and *Urbanisme*, books that he "devoured" and that were a "revelation for the young who were then working in the art schools.... All of a sudden, someone spoke clearly, a quite precise general line became apparent; few sentences and some photographic examples."[247] The book would be the reason for Le Corbusier's first invitation to Barcelona, where Josep Torres Clavé would paraphrase *Vers une architecture* in his 1929 lecture "La architectura moderna."[248] In Brazil, at the same moment, young architects got hold of it from native Europeans such as Grigori Warchavchik.[249]

Juggling with the Canon

The response to *Vers une architecture* would by no means be limited to architectural circles — art historians also used it for their own purposes, as Anthony Vidler has lucidly observed.[250] In his *Von Ledoux bis Le Corbusier*, Austrian historian Emil Kauffmann built in 1933 his interpretation of "autonomous" architecture on his reading of the book.[251] In 1949 Anthony Blunt would dwell upon it in his discussion of mannerism and, despite the problems of the Etchells translation, *Towards a New Architecture* would be widely used by Colin Rowe in his comparison of Le Corbusier's architecture and Palladianism.[252] He remarked that, as in the case of the Italian architect, the influence of Le Corbusier "has been principally achieved through the medium of the illustrated book."[253] Similarly, Banham would focus on the importance of the book itself. In December 1954, he asked Tony del Renzio to lecture on it at London's Institute of Contemporary Art as part of his seminar "Books and the Modern Movement" before discussing it at length in his *Theory and Design in the First Machine Age*.[254] And Vidler astutely reads the very structure of Banham's *Los Angeles* — with its alternating pattern of chapters devoted to the city's "ecologies" and to its architecture, and its final list of sources entitled "Towards a Drive-In Bibliography" — as a parody of Le Corbusier's book.[255]

The Long Life of a Manifesto

Le Corbusier's own passion for his first great book would last. On the occasion of its reissue in 1958, he dismissed the notion of introducing any "modern photographs." He maintained to his literary agent that "this book has no reason to exist except with its [photographic] documentation from 1919–1920."[256] A transparent Rhodoid jacket was placed over the original cover, carrying the inscription "written in 1920" (fig. 25). It also had a line engraving from the *Bulls* painting series and a Zip-A-Tone rectangle that partially obscured the original title and the ocean liner's gangway, a masking effect — or one of revelation — that maintained a distance from the 1923 cover.[257]

The success of *Vers une architecture* has continued. It has been translated into languages of the utmost diversity, which have multiplied since 1980.[258] The meaning ascribed to Le Corbusier's argument, of course, has evolved, even if there can be no doubt about the powerful effect of the reminders, and of the injunction to "open one's eyes," on at least three generations of architects. The book's pages have undermined the credibility of conservative academic precepts, determined the vocation of hundreds of young people, and been internalized so thoroughly as to result in unwitting plagiarism.

So the book offers an account not just of the personal conflicts of its author, and of his quest to reconcile his German and Latin cultures, but also of those of an entire generation. More than a personal bildungsroman — although it is certainly that too — *Vers une architecture* was an attempt to transcend the split between the values of the industrial age and those of classical culture, one that only a rhetorician as skillful as Le Corbusier could bring off. Overall, the impact of this provocative book has undoubtedly been even greater than that of the nonetheless pathbreaking buildings by its author.

Fig. 25. Le Corbusier
Design for the Rhodoid jacket of the first post–World War II edition of *Vers une architecture*, 1958
Paris, Fondation Le Corbusier

Notes

Abbreviations used in the notes:

FLC   Fondation Le Corbusier, Paris

GRI   Getty Research Institute, Los Angeles

IFA   Institut français d'architecture, Paris

1. Reyner Banham, *Theory and Design in the First Machine Age* (London: Architectural Press, 1960), 220.

2. Vincent Scully, preface to Robert Venturi, *Complexity and Contradiction in Architecture* (New York: Museum of Modern Art, 1966), 11.

3. Guillaume Apollinaire, "L'Esprit nouveau et les poètes," *Mercure de France*, n.s., 130 (1918): 385–96. The historian Edgar Quinet also used this title for his book about politics: *L'Esprit nouveau* (Paris: E. Dentu, 1875).

4. Amédée Ozenfant, *Mémoires 1886–1962* (Paris: Seghers, 1968), 113; Françoise Ducros, *Amédée Ozenfant* (Paris: Cercle d'Art, 2002), 64–65. Some texts are signed with individual pseudonyms, such as Vauvrecy, Julien Caron, and De Fayet for Ozenfant and Jeanneret; and Paul Boulard for Jeanneret. The texts about painting carry the double signature "Ozenfant-Jeanneret."

5. Carlo Olmo and Roberto Gabetti, *Le Corbusier e "L'Esprit nouveau"* (Turin: Einaudi, 1975); Stanislaus von Moos, ed., *L'Esprit nouveau: Le Corbusier et l'industrie 1920–1925*, exh. cat. (Strasbourg: Musées de la Ville, 1987).

6. Wassily Kandinsky and Franz Marc, eds., *Der Blaue Reiter* (Munich: R. Piper, 1912); Paul Schultze-Naumburg, *Kulturarbeiten: Herausgegeben vom Kunstwart*, 9 vols. (Munich: G. D. W. Callwey, [1904–17]).

7. "Francis Picabia et Dada," *L'Esprit nouveau* 2, no. 9 (1921): 1059–60.

8. A careful comparison of the initial *L'Esprit nouveau* articles with the successive versions of the book can be found in Le Corbusier, *Vers une architecture*, ed. Giovanni Maria Lupo and Paola Paschetto (Turin: Bottega d'Erasmo, 1983). The most comprehensive attempt at reconstructing the genesis of the book is Geoffrey Simmins, "New Lamps for Old: Tradition and Innovation in Le Corbusier's *Vers une architecture*" (Ph.D. diss., University of Toronto, 1987). Analyses from recent decades include: Peter Allison, "Le Corbusier, 'Architect or Revolutionary': A Reappraisal of Le Corbusier's First Book on Architecture," *Architectural Association Quarterly* 3, no. 2 (1971): 10–20; Martin Riehl, *Vers une architecture: Das moderne Bauprogramm des Le Corbusier* (Munich: Scaneg, 1992); and Jonathan Hale, "Towards a New Architecture," *Harvard Design Magazine*, no. 6 (1998): 66–67.

9. Jean Cocteau republished in 1926 his text of 1918, *Le coq et l'arlequin*, under the title *Le rappel à l'ordre* (Paris: Stock, 1926).

10. Charles-Édouard Jeanneret, *Étude sur le mouvement d'art décoratif en Allemagne* (La Chaux-de-Fonds: Haefeli, 1912).

11. Charles-Édouard Jeanneret, *La construction des villes: Genèse et devenir d'un ouvrage écrit de 1910 à 1915 et laissé inachevé*, ed. Marc E. Albert Emery (Lausanne: L'Age d'Homme, 1992). The most rigorous version is published in Christoph Schnoor, "La Construction des villes, Charles-Édouard Jeanneret's erstes städtebauliches Traktat von 1910/1911" (Ph.D. diss., Technische Universität, Berlin, 2003).

12. Charles-Édouard Jeanneret, "France ou Allemagne? Enquête sur un côté de l'activité artistique de deux peuples pendant une période historique (1870–1914); une oeuvre nécessaire de réhabilitation," MS E1(11)275, FLC.

13. See H. Allen Brooks, *Le Corbusier's Formative Years: Charles-Edouard Jeanneret at La Chaux-de-Fonds* (Chicago: Univ. of Chicago Press, 1997); Geoffrey H. Baker, *Le Corbusier — The Creative Search: The Formative Years of Charles-Edouard Jeanneret* (New York: Van Nostrand Reinhold, 1996); Stanislaus von Moos and Arthur Rüegg, eds., *Le Corbusier before Le Corbusier: Applied Arts, Architecture, Painting, Photography, 1907–1922*, exh. cat. (New Haven: Yale Univ. Press, 2002).

14. Le Corbusier, *Lettres à ses maîtres*, vol. 1, *Lettres à Auguste Perret*, ed. Marie-Jeanne Dumont (Paris: Éditions du Linteau, 2002).

15. Jean-Louis Cohen, "Le Corbusier's Nietzschean Metaphors," in Alexandre Kostka and Irving Wohlfarth, eds., *Nietzsche and "An Architecture of Our Minds"* (Los Angeles: Getty Research Institute for the History of Art and the Humanities, 1999), 311–32. Paul Venable Turner, *The Education of Le Corbusier* (New York: Garland, 1977), 236–37, was the first to report these readings.

16. De Fayct, "Toepffer, précurseur du cinéma," *L'Esprit nouveau* 2, nos. 11–12 (1921): 1336–43. Stanislaus von Moos, "Voyages en Zigzag," in Stanislaus von Moos and Arthur Rüegg, eds., *Le Corbusier before Le Corbusier: Applied Arts, Architecture, Painting, Photography, 1907–1922*, exh. cat. (New Haven: Yale Univ. Press, 2002), 22–44.

17. See the luminous analysis by Tim Benton, "From Jeanneret to Le Corbusier: Rusting Iron, Bricks and Coal, and the Modern Utopia," *Massilia* 3 (2003): 28–39.

18. On the sequencing of the articles and the chapters, see Guillemette Morel Journel, "Le Corbusier: un architecte écrivain de la modernité?" (architect's thesis, École d'architecture Paris-Villemin, 1983), 16–18.

19. Banham, *Theory and Design* (note 1), 220.

20. Le Corbusier, "Le voyage utile," in idem, *L'art décoratif d'aujourd'hui* (Paris: G. Crès, 1925), 216.

21. Sigfried Giedion, *Space, Time and Architecture* (Cambridge: Harvard Univ. Press, 1941), 146–48.

22. Le Corbusier, *Précisions sur un état présent de l'architecture et de l'urbanisme* (Paris: G. Crès, 1930), 35: "J'ai porté l'ingénieur sur le pavois. *Vers une architecture…* lui était voué pour une bonne part. C'était un peu par anticipation. J'allais pressentir bientôt 'le constructeur,' le nouvel homme des temps nouveaux."

23. Hermann Muthesius, *Stilarchitektur und Baukunst* (Mühlheim/Ruhr: Schimmelpfeng, 1902); translated as Hermann Muthesius, *Style-Architecture and Building-Art*, intro. and trans. Stanford Anderson (Santa Monica: Getty Center for the History of Art and the Humanities, 1994); Josef August Lux, *Ingenieurästhetik* (Munich: Gustav Lammers, 1910), 12–13.

24. Robert de la Sizeranne, "L'esthétique du fer," in idem, *Les questions esthétiques contemporaines* (Paris: Hachette, 1904), 4–50. This book is featured in the catalog of the La Chaux-de-Fonds art school library (call number 30).

25. Le Corbusier to William Ritter, 23 December 1913, R3(18)306, FLC: "les architectes sont des pantins"; "mon admiration va sans réserve aux ingénieurs qui

lancent leurs ponts phénoménaux, qui oeuvrent pour l'utile, le fort et le sain"; "je voudrais que lorsque par l'art nous voulons faire comme eux, de l'utile, ce soit en concevant la tâche si solennelle, si sérieuse, qu'alors, oui, nous osions redresser la tête et . . . être [non] plus des parasites, mais les suprêmes utiles."

26. Charles-Édouard Jeanneret, "Le Renouveau dans l'architecture," *L'Oeuvre* 1, no. 2 (1914): 34: "Nos Romains, nos Gothiques, nos Louis XIV, ce sont maintenant les ingénieurs."

27. Le Corbusier to Auguste Perret, 20 January 1914, E1(11)94, FLC; IFA; repr. in Le Corbusier, *Lettres à ses maîtres,* vol. 1 (note 14), 98: "fait voir en 1909 ou 1910 dans [son] album de photographies (des 9 x 9, je crois) un fameux et immense pont de fer qui doit être dans les Cévennes."

28. Le Corbusier to Auguste Perret, 27 November 1913, E1(11)86–87, FLC; IFA; repr. in Le Corbusier, *Lettres à ses maîtres,* vol. 1 (note 14), 87–88:

lorsque l'architecte aura mis dans la maison l'honnête expression du constructeur de paquebot, il semble que tout le fard et la crasse qui nous griment tomberont comme des écailles.

. . . Alors je rêverais d'être un constructeur de ponts ou un perceur de tunnels, ou un qui lutte contre un fleuve immense pour le barrer et former un lac ou un qui lance à travers nos Alpes ou à travers les steppes les deux rails d'un chemin de fer. Alors je serais sur la route de l'affranchissement.

29. Le Corbusier to Max Du Bois, [1914], E1(19)185, FLC: "les ingénieurs y auront la part belle et les architectes celle de crétins . . . qu'ils sont souvent."

30. Le Corbusier to William Ritter, 31 December 1917, G1(6)54–56, FLC.

31. Walter Gropius, "Die Entwicklung moderner Industriebaukunst," in *Die Kunst in Industrie und Handel. Jahrbuch des Deutschen Werkbundes, 1913* (Jena: Eugen Diederichs, 1913), 17–22. Le Corbusier owned a copy of the book; personal library of Le Corbusier, B2 , FLC.

32. Le Corbusier to Auguste Perret, 30 June 1915, E1(1)174, FLC; IFA; repr. in Le Corbusier, *Lettres à ses maîtres,* vol. 1 (note 14), 142. He also tells him that he has "fait venir . . . les maisons américaines de FLW" (had sent to him . . . the American houses of F[rank] L[loyd] W[right]).

33. Reyner Banham, *A Concrete Atlantis: U.S. Industrial Building and European Modern Architecture, 1900–1925* (Cambridge: MIT Press, 1986).

34. Le Corbusier to the Perret brothers, 26 March 1910, IFA; repr. in Le Corbusier, *Lettres à ses maîtres,* vol. 1 (note 14), 46–47: "perspective que [lui] ouvrait Monsieur Auguste d'un séjour à Chicago."

35. Le Corbusier to Auguste Perret, 3 June 1914, IFA; repr. in Le Corbusier, *Lettres à ses maîtres,* vol. 1 (note 14), 104: "les immenses bétonnages du Panama, les folles maisons du nouveau monde, le profond de cette vie toute moderne me fascinent."

36. Le Corbusier, *Vers une architecture* (Paris: G. Crès, 1923), 18, 17.

37. Ozenfant, *Mémoires 1886–1962* (note 4), 113:

Il y avait bien, par-ci par-là, en couronnement de ces puissantes batteries de cylindres monumentaux comme des donjons, quelques frontons à la grecque: l'ingénieur, ou quelque architecte traînant autour des tables à calcul, avait voulu 'embellir' le pur travail du technicien: comme si on pouvait embellir un oeuf!…J'effaçai à la gouache ces excroissances, et tout devint pur, ou plutôt le redevint.

38. Scarlett Reliquet and Philippe Reliquet, *Henri-Pierre Roché: L'enchanteur collectionneur* (Paris: Ramsay, 1999), 79–107, 159.

39. Le Corbusier, "1 silo Roché," handwritten note, B2(15)164, FLC: "Livre; illustrations nouvelles."

40. Le Corbusier, "remplacer l'usine de Gropius," handwritten note, B2(15), FLC: "Livre; illustrations nouvelles."

41. Typescript of "Esthétique de l'ingénieur," B2(15)77, FLC: "craignons les architectes américains. Preuve:…"

42. Julien-Azaïs Guadet, *Éléments et théorie de l'architecture*, vol. 1 of 4 (Paris: Librairie de la Construction Moderne, 1899).

43. Thierry Mandoul, "L'*Histoire de l'architecture* d'Auguste Choisy, entre raison et utopie" (Ph.D. diss., Université de Paris 8, 2004).

44. Sergei Eisenstein advanced a reading that parallels Choisy's: Sergei M. Eisenstein, "Montage and Architecture," *Assemblage* 10 (1989): 111–31. See also Richard A. Etlin, "Le Corbusier, Choisy and French Hellenism: The Search for a New Architecture," *Art Bulletin* 69, no. 2 (1987): 264–78.

45. Le Corbusier to Tony Garnier, 14 May 1919, E2(3)54, FLC: "tendance trop grécisante", "le premier qui ait *réalisé* l'entente de l'art avec notre magnifique époque." The earliest letter between Le Corbusier and Garnier to survive dates from 1915: Tony Garnier to Le Corbusier, 13 December 1915, B1(20)86, FLC.

46. Eugène Hénard, "Les alignements brisés: la question des fortifications et le boulevard de grande ceinture," in idem, *Etudes sur les transformations de Paris et autres écrits sur l'urbanisme*, vol. 1 (Paris: Librairies-Imprimeries réunies, 1903), 23–53. On the origin of pilotis (stilts), see Adolf Max Vogt, *Le Corbusier the Noble Savage: Toward an Archeology of Modernism* (Cambridge: MIT Press, 1998).

47. Auguste Perret, "Ce que j'ai appris à propos des villes de demain; c'est qu'il faudrait les construire dans des pays neufs," *L'Intransigeant*, 25 November 1920, 4; Francesco Passanti, "Le Corbusier et le gratte-ciel: aux origines du plan Voisin," in Jean-Louis Cohen and Hubert Damisch, eds., *Américanisme et modernité: L'idéal américain dans l'architecture* (Paris: Flammarion, 1993), 171–89.

48. This hypothesis is set forth in Winfried Nerdinger, "Standard et type: Le Corbusier et l'Allemagne 1920–1927," in Stanislaus von Moos, ed., *L'Esprit nouveau: Le Corbusier et l'industrie 1920–1925*, exh. cat. (Strasbourg: Musées de la Ville, 1987), 45; and Francesco Passanti, "Architecture: Proportion, Classicism, and Other Issues," in Stanislaus von Moos and Arthur Rüegg, eds., *Le Corbusier before Le Corbusier: Applied Arts, Architecture, Painting, Photography, 1907–1922*, exh. cat. (New Haven: Yale Univ. Press, 2002), 78.

49. Le Corbusier to Theodor Fischer, 18 April 1932, E2(2)267, FLC: "éléments architecturaux sains et constructifs."

50. Fritz Hoeber, *Peter Behrens* (Munich: Müller & Rentsch, 1913), 35; and Le Corbusier to Auguste Perret (note 35).

51. Postcard, L5(4)113, FLC; *Vers une architecture* (1923), 59.

52. Amédée Ozenfant and Charles-Édouard Jeanneret, "Sur la plastique I. Examen des conditions primordiales," *L'Esprit nouveau* 1, no. 1 (1920): 43.

53. *Vers une architecture* (1923), 62: "pas encore eu le plaisir de rencontrer d'architectes contemporains qui se soient occupés de cette question"; Hendrik Petrus Berlage to Le Corbusier, 30 December 1923, E1(7)112, FLC:

> Je me hâte de vous informer que, depuis 1890 déjà, cette question est étudiée en Hollande (initiateur 1. architecte de Groot) et avec un tel succès que beaucoup d'architectes commencèrent alors à dessiner leurs plans et façades d'après un tracé régulateur.
>
> Et comme exemple je vous informe que la nouvelle bourse à Amsterdam, 1897–1904, est construit [sic] selon le triangle 3, 4, 5.

Berlage nonetheless supported Le Corbusier's project for the League of Nations in 1927.

54. Le Corbusier to Hendrik Petrus Berlage, 11 January 1924, E1(7)113, FLC: "je connais depuis longtemps la bourse d'Amsterdam que j'ai toujours admirée."

55. Hendrik Petrus Berlage, *Grundlagen und Entwicklung der Architektur: Vier Vorträge gehalten im Kunstgewerbemuseum zu Zürich* (Rotterdam: W. L. & J. Brusse, 1908); translated in Hendrik Petrus Berlage, *Thoughts on Style, 1886–1909*, trans. Ian Boyd Whyte and Wim de Wit (Santa Monica: Getty Center for the History of Art and the Humanities, 1996), 185–252. Semper's remark is quoted on p. 187.

56. Le Corbusier, "Architecture d'époque machiniste," *Journal de psychologie* 23 (1926): 346: "élever"; "résille de diagonales"; "canevas"; "à ce compte-là toutes les broderies au point de croix seraient faites au tracé régulateur."

57. *Vers une architecture* (1923), 57, 27–28. In an undated preparatory note, he writes, "La rue de Rivoli est de l'architecture, le bd Raspail n'en est pas" (The Rue de Rivoli belongs to architecture, but not the Blvd. Raspail); A2(15)151, FLC.

58. *Vers une architecture* (1923), 19.

59. Le Corbusier to Auguste Perret, 14 December 1915, IFA; repr. in Le Corbusier, *Lettres à ses maîtres*, vol. 1 (note 14), 151–54. Le Corbusier does mention them in his introduction to O. Storonov and W. Boesiger, eds., *Le Corbusier und Pierre Jeanneret: Ihr gesamtes Werk von 1910 – 1929* (Zurich: Girsberger, 1930).

60. Le Corbusier to Auguste Perret, 3 November 1914, IFA; repr. in *Lettres à ses maîtres*, vol. 1 (note 14), 121–24. He also mentions his readings of the poet in a letter to Amédée Ozenfant, 28 July 1918, G1(6)182, FLC.

61. Stéphane Mallarmé, "Le phénomène futur," in idem, *Oeuvres complètes*, ed. Bertrand Marchal, 2 vols. (Paris: Gallimard, Bibliothèque de la Pléiade, 1998), 1:413–14: "femme d'autrefois"; "montreur de choses passées." The poem ends thusly:

> Quand tous auront contemplé la noble créature, vestige de quelque époque déjà maudite, les uns indifférents, car ils n'auront pas eu la force de comprendre, mais d'autres navrés et la paupière humide de larmes résignées se regarderont; tandis que les poètes de ces temps, sentant se rallumer leurs yeux éteints, s'achemineront vers leur lampe, le cerveau ivre un instant d'une gloire confuse, hantés du Rythme et dans l'oubli d'exister à une époque qui survit à la beauté.

The prose poem was first published in the collection *Divagations* (Paris: Fasquelle, 1897), 15–16. Jeanneret had already mentioned Mallarmé in a letter of 1911 to William Ritter. See Passanti, "Architecture" (note 48), 88, 291 nn. 90–91. In October 1914 in La Chaux-de-Fonds, he had bought an anthology featuring the poem: *Vers et proses* (Paris: Librairie académique Perrin, 1912); J 186, FLC.

62. Georges Rozet, "Les yeux qui ne voient plus," *L'Oeuvre*, 5 January 1919. This article was brought to my attention by Francesco Passanti.

63. Ozenfant et Jeanneret, "Formation de l'optique moderne," *L'Esprit nouveau* 5, no. 21 (1924); the journal also published a series of articles by psychophysiologist Charles Henry; see Charles Henry, "La lumière, la couleur et la forme," *L'Esprit nouveau* 2, no. 6 (1921): 605–23; no. 7 (1921): 728–36; no. 8 (1921): 948–58; and no. 9 (1921): 1068–75. On these issues, see Nina Rosenblatt, "Photogenic Neurasthenia: Aesthetics, Modernism and Mass Society in France, 1889–1929" (Ph.D. diss., Columbia University, 1997), 90–141.

64. Lux, "Das Neue Auge," in idem, *Ingenieurästhetik* (Munich: Gustav Lammers, 1910), 8.

65. *Jahrbuch des Deutschen Werkbundes, 1914. Der Verkehr* (Jena: Diedrichs, 1914).

66. Paul Souriau, *L'esthétique du mouvement* (Paris: Félix Alcan, 1889); *La beauté rationnelle* (Paris: Félix Alcan, 1904), no. 13 in the catalog of the La Chaux-de-Fonds art school library.

67. Olmo and Gabetti, *Le Corbusier e "L'Esprit nouveau"* (note 5), 9, 10, 43, 119–21.

68. Le Corbusier to Perret (note 32): "l'honnête expression du constructeur de paquebots." Camille Mauclair, *Trois crises de l'art actuel* (Paris: Fasquelle, 1906), 222: "cette maison à locataires se présente comme … un paquebot prêt à partir." Mauclair's book was assigned no. 53 in the La Chaux-de-Fonds art school library catalog.

69. Le Corbusier to William Ritter, 7 April 1922, R3(19)391, FLC: "vous y verrez mes idées sur l'architecture en vous souvenant qu'à l'école à 20 ans on m'avait surnommé 'Paquebot.' Ça n'a pas changé."

70. Felix Philipp Ingold, *Literatur und Aviatik. Europäische Flugdichtung 1909–1927, mit einem Exkurs über die Flugidee in der Modernen Malerei und Architektur* (Basel: Birkhäuser, 1978); Joseph J. Corn, *The Winged Gospel: America's Romance with Aviation, 1900–1950* (New York: Oxford Univ. Press, 1983).

71. Le Corbusier, *Sur les quatre routes* (Paris: Gallimard, 1941), 108–9: "la chimère fut capturée par les hommes et conduite au-dessus de la ville"; 112: "du point de vue de l'architecture, dans l'état d'esprit de l'inventeur d'avions."

72. Ducros, *Amédée Ozenfant* (note 4), 65–67.

73. Amédée Ozenfant to Le Corbusier, 13 August 1924, E2(17)490, FLC: "vous aimiez le paquebot, moi l'auto…. Ma familiarité plus grande avec la mécanique et votre goût pour la construction se sont vite entendus."

74. The museum curator Walter Riezler discussed in Cologne the Parthenon as an expression of type; see Francesco Passanti, "The Vernacular, Modernism, and Le Corbusier," *Journal of the Society of Architectural Historians* 56, no. 4 (1997): 443.

75. Beatriz Colomina, *Privacy and Publicity: Modern Architecture as Mass Media* (Cambridge: MIT Press, 1994); von Moos, ed., *L'Esprit nouveau* (note 5).

76. This project from 1923 would be adopted by the French Chambre des députés (Chamber of deputies) in 1928.

77. *Vers une architecture* (1923), 126, 128: "châssis superbe"; "carrosseries déplorables"; "[ne] connaissaient rien."

78. Le Corbusier here reused the best part, beginning on p. 43, of Ozenfant and Jeanneret, "Sur la plastique" (note 52).

79. Le Corbusier to William Ritter, 9 April 1915, R3(18)420, FLC.

80. Le Corbusier to Amédée Ozenfant, postcard, [1921], E2(17)483, FLC:

Vous savez qu'il y a dix ans Michel-Ange, pour moi, mettait à la porte Raphaël. J'aurais eu de grandes joies à vérifier avec vous cette loi implacable du monde, dans une intimité que j'aurai tout fait pour rétablir.

Pour cette fois voyons Rome pour soi même. Il n'y aura pas eu pour nous la leçon de Rome.

81. Le Corbusier, sketch for "L'illusion des plans," n.d., B2(15)104, FLC.

82. Charles Blanc, *Grammaire des arts du dessin* (Paris: Renouard, 1867).

83. Ernest Renan, *Prière sur l'Acropole* (Paris: A. Ferroud, 1920; original ed., Paris: E. Pelletan, 1899), 6. The copy purchased by Jeanneret in Athens is in the FLC: J 231, FLC.

84. Le Corbusier to William Ritter, 1 July 1920, R3(19)366, FLC: "le Parthénon, ce drame."

85. Maxime Collignon, *Le Parthénon: L'histoire, l'architecture et la sculpture*, with photographs by Frédéric Boissonnas and W.-A. Mansell (Paris: Librairie Centrale d'art & d'architecture, 1910–12); most plates reproduced in the book can be found in Le Corbusier's copy in the FLC. *L'Acropole d'Athènes, le Parthénon*, intro. Gustave Fougères (Paris: Albert Morancé, 1910).

86. Charles Maurras, *Athènes antique* (Paris: De Boccard, 1918), 55: "j'ai peine à comprendre qu'on ait méconnu cette force."

87. As Dan Sherer remarks in a perceptive article, Le Corbusier had no archaeological knowledge of the use of models for the definition of proportions: Dan Sherer, "Le Corbusier's Discovery of Palladio in 1922 and the Modernist Transformation of the Classical Code," *Perspecta* 35 (2004): 24.

88. See also the discussion of this term in "From the Translator" in the present volume. Jeanneret was for many years interested in this issue and had mentioned the term *modeling* (*modeler*) in one of his letters to Charles L'Eplattenier, repr. in Le Corbusier, *Lettres à ses maîtres*, vol. 2, *Lettres à Charles L'Eplattenier*, ed. Marie-Jeanne Dumont (Paris: Éditions du Linteau, 2006), 171.

89. Le Corbusier to Louis Bonnier, 19 March 1924, E1(9)11, FLC:

J'ai rassemblé mes souvenirs. Le mot n'est pas employé en Suisse. Du moins, je ne l'y ai pas entendu. Mais, ayant passé quelques semaines sur l'acropole à Athènes, le sens de la modénature m'a frappé et c'est à ce moment-là que je dois avoir recherché le mot correspondant à la chose.

....Ce mot mérite d'entrer dans la langue pratique de l'architecture signifiant une chose capitale de l'art architectural.

Bonnier would apologize on 2 March, reenacting his reluctance to use an "obsolete" (*hors d'usage*) term; A2(5)35, FLC.

90. Auguste Choisy, *Histoire de l'architecture*, 2 vols. (Paris: Gauthier-Villars, 1899), 1:48: "l'art abstrait d'accentuer les masses."

91. Antoine Chrysostome Quatremère de Quincy, *Dictionnaire historique d'architecture: Comprenant dans son plan les notions historiques, descriptives, archéologiques, biographiques, théoriques, didactiques et pratiques de cet art*, 2 vols. (Paris: Librairie d'Adrien le Clère, 1832), 2:121: "l'assemblage et la distribution des membres, des profils ou des moulures d'une ordonnance." Quatremère mentions as a precedent Pierre-François Hugues d'Harcanville, *Recueil d'antiquités étrusques, grecques et romaines*, 4 vols. (Paris: chez l'auteur, 1785–88), 1:50, who mentions the "rules of contour modulation" (*les règles de la modénature*).

92. Maurras, *Athènes antique* (note 86), 59: "immense hangar de marbre."

93. Friedrich Nietzsche, *The Gay Science*, ed. Bernard Williams, trans. Josefine Nauckhoff, poems trans. Adrian Del Caro (Cambridge: Cambridge Univ. Press, 2001), 8–9.

94. Le Corbusier, "Supprimer maisons Auguste," handwritten note in "Livre; illustrations nouvelles," B2(15)164, FLC.

95. *Vers une architecture* (1923), 206. On this project, see Pierre-Alain Croset, "Immeubles-villas, les origines d'un type," in Jacques Lucan, ed., *Le Corbusier (1887–1965), une encyclopédie*, exh. cat. (Paris: Centre Georges Pompidou, 1987), 178–89.

96. Adolf Loos, "L'architecture et le style moderne," *Les Cahiers d'aujourd'hui* 1, no. 2 (1912): 82–92.

97. Le Corbusier, *Pour bâtir: Standardiser et Tayloriser*, supplement to the *Bulletin du Redressement français* 3, no. 9 (1928): 1–8. On this point, see Jean-Louis Cohen, *Scenes of the World to Come: European Architecture and the American Challenge, 1893–1960*, exh. cat. (Paris: Flammarion, 1995), 69–71; and Mary McLeod, "'Architecture or Revolution': Taylorism, Technology, and Social Change," *Art Journal* 43, no. 2 (1983): 132–43.

98. Le Corbusier to Monsieur Hostache, 23 March 1922, B2(15)13, FLC: "sur des gratte-ciels américains, sur des vues de cités-jardins américaines (Los Angeles, Chicago ou autres) ainsi que sur des usines avec jardins."

99. On the planned publication of "Architecture or Revolution," see A1(5)304, FLC.

100. Antoine Picon, *Les Saint-Simoniens* (Paris: Belin, 2003).

101. Le Corbusier to William Ritter, [1915], R3(18)386, FLC.

102. Le Corbusier, "Architecture ou révolution," [1922], B2(15)153, FLC: "il y a trop de quartiers misérables, honteux, scandaleux dans les vieilles villes vermoulues et impossibles à désinfecter." A propaganda leaflet for *L'Esprit nouveau* printed after the issue 11–12 announcing the forthcoming publication of "Architecture ou révolution" reads as a warning: "the housing shortage will bring to revolution. Be alert to housing," A1(1)182, FLC: "la crise des logements amènera à la révolution. Préoccupez-vous de l'habitation."

103. Le Corbusier, typescript of "Architecture ou révolution," B2(15)174, FLC: "on peut éviter la révolution."

104. In this article, Pavel Janák criticizes Otto Wagner's *Moderne Architektur*: "Od moderní architektury k architektuře," *Styl* 2 (1910): 105–9.

105. Le Corbusier, "Introduction à la seconde édition," in idem, *Vers une architecture* (Paris: G. Crès, 1924), vi: "à l'emporte-pièce."

106. Françoise Bradfer, *Le travail d'écriture chez l'architecte; l'invention de Le Corbusier ou l'accomplissement de la mémoire: Instrumentalisation et opérationnalité de l'écriture* (Louvain-la-Neuve: Université Catholique, 2002), 75–85.

107. Jean-Claude Garcias, "Paradoxes: la rhétorique de Le Corbusier, ou les paradoxes de l'autodidaxie," in Jacques Lucan, ed., *Le Corbusier (1887–1965), une encyclopédie,* exh. cat. (Paris: Centre Georges Pompidou, 1987), 289–91.

108. Guillemette Morel Journel, "Rhétorique de Le Corbusier dans *Vers une architecture*" (master's thesis, Université de Paris 4, 1984); Guillemette Morel Journel, "Le Corbusier, structure rhétorique et volonté littéraire," in *Le Corbusier, écritures: Rencontres des 18 et 19 juin 1993* (Paris: Fondation Le Corbusier, 1993), 15–29.

109. *Vers une architecture* (1923), 210: "coquet."

110. Morel Journel, "Le Corbusier" (note 18), 33–34, 97.

111. Guillemette Morel Journel, "Le Corbusier's Binary Figures," *Daidalos* 64 (1997): 24–29.

112. Morel Journel, "Le Corbusier" (note 18), 70, has inventoried seventeen distinct variants.

113. Morel Journel, "Rhétorique de Le Corbusier" (note 108), 161–65.

114. The *Magasin pittoresque* is mentioned in Catherine de Smet, "Le livre comme synthèse des arts; éditions et design graphique chez Le Corbusier, 1945–1965" (Ph.D. diss., École des hautes études en sciences sociales, Paris, 2002); and Catherine de Smet, *Le Corbusier, Builder of Books* (Baden: Lars Müller, 2005). See also Marie-Victoire de Vaubernier, "Le livre d'architecte: L'exemple de Le Corbusier" (D.E.A. d'histoire de l'art, Université de Paris 10, 1990); and idem, "Le Corbusier, éditeur," in *Le Corbusier, écritures: Rencontres des 18 et 19 juin 1993* (Paris: Fondation Le Corbusier, 1993), 31–45.

115. Le Corbusier to Auguste Perret, [September 1916], IFA; repr. in Le Corbusier, *Lettres à ses maîtres,* vol. 1 (note 14), 182–84. See Jean-Louis Cohen, "'France ou Allemagne?' Un zigzag éditorial de Charles-Édouard Jeanneret," in Bruno Maurer, ed., *Festschrift für Stanislaus von Moos* (Zurich: gta, 2005), 74–92.

116. A very partial investigation of this point is found in Barbara Mazza, *Le Corbusier e la fotografia: La vérité blanche* (Florence: Firenze Univ. Press, 2002); and Geoffrey Simmins, "New Lamps for Old" (note 8).

117. *Vers une architecture* (1923), 132; see the "Editor's and Translator's Notes."

118. *Vers une architecture* (1923), 98, 139; see the "Editor's and Translator's Notes."

119. *Vers une architecture* (1923), 129–31; see the "Editor's and Translator's Notes." Le Corbusier's sketch for this "Photoshop" manipulation *ante literam* is found in B2(15)87, FLC, 13.

120. Le Corbusier, preface to the 1958 reprint of *Vers une architecture,* 3rd ed.

(Paris: Vincent et Fréal, 1958), v: "Les maquettes de mes articles (alors réunis) provo-quaient l'étonnement, l'indignation de l'imprimerie Arrault à Tours (notre imprimeur); ils disaient, eux parlant de moi: 'c'est un fou!' Déjà! Et à propos de typographie et de métier (typographie). *Vers une architecture* (1920–21) témoigne d'un esprit propre."

121. Le Corbusier, *L'Esprit nouveau* 2, no. 10 (1921): 1147n: "leur signification demeure." This caption is absent from the book, although the image is still in the wrong place. He would keep the images in place, despite his intention of correcting the misfit; see Le Corbusier, "Livre; illustrations nouvelles," handwritten note, B2(15)164, FLC.

122. Stéphane Mallarmé, "La Pipe," in idem, *Oeuvres complètes*, ed. Bertrand Marchal, 2 vols. (Paris: Gallimard, Bibliothèque de la Pléiade, 1998), 1:419–20.

123. Le Corbusier to George Besson, 4 January 1922, A2(11)17, FLC. Le Corbusier would again use an illustration of a pipe (an English one this time) in the opening of the chapter "Usurpation le folklore" in Le Corbusier, *L'art décoratif d'aujourd'hui* (Paris: G. Crès, 1925), 27.

124. Lewis Mumford, *Technics and Civilization* (London: Routledge, 1934), 352.

125. Élie Faure, "La Ville radieuse," *L'architecture d'aujourd'hui* 6, no. 11 (1935): 34:

Rappelez-vous cette présentation singulière, chaotique à première vue, mais ordon-née avec tant de malice. Rappelez-vous ces illustrations originales par photogra-phies imprévues, tantôt belles, tantôt cocasses, vues aériennes, images de roues et de moteurs, de vaisselles périmées, de meubles "de style", de pipes, de récepteurs télé-phoniques, ou bien par croquis à la plume, charmants parfois, et soignés, d'autre fois lâchés de verve, mais s'attachant toujours à solliciter la rigueur d'un raison nement qui fixe la pensée du lecteur comme avec un clou de fortune. Il le secoue, le chatouille, le sachant apathique et gourd. Il le pince sans rire, et ainsi l'indigne après l'avoir épouvanté.

In Élie Faure, *L'esprit des formes* (Paris: G. Crès, 1927), Faure reproduces an ocean liner (fig. 71), an airplane (fig. 168), and a Freyssinet hangar (fig. 215); he, too, took pride in inserting photographs of airplanes into his books, and he published one called *L'avion* (Villefranche: J. Bonthoux, 1937).

126. Paul Valéry to Le Corbusier, Paris, n.d., T2(20)412, FLC (typed copy): "enchaînement"; "la pureté ne peut même pas commencer si vous ne l'introduisez par les exemples épars qu'on trouve dans le passé." This was proudly reproduced by Le Corbusier in the new edition of *L'art décoratif d'aujourd'hui* (Paris: Vincent & Fréal, 1959), vi.

127. Paul Valéry, "Les deux vertus d'un livre" [1926], in idem, *Oeuvres*, 2 vols. (Paris: Gallimard, Bibliothèque de la Pléiade, 1960), 2:1246–50; cited passage, 1249: "une parfaite *machine à lire*."

128. Advertisement in Amédée Ozenfant, *Après le cubisme* (Paris: Editions des Commentaires, 1918), unpaginated; Amédée Ozenfant and Charles-Édouard Jeanneret, "Les Idées d'esprit nouveau dans les livres et la presse," *L'Esprit nouveau* 2, nos. 11–12 (1921): 1344.

129. Le Corbusier to his parents, 9 January 1919, R1(6)49, FLC: "un nouveau livre de commandé, qui s'appellera *Vers une architecture* qui sera une chose d'avant-garde."

130. Le Corbusier to Paul Laffitte, 17 February 1922, B2(7)18, FLC.

131. Le Corbusier to William Ritter, 7 April 1922, R3(19)391, FLC: "'Architecture et révolution'"; "suite des articles dans l'EN."

132. Jean Petit, *Le Corbusier lui-même* (Geneva: Rousseau, 1970), 57.

133. Le Corbusier to Georges Crès, 21 April 1922, A1(4)10, FLC.

134. Le Corbusier to George Besson, 4 January 1922, A2(11)17, FLC: "manuscrit définitif."

135. Georges Crès to Le Corbusier, 21 December 1922, B2(15)10, FLC: "un ouvrage intitulé 'l'architecture nouvelle.'"

136. Invoice from *L'Esprit nouveau* to Georges Crès, 9 January 1923, A(1)10, FLC.

137. Le Corbusier to George Besson, 3 July 1923, B2(15)16, FLC.

138. Georges Crès to Le Corbusier, 7 April 1924, A1(13)312, FLC.

139. Le Corbusier, "Introduction à la seconde édition" (note 105), vi. See Josep Quetglas, "With the Audience in Suspense," pamphlet accompanying the exhibition *Le Corbusier at Princeton 14–16 November 1935* (Princeton: Princeton University School of Architecture, 2001).

140. Le Corbusier to Georges Crès, 6 December 1928, T1(9)2, FLC.

141. Boesiger and Storonov, eds., *Le Corbusier und Pierre Jeanneret* (note 59).

142. Prospectus for *Vers une architecture*, 1923, B2(15)17, FLC: "ce livre est implacable. Il ne ressemble à aucun autre"; "outillage et esprit moderne sont au point limite de fusion; une grande période d'architecture s'ouvre. On va *vers une architecture.*"

143. Prospectus for *Vers une architecture* (note 142): "dans leur intérêt, tenues d'exiger."

144. Paul Budry, "Vers une architecture, par Le Corbusier-Saugnier," *L'Esprit nouveau* 4, no. 19 (1923): unpaginated: "[les] pures carènes de paquebots…recèlent d'immondes salons copiés sur la gare d'Orsay"; "dans les Goliath, dining et sleeping-cars, les cuivres ont des formes de pavots"; "[les] Américains à silos achètent…des basiliques romanes à planter dans leurs jardins à l'anglaise."

145. Budry, "Vers une architecture" (note 144): "[les Grecs avaient] leurs Tanagras et leurs bicoques au pied du Parthénon"; "[le propos du livre est] positif et métallique."

146. Budry, "Vers une architecture" (note 144): "ce raisonnement sur l'auto déclassera la *Prière sur l'Acropole.*"

147. Amédée Ozenfant, "Vers une architecture," *L'Esprit nouveau* 4, no. 19 (1923: unpaginated: "[un] cours d'architecture comme jamais on n'en fit"; "lumineuse démonstration"; "réaliste mais ailé"; "vieux murs mélancoliques à casser les bras"; "de nouvelles coquilles dignes des êtres vraiment nouveaux, c'est-à-dire lucides, poètes; complets enfin"; "son art est digne des volontés puristes."

148. Le Corbusier to Amédée Ozenfant, autograph dedication, 23 June 1923, photocopy of the false title page, E2(17)488, FLC: "ce livre vous est dédié en témoignage de notre amitié et en vertu de notre travail commun."

149. Le Corbusier to Amédée Ozenfant, [June 1924], with annotation by Ozenfant dated 24 June 1924, E2(17)521, FLC: "les preuves avec la dédicace rayée."

150. Le Corbusier to Amédée Ozenfant, 8 August 1924, E2(17)489, FLC: "vous auriez voulu que le livre Architecture soit de vous aussi."

151. Le Corbusier to Amédée Ozenfant, 13 August 1924, E2(17)490, FLC: |"capitale."

152. Le Corbusier to Amédée Ozenfant, 11 March 1925, E2(17)496, FLC: "fissurée." In 1929, Le Corbusier claimed that Ozenfant's name had been "restored" to the guard page; Le Corbusier, 22 March 1929, E2(17)506, FLC.

153. Amédée Ozenfant to Le Corbusier, 13 March 1926, E2(17)497, FLC:

Certes je ne l'ai pas rédigé, mais ce que vous y dites est la traduction de ce que vous et moi, vous autant que moi, c'est-à-dire *nous* disions et pensions pendant les longues années où nous collaborâmes: je n'ai jamais prétendu autre chose. D'ailleurs je n'attache aucune vanité d'auteur à des idées qui ne sont ni de vous ni de moi, mais de Loos et de Perret, ainsi que la lecture de "Ornement et crime"... le prouve; et pour ce qui est des machines, bien avant de vous connaître nous en causions presque quotidiennement avec notre ancien maître Auguste Perret et si je me suis si bien entendu avec vous, c'est que Perret (c'est Perret qui m'a fait vous connaître) — Perret vous et moi avions des idées communes.

154. Le Corbusier to Amédée Ozenfant, caricature enclosed in letter, 8 July 1932, E2(17)510, FLC (copy; original in a private collection): "alors, Corbu s'étant bien gavé, mordit le sein de sa nourrice!"

155. Amédée Ozenfant to Le Corbusier, 7 December 1928, E2(17)504, FLC: "il n'est pas d'usage qu'un des signataires de l'ouvrage dédie l'ouvrage à l'autre."

156. Le Corbusier to Christian Zervos, 6 July 1936, R3(9)87, FLC.

157. Ozenfant, *Mémoires 1886–1962* (note 4), 142–43: "Il voulait être seul. Je me retirai.... Il fut doué pour bien des choses, mais pas pour la reconnaissance, voilà tout."

158. Le Corbusier to Sigfried Giedion, 4 March 1927, 43K 1927 03-19, Giedion Archive, Institut für Geschichte und Theorie der Architektur, Eidgenössische Technische Hochschule Zürich.

159. Le Corbusier, "Température, à l'occasion de la troisième édition," in idem, *Vers une architecture* (Paris: G. Crès, 1928): xiv, xvi.

160. Ilya Ehrenburg to Le Corbusier, Berlin, 31 October [1923], A1(4)20, FLC. Petit mentions this initiative; see Petit, *Le Corbusier lui-même* (note 132), 57.

161. Ilya Ehrenburg to Le Corbusier, 12 March 1922, E2(1)52, FLC.

162. *Život II, Sborník nové krásy* (1922); and Karel Teige, "K nové architektuře," *Stavba* 2 (1923): 179–83; an English translation can be found in Karel Teige, *Modern Architecture in Czechoslovakia and Other Writings*, intro. Jean-Louis Cohen, trans. Irena Žantovská Murray and David Britt (Los Angeles: Getty Research Institute, 2000), 309–15. Le Corbusier's views are also analyzed in Oldrich Stary, "Vyvoj k nové architekture," *Stavba* 3 (1924–25): 171–80, 187–203, 205–18.

163. Karel Teige to Le Corbusier, 22 May 1925, A1(7)459, FLC.

164. The earliest of these publications is: Nakamura Junpei, "Furansu gendai toshi kenkyojo ni tsuite" (Concerning the contemporary French city research center), *Kenchiku Shincho* (New architectural currents) 5 (1924); other illustrated extracts appeared in *Kokusai Kenchiku* (International architecture) (May and June 1929), and an assessment of the translations was published by the architect and critic Kurata

Chikatada in *Kokusai Kenchiku* 5 (1929). See the discussion in Sasaki Hiroshi, *Kysho e no shokei: Re corubyujie ni miserareta nihon no kenchikuka tachi* [Ringing the bell for the master: Japanese architects bewitched by Le Corbusier] (Tokyo: Sagami, 2000).

165. Le Corbusier, *Kenchiku geijutse* [Toward artistic architecture], trans. Miyazaki Kanemitsu (Tokyo: Koseisha, 1929).

166. Le Corbusier, *Hacia una arquitectura*, trans. Luis A. Romero (Buenos Aires: El Distribuidor Americano, 1939).

167. Text preserved in the "Gebäudelehre Villen Wohnhäuser, Notizen z. Vortrage Sommersemester 25" file, Moser Archive, Institut für Geschichte und Theorie der Architektur, Eidgenössische Technische Hochschule Zürich. Moser states in his lecture of 27 July 1925: "*Vers une architecture*, welches so grosse Bedeutung gewonnen und so viel Klarheit in die Zeitausfassungen gebraucht hat."

168. Le Corbusier to Alexander Dorner, 19 February 1924, F2(14)257, FLC. On 21 February, Le Corbusier asked Crès to send him a copy; E1(17)97, FLC.

169. Roger Ginsburger to Le Corbusier, 21 January 1924, E1(17)99, FLC; 16 February 1923, E2(3)298, FLC; and 22 March 1923, E2(3)300, FLC. Le Corbusier to Roger Ginsburger, 12 February 1924, E2(3)297, FLC; and 21 February 1924, E2(3)299, FLC: "un livre qui trouverait l'intérêt le plus profond dans les pays de langue allemande et qui aiderait à éliminer de la nouvelle architecture de ces pays bien des tendances vers le décoratif et l'artificiel."

170. Le Corbusier, *Kommende Baukunst*, trans. and preface Hans Hildebrandt (Stuttgart: Deutsche Verlags-Anstalt, 1926); and Walther Rathenau, *Von kommenden Dingen* (Berlin: S. Fischer, 1918). This link was suggested to me by Stanislaus von Moos.

171. List of subscribers, A2(8)336, FLC; Le Corbusier to Hans Hildebrandt, [1923], Hans and Lily Hildebrandt Papers, 850676, box 41, folder 38, GRI.

172. Hans Hildebrandt to Le Corbusier, 26 August 1924, E2(4)522, FLC.

173. Le Corbusier to Hans Hildebrandt, 2 September 1924 (note 171):

Wasmuth . . . avait répondu que ce livre n'apportait rien de neuf en Allemagne où ces idées sont déjà connues depuis longtemps et où elles ont été largement expérimentées. Or telle n'est pas mon idée: depuis quarante ans l'Allemagne a reconstruit des villes; on a, à cette occasion, fait des théories et "*recherché le moderne*." Mais à mon avis on n'est pas allé au fond des choses de l'architecture et l'on a travaillé en surface: on a fait des style modernes (Olbrich, Behrens, Fischer, Paul, etc.). Et l'on continue aujourd'hui, sur des formules plus près de la construction, mais là encore, on est sentimental et l'on fait des démonstrations de style moderne, on fait des objets de parade moderne. En France évidemment mon livre au contraire devait frapper plus violemment—et durement peut-être—les professionels de l'architecture; mais par ailleurs il touchait toute une couche de gens exercés à l'esprit moderne par la pratique et le sens qu'ils avaient de la construction. Mais persuasion est que l'architecture moderne naîtra en France. Je ne voudrais pas avoir l'air exclusif, mais la carrière d'un Behrens est typique, celle de Poelzig est démonstrative, etc.

Crès later attempted to convince Wasmuth to publish a translation of *Urbanisme*: Le Corbusier to Gertrud Grohman, 18 November 1925, B3(6)102, FLC.

174. Le Corbusier to Hans Hildebrandt, [autumn 1924], E2(4)526, FLC; and 22 November 1924 (note 171).

175. Le Corbusier to Hans Hildebrandt, 31 December 1924; E2(04)528, FLC.

176. Le Corbusier to Hans Hildebrandt, 2 March 1925, E2(04)532, FLC; Hans Hildebrandt to Le Corbusier, 15 January 1925, E2(04)589, FLC; Le Corbusier to Hans Hildebrandt, 26 February 1925 (note 171); and Le Corbusier to Hans Hildebrandt, postcard, 4 December 1926 (note 171).

177. Le Corbusier to Hans Hildebrandt, 26 March 1925 (note 171):

je trouve qu'il est indispensable que la typographie de l'ouvrage soit tout à fait semblable à celle de l'édition française et vous m'obligeriez en demandant à votre imprimeur de me soumettre un échantillon des caractères qu'il emploiera; il est très important que ce livre ait sa présentation typographique conforme à l'esprit du texte.

178. Hans Hildebrandt to Le Corbusier, 6 November 1925 (note 171), with autograph annotations by Le Corbusier on the original that he sent back to Hildebrandt: "poison mondain."

179. Le Corbusier to Hans Hildebrandt, 17 April 1926 (note 171): "Ozenfant se persuade de jour en jour qu'il a pensé et dit ce que j'ai écrit, à un tel point que j'avais été conduit à lui dédier V[ers] u[ne] Arch[itecture] afin d'ôter ainsi toute vraisemblance à cette prétention."

180. Le Corbusier to Hans Hildebrandt, 22 December 1936 (note 171): "de l'argot d'atelier"; contrary to what an "ancien ami ... pratiquant le mensonge avec un tel sang-froid qu'il [lui] a été impossible de continuer à partager les soucis et les plaisirs d'une entreprise avec lui" had maintained.

181. Muthesius, *Stilarchitektur und Baukunst* (note 23).

182. Le Corbusier, *Ausblick auf eine Architektur*, rev. trans. Eva Gärtner (Frankfurt: Ullstein, 1963). Includes Le Corbusier's preface to the 1958 edition.

183. Hans Hildebrandt to Le Corbusier, 6 November 1925 (note 171): "lettres en bloc des titres."

184. Le Corbusier to Hans Hildebrandt, 24 July 1926 (note 171): "le dollar leur permet des conditions qui me consolent de celles faites par Deutsch Verlag [sic]."

185. G. Crès to Le Corbusier, 8 February 1924, B1(17)96, FLC.

186. Amédée Ozenfant, *Foundations of Modern Art*, trans. John Rodker (London: John Rodker, 1931); original ed., *Art* (Paris: Paul Budry, 1928). Rodker's name appears on the list of subscribers to *L'Esprit nouveau*, A2(9)532, FLC, and he published "La littérature anglaise d'aujourd'hui," *L'Esprit nouveau* 2, no. 4 (1921): 476–77. On Rodker (1894–1955), see James Dunnett, "Words of Wisdom," *Building Design*, no. 838 (1987): 18–19.

187. On Etchells (1886–1973), see the obituary by John Betjeman, *The Architectural Review*, no. 154 (1973): 271, 273; and Dinah Adams, "Frederick Etchells, Artist and Architect" (diploma thesis, The Architectural Association, London, 1977).

188. "Crawford's, nos. 232–34, High Holborn, London," *The Architectural Review*, no. 69 (1931): 51.

189. G. W. O. Addleshaw and Frederick Etchells, *The Architectural Setting of Anglican Worship* (London: Faber & Faber, 1948).

190. Frederick Etchells, "Le Corbusier: A Pioneer of Modern European Architecture," *Studio*, no. 96 (1928): 156–63. Even before the term was used by Hitchcock, it figured in an article published the very same year: "Modern Architecture. II. The New Pioneers," *The Architectural Record* 63, no. 5 (1928), 452–60.

191. Le Corbusier, *Towards a New Architecture*, trans. and intro Frederick Etchells (London: John Rodker, 1927), xvi, 16 n.1.

192. Mardges Bacon, *Le Corbusier in America: Travels in the Land of the Timids* (Cambridge: MIT Press, 2001), 331.

193. Henry-Russell Hitchcock and Philip Johnson, *The International Style: Architecture since 1922* (New York: W. W. Norton, 1932), 40–49.

194. Le Corbusier, *Vers une architecture* (1924), 196; Le Corbusier, *Towards a New Architecture* (note 191), 263.

195. The fiftieth anniversary of its publication was commemorated by Phil Windsor, "How Wrong Was Corbusier?" *The Architect* 7 (1977): 36–37.

196. Le Corbusier to A. Yvonneau, 5 January 1923, R3(9)49, FLC. Yvonneau asks him to design buildings in Blois.

197. Henri Frugès to Le Corbusier, 3 November 1923, H1(17)1, FLC.

198. Le Corbusier to Marcel Poëte, 10 November 1923, A2(15)19, FLC; and Le Corbusier to Eduard Beneš, 21 October 1923, R(09)151, FLC.

199. Jacques-Émile Blanche to Le Corbusier, postcard, 1 August 1925, E1(8)24, FLC.

200. Joseph Abram (untitled paper presented at the IFA, 24 November 2001).

201. Guillaume Baderre, "M. Auguste Perret nous parle de l'architecture au Salon d'automne," *Paris-Journal*, 7 December 1923. This occasioned Le Corbusier's break with his elder colleague; see Le Corbusier to Auguste Perret, 13 December 1923, E1(11)239, FLC; repr. in Le Corbusier, *Lettres à ses maîtres*, vol. 1 (note 14), 212–15. On the conflict between the positions expressed in *Vers une architecture* and by Perret, see Peter Collins, *Concrete: The Vision of a New Architecture; A Study of Auguste Perret and His Precursors* (London: Faber & Faber, 1959), 186, 213, 219.

202. Pol Abraham, "'Vers une architecture' par Le Corbusier-Saugnier," *L'Architecte* 1, no. 2 (1924): 9–12.

203. Michel Roux-Spitz declared to Le Corbusier that he was a "reader of your book on architecture"; see Michel Roux-Spitz to Le Corbusier, 2 April 1924, A1(10)289, FLC: "lecteur de votre ouvrage sur l'architecture."

204. André Lurçat, *Architecture* (Paris: Au Sans Pareil, 1929), 164, 170: "la plus subtile et la plus difficile, science de l'architecte." See Jean-Louis Cohen, *André Lurçat (1894–1970), autocritique d'un moderne* (Paris: Institut français d'architecture, 1995), 94–103.

205. Miloutine Borissavliévitch, *Les théories de l'architecture* (Paris: Payot, 1926), 11: "Livre curieux, mais qui n'est pas une 'Esthétique.'"

206. Élie Faure, *Histoire de l'art*, vol. 4, *L'art moderne*, in idem, *Oeuvres complètes*, 3 vols. (Paris: Pauvert, 1964), 2:15; original ed. (Paris: G. Crès, 1923), xvii: "la machine, qui est architecture … est universelle"; "l'usine et la machine vont donner à la face de la planète la forme unique de l'esprit."

207. Faure, *L'esprit des formes* (note 125), 98: "admirer la nécessité bienfaisante

de l'effort"; "à substituer partout l'abstraction géometrique anthropocentriste à l'empirisme climatique et ethnique."

208. Élie Faure to Frantz Jourdain, n.d., Élie Faure, *Oeuvres complètes,* 3 vols. (Paris: Pauvert, 1964), 3:1114–15: "bien plutôt comme un métaphysicien que comme un architecte, un praticien"; "[il] combat la marotte Lecorbusiéresque (si je puis dire) du tracé régulateur" and "l'*industrialisation excessive* de l'architecture."

209. Marie Dormoy, *L'architecture française* (Boulogne: Éditions de "l'Architecture d'aujourd'hui," 1938), unpaginated: "violent réquisitoire contre le pastiche, la copie, l'inintelligence dans l'emploi des moyens techniques maintenant à notre disposition"; "purifié l'air"; "dissimulation de la construction"; "place prépondérante."

210. Adolf Behne, "Architekten," *Frühlicht* 2 (1921–22): 57; Adolf Behne, "Junge französische Architektur," *Sozialistische Monatshefte* 58, nos. 12–13 (1922): 512–17.

211. Paul Westheim, "Architektur in Frankreich, Le Corbusier-Saugnier," *Wasmuths Monatshefte für Baukunst* 7, nos. 3–4 (1923): 69–82: "einen entschlossenen Kampf"; "schlagende Abbildungsbeispielen"; "Glorifizierung des technischen Denkens und des Ingenieurschaffens"; "rückhaltlosen Begeisterung"; "Ingenieursachlichkeit"; "ist plastische Gestaltung, ist geistige Spekulation, ist höhere Mathematik."

212. Walter Gropius to Le Corbusier, 13 November 1923, R3(4)381, FLC.

213. Walter Gropius to Le Corbusier, 17 March 1924, E2(11)15, FLC: "Sie haben im Wesentlichen gegen meine Bauhaus-Intentionen Stellung genommen. Ich habe noch keinen Veröffentlichung gelesen, die im Grundkern dem so nahe kommt, was ich selbst gedacht und geschrieben habe, als Ihr Buch."; Le Corbusier, "Curiosité? Non: anomalie!" *L'Esprit nouveau* 2, no. 9 (1921): 1016–17; and Le Corbusier, "Pédagogie," *L'Esprit nouveau* 4, no. 19 (1923).

214. G. Rietveld, "Nieuwe Zakelijkheid in de Nederlandsche architectuur," *De Vrije Bladen* 9, no. 7 (1932): 1–27; repr. in Marijke Küper and Ida van Zijl, eds., *Gerrit Th[omas] Rietveld: The Complete Works* (Utrecht: Centraal Museum, 1992), 33–39. On the Dutch reception of Le Corbusier, see Robert Mens, "Le Corbusier en de Nederlandse architectuur (1920–1940)," in Paul Blom, ed., *La France aux Pays-Bas: Invloeden in het verleden* (Vianen: Kwadraat, 1985), 241–77; Robert Mens, "Documenten rondom Le Corbusier, 1920–1965," in Robert Mens, Bart Lootsma, and Jos Bosman, *Le Corbusier en Nederland* (Utrecht: Kwadraat, 1985), 9–84.

215. W. van Gelderen, "Le Corbusier: schilder, schrijver, architect en stedebouwer," *Bouw* (1947): 32.

216. Alfred Boeken, "Over den architect Le Corbusier," *Bouwkundig Weekblad Architectura* 5, no. 15 (1930): 122; and Alfred Boeken, *Architectuur* (Amsterdam: Van Holkema & Warendorf N.V., 1936). See also his correspondence: Alfred Boeken to Le Corbusier, postcard, 13 March 1924, E1(08)73, FLC; and Le Corbusier to Alfred Boeken, 18 March 1924, FLC, E1(08)74.

217. Nina Yavorskaia, "Corbusier-Saugnier, K voprosam arkhitektury," *Pechat i Revolyutsiia,* no. 55 (1924): 296–97. See Jean-Louis Cohen, *Le Corbusier and the Mystique of the USSR* (Princeton: Princeton Univ. Press, 1992), 22–24.

218. Moisei Ginzburg, *Stil' i epokha, prohblemy sovremennoi arkhitektury* (Moscow: Gosudarstvennoi Izdatelstvo, 1924); translated as *Style and Epoch,* ed. and trans. Anatole Senkevitch Jr. (Cambridge: MIT Press, 1982).

219. See the copy of Moisei Ginzburg, *Stil' i epokha,* inscribed with a dedication to "Monsieur Le Corbusier-Saugnier": V 191, FLC.

220. Theo van Doesburg and Cor van Eesteren, "Vers une construction collective," *De Stijl* 6, nos. 6–7 (1924): 89–92; Theo van Doesburg, "Tot een beeldende Architectuur, *De Stijl* 6, nos. 6–7 (1924): 78–83.

221. On the relations between Le Corbusier and van Doesburg, see Yve-Alain Bois and Nancy Troy, "De Stijl et l'architecture à Paris," in Bruno Reichlin and Yve-Alain Bois, eds., *De Stijl et l'architecture en France* (Liège: Mardaga, 1985), 25–90.

222. J. J. P. Oud, "'Vers une architecture' van Le Corbusier-Saugnier," *Bouwkundig Weekblad* 45, no. 9 (1924): 90–94.

223. Theo van Doesburg, "Alphabetische informatie," *De Stijl* 6, no. 8 (1924): 107–10.

224. Frank Lloyd Wright, "In the Cause of Architecture: Purely Personal" (1928), in Bruce Brooks Pfeiffer, ed., *The Collected Writings of Frank Lloyd Wright,* 5 vols. (New York: Rizzoli in association with the Frank Lloyd Wright Foundation, 1992), 1:255–58.

225. Frank Lloyd Wright, "Towards a New Architecture," *World Unity* 2, no. 6 (1928): 393–95; published in Pfeiffer, ed., *Collected Writings* (note 224), 1:317–18.

226. Frank Lloyd Wright, "Modern Architecture, Being the Kahn Lectures; 4: The Cardboard House," in Bruce Brooks Pfeiffer, ed., *The Collected Writings of Frank Lloyd Wright,* 5 vols. (New York: Rizzoli in association with the Frank Lloyd Wright Foundation, 1992), 2:51–59.

227. Lewis Mumford, *The Human Prospect* (Boston: Beacon, 1955), 213.

228. Richard Buckminster Fuller, "Universal Architecture," *Shelter* 2, no. 1 (1932): 22–23; Richard Buckminster Fuller, *Utopia or Oblivion, the Prospects for Humanity* (Toronto: Bantam, 1969), 408.

229. Steen Eiler Rasmussen, "Le Corbusier, die kommende Baukunst?" *Wasmuths Monatshefte für Baukunst* 10, no. 9 (1926): 381, 386.

230. Alexei Shchusev, untitled article, *Stroitelnnaia Promyshlennost* 2, no. 12 (1924): 760–62.

231. Alexander de Senger, *Le Cheval de Troie du bolchvisme* (Bienne: Editions du Chandelier, 1931).

232. Mario Manieri Elia, "La 'scuola romana' l'altro ieri e oggi," in *Principi e metodi della storia dell'architettura e l'eredita della 'scuola romana'* (Rome: Centro Stampa Ateneo, 1995), 57.

233. Marcello Piacentini, "Esthétique de l'ingénieur. Maisons en série. Articolo di Le Corbusier-Saugnier in uno degli ultimi numeri de *L'Esprit nouveau,*" *Architettura e arti decorative* 2, no. 6 (1922–23): 220, 222–23.

234. Paul-Philippe Cret, "The Architect as Collaborator with the Engineer," *Architectural Forum* 49, no. 1 (1928): 101.

235. A. S. G. Butler, "M. Le Corbusier's Book," *RIBA Journal* 35, ser. 3, no. 8 (1928): 269.

236. Edwin Lutyens, "The Robotism of Architecture," *The Observer,* 29 January 1928.

237. Julius Posener, *Fast so alt wie das Jahrhundert* (Berlin: Siedler, 1990), 196.

238. Carlo Enrico Rava to Le Corbusier, 20 January 1927, E2(20)156, FLC.

239. Gruppo "7," "Architettura," *La Rassegna italiana*, no. 103 (1926): 849.

240. Carla Sonego, "Carlo Scarpa, gli anni di formazione" (diploma thesis, Istituto universitario di architettura di Venezia, 1995), 99.

241. J. M. Richards, *Memoirs of an Unjust Fella* (London: Weidenfeld & Nicholson, 1980), 43.

242. Maxwell Fry, quoted in "Le Corbusier—His Impact on Four Generations," *RIBA Journal* 72, no. 10 (1965): 497.

243. John Summerson, "This Age in Architecture," *The Bookman* 83, no. 493 (1932): 13–14; John Summerson, "Modernity in Architecture: An Appeal for the New Style," *The Scotsman*, 21 February 1930.

244. Tange Kenzô, "Michelangelo shô—Le Corbusier ron he no josetu toschite" [Homage to Michelangelo: Introduction to the Study of Le Corbusier], *Gendai Kenchiku* (December 1939); unpublished translation by Benoit Jacquet.

245. Henry-Russell Hitchcock, "The Architect's Library: *Towards a New Architecture*," *The Architectural Record* 63, no. 1 (1928): 90–91. Rhys Carpenter was a professor at Bryn Mawr College and an archaeologist who had published at that time; see Rhys Carpenter, *The Esthetic Basis of the Greek Art of the Fifth and Fourth Centuries B.C.* (New York: Longmans, Greens, 1921).

246. Max Abramovitz, interview with Mardges Bacon, 1987; quoted in Bacon, *Le Corbusier in America* (note 192), 92.

247. "La position de Le Corbusier et Jeanneret dans l'évolution de l'architecture d'aujourd'hui, opinion de J. Ll. Sert," *L'architecture d'aujourd'hui* 4, no. 10 (1933): 11: "dévoré"; "une révélation pour les jeunes qui travaillaient alors dans les écoles des Beaux-arts.... Tout d'un coup, quelqu'un qui parlait clairement, une ligne générale bien précise se montrait. Peu de phrases et quelques exemples photographiques"; Jordi Oliveras y Samitier, "Le Corbusier a Barcelona; les viatges de Le Corbusier a Barcelona i els viatges per Espanya," in Fernando Marzá, ed., *Le Corbusier y Barcelona* (Barcelona: Fundació Caixa de Catalunya, 1988), 19; John Peter, *The Oral History of Modern Architecture: Interviews with the Greatest Architects of the Twentieth Century* (New York: Abrams, 1994), 249.

248. Josep Torres Clavé, "La arquitectura moderna" (lecture, Sala Niu d'Art, Barcelona, 22 December 1929), published in Ramon Torres Clavé, *Torres Clavé* (Barcelona: UPC/Santa & Colle, 1994), 249.

249. Ugo Segawa, *Arquiteturas no Brasil 1900–1990* (São Paulo: EDUSP, 1999), 51–52, 77–78.

250. See Anthony Vidler, "Histories of the Immediate Present: Inventing Architectural Modernism, 1930–1975" (Ph.D. diss., Technische Universiteit, Delft, 2005), 47.

251. Emil Kauffmann, *Von Ledoux bis Le Corbusier. Ursprung und Entwicklung der autonomen Architektur* (Vienna: Rolf Passer, 1933), 63.

252. Anthony Blunt, "Mannerism in Architecture," *Journal of the RIBA* 56, ser. 3, no. 5 (1949): 199; Vidler, "Histories of the Immediate Present" (note 250), 91.

253. Colin Rowe, *As I Was Saying: Recollections and Miscellaneous Essays*, vol. 1 (Cambridge: MIT Press, 1996), 137; Vidler, "Histories of the Immediate Present" (note 250), 89.

254. Graham Whitham, "Chronology," in David Robbins, ed., *The Independent Group: Postwar Britain and the Aesthetics of Plenty* (Cambridge: MIT Press, 1990), 27.

255. Reyner Banham, *Los Angeles: The Architecture of Four Ecologies* (London: Penguin, 1971). Vidler, "Histories of the Immediate Present" (note 250), 151–57.

256. Le Corbusier to Hélène Strassova, note, 5 February 1955, G2(18)132, FLC.

257. See de Smet, "Le livre comme synthèse des arts" (note 114), 318–24.

258. Since 1990, translations have been published in Portuguese, Hungarian, Finnish, Greek, Turkish, Norwegian, Czech, Korean, Hebrew, and Dutch.

COLLECTION DE "L'ESPRIT NOUVEAU"

LE CORBUSIER

VERS UNE ARCHITECTURE

NOUVELLE ÉDITION REVUE ET AUGMENTÉE

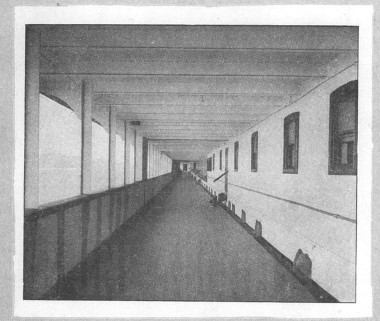

LES ÉDITIONS G. CRÈS ET Cie

11, RUE DE SÈVRES (VIe)

PARIS

2e ÉDITION

INTRODUCTION TO THE SECOND EDITION

When, less than a year ago, the first edition of this work appeared, interest in architectural things was stirring everywhere. Most of these chapters, published previously as articles in *L'Esprit nouveau,* made for a sudden stocktaking: people talked, liked to talk, wanted to be able to talk Architecture. The consequence of a profound social movement. A general passion for architecture had likewise arisen in the eighteenth century: bourgeois designed architecture, senior civil servants too, Blondel, Claude Perrault, the Porte Saint-Denis, the Louvre colonnade. And the country was completely covered with works attesting to this spirit.

The way the present book made an impact not only on professionals but also on the public confirms the advent of an architectural cycle. A public indifferent to studio questions concerns itself only with the idea of a new architecture that affords it a comfort already glimpsed in different terms (automotive tourism, ocean cruises, etc.), but above all the satisfaction of a new feeling. What is this new feeling and where does it come from? It is the bursting forth, after an extended germination, of the architectural meaning of the era. A new era — fallow spiritual territory — with a need to build *its house. A house that will be this human boundary that encloses us and separates us from antagonistic natural phenomena, giving us, we men, our human milieu.* The need to fulfill an instinctive aspiration, to realize a natural function. To do architecture! This is not just a matter of the technical work of professionals. It is characteristic changes of direction, impulsive movements of the shared idea, that demonstrate in what mode it means to organize its acts.

Thus does architecture become a mirror of the times.

The architecture of today concerns itself with the house, with the ordinary and common house for normal and common men. It lets palaces alone. Here is a sign of the times.

To study the house for the common man, for "all and sundry," is to recover human foundations: the human scale, the typical need, the typical function, the *typical emotion*. There you have it! That's crucial, that's everything. A period of dignity comes into view, one in which man has left pomp behind!

* * *

This book is written in bold strokes. How to talk about architecture with elegant detachment, about architecture as resulting from the spirit of an era, at a time when this spirit is still obscured by the unbearable rags of a dying era?

Why this way, of course: to pass beyond the leaden sheath that crushes, by hurling darts that pierce it, so many pickax blows that make holes in the heavy sheath. By making holes. So, a hole here, a hole there. Here are views! We have views beyond the stifling leaden sheath. By offering views, by breaking through. A useful, efficient strategy. I have rallied to this tactic, all but inescapable anyway.

This book being printed a second time, it was still necessary to complete it, it was necessary to expand the terrain around the breakthroughs already achieved. To do so in this new edition would have amounted to making another book. So I have left this one intact and I have made two other books that are like right and left wings. Simultaneously with the new edition of *Vers une architecture,* the same press will publish *Urbanisme* and *L'art décoratif d'aujour-d'hui,* two cycles of ideas that, in the course of the past year, I covered in *L'Esprit nouveau,* this review of contemporary activity that puts the many faces of the modern event side by side and makes out of them a figure that is clear, concordant, convincing, a figure whose firm male face calls forth our sympathy, calls forth our support and the efficient work of our hands and our minds.

Thus *Vers une architecture,* issued just last year, continues its journey this year flanked by two far-flung supports — on one side, the urban architectural phenomenon, whereby architecture situates itself; on the other side, what has come to be called by the sad phrase "decorative art" — whereby we ought to find, at hand and accompanying all our actions, the constant presence of an architectural spirit keeping us as much under the spell of the senses as in a state of virile dignity.

November 1924

ARGUMENT

AESTHETIC OF THE ENGINEER
ARCHITECTURE

Aesthetic of the Engineer, Architecture: two things firmly allied, sequential, the one in full flower, the other in painful regression.

The engineer, inspired by the law of Economy and guided by calculations, puts us in accord with universal laws. He attains harmony.

The architect, through the ordonnance of forms, realizes an order that is a pure creation of his mind; through forms, he affects our senses intensely, provoking plastic emotions; through the relationships that he creates, he stirs in us deep resonances, he gives us the measure of an order that we sense to be in accord with that of the world, he determines the diverse movements of our minds and our hearts; it is then that we experience beauty.

THREE REMINDERS TO ARCHITECTS

VOLUME

Our eyes are made for seeing forms in light.

Primary forms are beautiful forms because they are clearly legible.

The architects of today no longer make simple forms.

Relying on calculations, engineers use geometric forms, satisfying our eyes through geometry and our minds through mathematics; their works are on the way to great art.

A volume is enveloped by a surface, a surface that is divided according to the generators and the directing vectors of the volume, accentuating the individuality of this volume.

Architects today are afraid of the geometric constituents of surfaces.

The great problems of modern construction will be solved through geometry.

Under strict obligation to an imperative program, engineers use the directing vectors and accentuators of forms. They create limpid and impressive plastic facts.

PLAN

The plan is the generator.

Without a plan, there is disorder, arbitrariness.

The plan carries within it the essence of the sensation.

The great problems of tomorrow, dictated by collective needs, pose the question of the plan anew.

Modern life demands, awaits a new plan for the house and for the city.

REGULATING LINES

Of the fateful birth of architecture.

The obligation to order. The regulating line is a guarantee against arbitrariness. It brings satisfaction to the mind.

The regulating line is a means; it is not a formula. Its choices and its expressive modalities are integral parts of architectural creation.

EYES THAT DO NOT SEE

LINERS

A great era has just begun.

There exists a new spirit.

There exists a host of works in this new spirit, they are encountered above all in industrial production.

Architecture suffocates in routine.

The "styles" are a lie. Style is a unity of principle that animates all the works of an era and results from a distinctive state of mind.

Our era fixes its style every day.

Our eyes, unfortunately, arc not yet able to discern it.

AIRPLANES

The airplane is a product of high selection.

The lesson of the airplane is in the logic that governed the statement of the problem and its realization.

The problem of the house has not been posed.

Current architectural things do not answer to our needs.

Yet there are standards for the dwelling.

The mechanical carries within it the economic factor that selects.

The house is a machine for living in.

AUTOMOBILES

We must see to the establishment of standards so we can face up to the problem of perfection.

The Parthenon is a product of selection applied to a standard.

Architecture works on standards.

Standards are a matter of logic, of analysis, of scrupulous study; they are based on a problem well posed. Experimentation fixes the standard definitively.

ARCHITECTURE

THE LESSON OF ROME

Architecture is the use of raw materials to establish stirring relationships.

Architecture goes beyond utilitarian things.

Architecture is a plastic thing.

Spirit of order, unity of intention.

The sense of relationships; architecture organizes quantities.

Passion can make drama out of inert stone.

The plan proceeds from the inside out; the exterior is the result of an interior.

The elements of architecture are light and shadow, walls and space.

Ordonnance is the hierarchy of goals, the classification of intentions.

Man sees architectural things with eyes that are 1 meter 70 from the ground. We can reckon only with goals accessible to the eye, with intentions that take the elements of architecture into account. If we reckon with intentions that do not belong to the language of architecture, we end up with an illusory plan; we break the rules of the plan through faulty conception or a penchant for vain things.

PURE CREATION OF THE MIND

Contour modulation is the touchstone of the architect.

The latter reveals himself as artist or mere engineer.

Contour modulation is free of all constraint.

It is no longer a question of routine, nor of traditions, nor of construction methods, nor of adaptation to utilitarian needs.

Contour modulation is a pure creation of the mind; it calls for the plastic artist.

MASS-PRODUCTION HOUSING

A great era has just begun.

There exists a new spirit.

Industry, invading like a river that rolls to its destiny, brings us new tools adapted to this new era animated by a new spirit.

The law of Economy necessarily governs our actions and our conceptions.

The problem of the house is a problem of the era. Social equilibrium depends on it today. The first obligation of architecture, in an era of renewal, is to bring about a revision of values, a revision of the constitutive elements of the house.

Mass production is based on analysis and experimentation.

Heavy industry should turn its attention to building and standardize the elements of the house.

We must create a mass-production state of mind,

A state of mind for building mass-production housing,

A state of mind for living in mass-production housing,

A state of mind for conceiving mass-production housing.

If we wrest from our hearts and minds static conceptions of the house and envision the question from a critical and objective point of view, we will come to the house-tool, the mass-production house that is healthy (morally, too) and beautiful from the aesthetic of the work tools that go with our existence.

Beautiful too from all the life that the artistic sense can bring to strict and pure organs.

ARCHITECTURE OR REVOLUTION

In every domain of industry, new problems have been posed and tools capable of solving them have been created. If we set this fact against the past, there is revolution.

In building, the factory production of standardized parts has begun; on the basis of new economic necessities, part elements and ensemble elements have been created; conclusive realizations have been achieved in parts and in ensembles. If we set ourselves against the past, there is revolution in the methods and the magnitude of enterprises.

Whereas the history of architecture evolves slowly over the centuries in terms of structure and decor, in the last fifty years iron and cement have brought gains that are the index of a great power to build and the index of an architecture whose code is in upheaval. If we set ourselves against the past, we determine that the "styles" no longer exist for us, that the style of an era has been elaborated; there has been a revolution.

Consciously or unconsciously, minds have become aware of these events; consciously or unconsciously, needs are born.

The social mechanism, deeply disturbed, oscillates between improvements of historical importance and catastrophe.

It is the primal instinct of every living thing to secure a shelter. The various working classes of society no longer have suitable shelter, neither laborers nor intellectuals.

It is a question of building that is key to the equilibrium upset today: architecture or revolution.

Garabit Bridge (Eiffel, engineer)

AESTHETIC OF THE ENGINEER ARCHITECTURE

Aesthetic of the Engineer, Architecture: two things firmly allied, sequential, the one in full flower, the other in painful regression.

The engineer, inspired by the law of Economy and guided by calculations, puts us in accord with universal laws. He attains harmony.

The architect, through the ordonnance of forms, realizes an order that is a pure creation of his mind; through forms, he affects our senses intensely, provoking plastic emotions; through the relationships that he creates, he stirs in us deep resonances, he gives us the measure of an order that we sense to be in accord with that of the world, he determines the diverse movements of our minds and our hearts; it is then that we experience beauty.

Aesthetic of the Engineer, Architecture: two things firmly allied, sequential, the one in full flower, the other in painful regression.

————————

A question of morality. Lying is intolerable. We perish by lying.

Architecture is one of the most urgent needs of man, since the house has always been the indispensable and first tool that he forged for himself. The tools of man mark the stages of civilization, the Stone Age, the Bronze Age, the Iron Age. Tools advance by successive improvements; they are the sum of the work of generations. Tools are direct and immediate expressions of progress; tools are necessary helpmates; they are liberators, too. We throw old tools onto the scrap heap: the blunderbuss, the culverin, the carriage, and the old locomotive. This gesture is a manifestation of health, of moral health, also of morality; we do not have the right to produce badly because of bad tools; we do not have the right to use up our strength, our health and our courage because of bad tools; we throw out, we replace.

———————

But men live in old houses and have not yet dreamed of building their own houses. The home is dear to their hearts, always has been. So much so that they established a sacred cult of the home. A *roof!* other household gods. Religions are built on dogmas, dogmas do not change; civilizations change; religions crumble to dust. Houses have not changed. The religion of houses has remained identical for centuries. The house will crumble.

———————

A man who practices a religion and does not believe in it is a coward; he is unhappy. We are unhappy living in unworthy houses because they ruin our health and our morale. We have become sedentary beings, that is our lot. The house eats away at us in our immobility, like consumption. We will soon need too many sanatoria. We are unhappy. Our houses disgust us; we flee from them and frequent cafés and dance halls; or we gather glum and skulking in houses like sad animals. We become demoralized.

———————

Engineers construct the tools of their time. Everything, except the houses and rotten boudoirs.

———————

There is a great national school for architects and there are, in all countries, national, regional, municipal schools for architects that muddle young minds and teach them the falsehood, fakery, obsequiousness of courtiers. National schools!

Engineers are healthy and virile, active and useful, moral and joyful. Architects are disenchanted and idle, boastful or morose. That is because they will soon have nothing to do. *We have no more money* to pile up historical keepsakes. We need to cleanse ourselves.

Engineers are equipped for this and they will build.

———————

Nevertheless there is ARCHITECTURE. An admirable thing, the most beautiful. The product of happy peoples and what happy peoples produce.

Happy cities have architecture.

Architecture is in the telephone and in the Parthenon. How comfortable it might be in our houses! Our houses make streets and streets make cities and cities, they're individuals who take on a soul, who feel, suffer, and admire. How well architecture might be in the streets and in the whole city!

––––––––––

The diagnosis is clear.

Engineers make architecture, since they use calculations that issue from the laws of nature, and their works make us feel HARMONY. So there is an aesthetic of the engineer, because when doing calculations, it is necessary to qualify certain terms of the equation, and what intervenes is taste. Now when one does calculations, one is in a pure state of mind and, in that state of mind, taste follows reliable paths.

Architects issuing from the Schools, those hothouses where they fabricate blue hydrangeas and green chrysanthemums, where they cultivate unclean orchids, enter the city with the minds of milkmen who would sell their milk mixed with vitriol, with poison.

People still believe, here and there, in architects, just as people blindly believe in doctors. Houses have to stand up! Art, according to Larousse, is the application of knowledge to the realization of a conception. But today it is engineers who *know how,* who know how to make things stand up, how to heat, how to ventilate, how to illuminate. Isn't that so?

The diagnosis: to begin at the beginning, the engineer who proceeds from knowledge shows the way and grasps the truth. Architecture, which is a thing of plastic emotion, should, in its domain, ALSO BEGIN AT THE BEGINNING, and USE ELEMENTS CAPABLE OF STRIKING OUR SENSES, OF SATISFYING OUR VISUAL DESIRES, and arrange them in such a way THAT THE SIGHT OF THEM CLEARLY AFFECTS US through finesse or brutality, tumult or serenity, indifference or interest. These elements are plastic elements, forms that our eyes see clearly, that our minds measure. These forms, which are primary or subtle, supple or brutal, act on our senses physiologically (sphere, cone, cylinder, horizontal, vertical, oblique, etc.) and shake them up. Being affected, we are able to perceive beyond raw sensation; then certain relations will come into being that act on our consciousness and put us in a state of bliss (consonance with the laws of the universe that govern us and to which all of our acts are subject), in which man makes full use of his gifts of memory, of examination, of reasoning, of creation.

Architecture today no longer remembers what got it started.

Architects make styles or talk structure to excessive length; the client and the public respond according to visual habit and reason on the basis of an inadequate education. Our exterior world has been formidably transformed in its appearance and its use owing to the machine. We have a new vision and a new social life, but we have not adapted the house accordingly.

———

So there is reason to pose the problem of the house, the street, and the city and to compare the architect and the engineer.

For the architect, we wrote "THREE REMINDERS":

VOLUME, which is the element through which our senses perceive and measure and are fully affected.

SURFACE, which is the envelope of the volume and which can annihilate sensation or amplify it.

PLAN, which is the generator of volume and surface and which irrevocably determines everything.

Then, still for the architect, "REGULATING LINES," showing one of the means whereby architecture achieves that sensory mathematics that gives us a beneficial perception of order. We wanted to set out some facts here that are worth more than dissertations on the soul of stones. We remained within the physics of the work, *within knowledge.*

We thought about the inhabitants of the house and about the crowds of the city. We know well that much of the current misfortune of architecture is due to the *client,* to he who commissions, chooses, corrects, and pays. For him, we wrote: "EYES THAT DO NOT SEE."

We know too many great industrialists, bankers, and merchants who say to us: "Sorry, I'm just a businessman, I live totally outside the arts, I'm a philistine." We protested and said to them:

"All your energies are directed toward the magnificent goal of forging the tools of an era and creating throughout the world that host of very beautiful things wherein reigns the law of Economy, mathematical calculation combined with boldness and imagination. Look at what you have done; it is, strictly speaking, beautiful."

These same industrialists, bankers, and merchants, we have seen them away from their businesses, in their homes, where everything seemed to thwart their being — walls too close together, clutters of useless and disparate objects, and a repulsive spirit that presided over so many falsehoods by way of Aubusson and the Salon d'automne, in all manner of styles and ridiculous trinkets. They seemed sheepish and diminished, like tigers in a cage; one sensed clearly that they were happier at the factory or their bank. In the name of the liner, the airplane, and the automobile, we demanded logic, boldness, harmony, perfection.

Our meaning is clear. These are evident truths. It is no trifling matter to hasten the cleansing.

It will be agreeable finally to talk ARCHITECTURE after so many silos, factories, machines, and skyscrapers. ARCHITECTURE is an artistic fact, an emotional phenomenon that is outside questions of construction, beyond them. Construction: THAT'S FOR MAKING THINGS HOLD TOGETHER; Architecture: THAT'S FOR STIRRING EMOTION. Architectural emotion: that's when the work resounds inside us in tune with a universe whose laws we are subject to, recognize, and admire. When certain relationships are achieved, we are apprehended by the work. Architecture is a matter of "relationships," a "pure creation of the mind."

Today, painting has gotten ahead of the other arts.

It is the first to become attuned to the era (1). Modern painting has left the wall, tapestries, and decorative urns to enclose itself within a frame, nourished, filled with facts, far from a figuration that distracts; it lends itself to meditation. Art no

(1) We have in mind the crucial advances brought about by cubism and subsequent experiment, not the lamentable decline that for two years has taken hold of painters thrown into disarray by the slump and indoctrinated by critics as ill informed as they are insensitive (1921).

longer tells stories, it prompts meditation; after labor, it is good to meditate.

On the one hand, masses of people await decent dwelling places, and this is among the most fiercely pressing questions of the day.

On the other hand, the man of initiative, of action, of thought, the FOREMAN, demands that his meditation be sheltered in a space that is serene and solid, a matter essential to the health of elites.

Painters and sculptors, champions of the art of today, you who have to endure so much mockery and who suffer from so much indifference, cleanse our houses, join together so that we might rebuild the cities. Then your works will find their place within the framework of the era and everywhere you will be accepted and understood. Tell yourselves that architecture needs your attention. Be mindful of architecture.

PISA.

Grain silo.

THREE REMINDERS TO
ARCHITECTS

I

VOLUME

Our eyes are made for seeing forms in light.
Primary forms are beautiful forms because they are clearly legible.
The architects of today no longer make simple forms.
Relying on calculations, engineers use geometric forms, satisfying our eyes through geometry and our minds through mathematics; their works are on the way to great art.

Grain silo.

Architecture has nothing to do with the "styles."

Louis XV, XVI, XIV and Gothic are to architecture what feathers are to a woman's head; they are pretty sometimes, but not always, and nothing more.

Architecture has graver ends; capable of sublimity, it touches the most brutal instincts through its objectivity; it appeals to the highest of the faculties, through its very abstraction. Architectural abstraction has the distinctive and magnificent quality that, while being rooted in brute fact, it spiritualizes this, because brute fact is nothing other than the materialization, the symbol of a possible idea. Brute fact is amenable to ideas only through an order that is projected onto it. The emotions aroused by architecture emanate from physical conditions that are ineluctable, irrefutable, forgotten today.

Volume and surface are the elements through which architecture manifests itself. Volume and surface are determined by the plan. It is the plan that is the generator. So much the worse for those who lack imagination!

Architecture is the masterful, correct, and magnificent play of volumes brought together in light. Our eyes were made for seeing forms in light; shadow and light reveal forms; cubes, cones, spheres, cylinders, and pyramids are the great primary forms that light reveals well; the image is clear and tangible for us, without ambiguity. That is why these are *beautiful forms, the most beautiful forms.* Everyone is in agreement about this: children, savages, and metaphysicians. It is the very condition of the plastic arts.

Egyptian, Greek, and Roman architecture is an architecture

Grain silos and elevators in Canada.

Grain silos and elevators in the United States.

of prisms, cubes, and cylinders, of trihedrons and spheres: the Pyramids, the Temple of Luxor, the Parthenon, the Colosseum, Hadrian's Villa.

Gothic architecture is not, fundamentally, based on spheres, cones, and cylinders. Only the naves express a simple form, but with a complex, second-order geometry (intersecting rib vaults). That is why a cathedral is not very beautiful and why we seek in it compensations of a subjective order, outside the formal one. A cathedral interests us as an ingenious solution to a difficult problem, but one whose givens were badly formulated because they do not proceed from the great primary forms. *The cathedral is not a plastic work; it is a drama: the fight against gravity, sensation on the order of feeling.*

The Pyramids, the Towers of Babylon, the Gates of Samarkand, the Parthenon, the Colosseum, the Pantheon, the Pont du Gard, Hagia Sophia in Constantinople, the mosques of Istanbul, the Tower of Pisa, the domes of Brunelleschi and Michelangelo, the Pont-Royal, the Invalides: these are architecture.

The train station on the quai d'Orsay, the Grand Palais: these are not architecture.

The *architects* of the present day, lost in the sterile "pochés" of

their plans, rinceaux, pilasters, and lead roofs, have not learned to conceive primary volumes. They were never taught this at the École des Beaux-Arts.

Not pursuing an architectural idea, but simply guided by the results of calculations (derived from the principles that govern our universe) and the conception of A VIABLE ORGAN, *today's* ENGINEERS *make use of the primary elements and, coordinating them according to rules, stir in us architectural emotions, thus making the work of humanity resonate with the universal order.*

Here are American silos, magnificent FIRST FRUITS *of the new age.* AMERICAN ENGINEERS AND THEIR CALCULATIONS CRUSH AN EXPIRING ARCHITECTURE.

THREE REMINDERS TO ARCHITECTS

II

SURFACE

A volume is enveloped by a surface, a surface that is divided according to the generators and the directing vectors of the volume, accentuating the individuality of this volume.

Architects today are afraid of the geometric constituents of surfaces.

The great problems of modern construction will be solved with geometry.

Under strict obligation to an imperative program, engineers use the directing vectors and accentuators of forms. They create limpid and impressive plastic facts.

Architecture has nothing to do with the "styles."

Louis XV, XIV, XVI and Gothic are to architecture what feathers are to a woman's head; they are pretty sometimes, but not always, and nothing more.

SECOND REMINDER: SURFACE

Architecture being the masterful, correct, and magnificent play of volumes brought together in light, it is the architect's task to bring the surfaces that envelop these volumes to life, without their becoming parasites that consume the volume and absorb it to their profit: the sad story of the present day.

To let a volume retain the splendor of its form in light but, on the other hand, to appropriate its surface for tasks that are often utilitarian: that is to find, in the divisions imposed on the surface, the *accentuators,* the *generators* of the form. In other words, an architecture is a house, temple, or factory. The surface of the temple or factory is, most of the time, a wall pierced by holes that

are doors and windows; these holes are often the destroyers of form; it is necessary to make them into accentuators of form. If spheres, cones, and cylinders are the essentials of architecture, the generators and accentuators of these forms are based in pure geometry. But this geometry alarms the architects of today. Architects

today don't dare make the Pitti Palace or the rue de Rivoli; they make the boulevard Raspail.

Let us situate the present observations on the terrain of current needs: we need cities that are laid out in a useful way and whose volumes are beautiful (urban plans). We need streets where the cleanliness, the suitability to housing needs, the application of the mass-production spirit to construction, the grandeur of intention,

the serenity of the whole ravish the mind and make for the charm of things felicitously born.

To model the smooth surface of a simple primary form is automatically to make the competition from the volume itself spring to the fore: contradictory intentions — boulevard Raspail.

To model the surface of volumes that are complex and symphonically related is to *modulate* and to remain within the volume: a rare problem — the Invalides by Mansart.

A problem of the era and of contemporary aesthetics: everything leads to the reinstatement of simple volumes: streets, factories, department stores, all the problems that will be presented tomorrow in synthetic forms, in general views such as no other era has ever known. Surfaces, pierced due to practical necessity, should follow the accentuators and the generators of these simple forms. These accentuators are, in practice, the checkerboard or grid — American factories. But this geometry causes fear!

Not following an architectural idea but simply guided by the needs of an imperative program, the engineers of today arrive at the accentuators and generators of volumes: they show the way and create facts that are plastic, clear, and limpid, bringing calm to the eyes and, to the mind, the joys of geometry.

Such are factories, the reassuring first fruits of the new age.

The engineers of today find themselves in accord with the principles that Bramante and Raphael applied long ago.

———————

NB — Let us heed the advice of American engineers. But let us fear American *architects*. Proof:

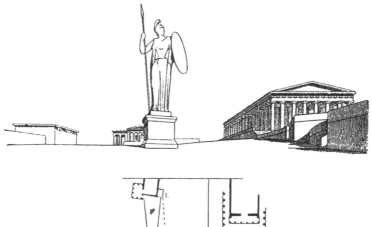

THREE REMINDERS TO
ARCHITECTS

III

PLAN

THE ACROPOLIS IN ATHENS. View of the Parthenon, the Erechtheum, and the Athena
Parthenos from the Propylaea. It must not be forgotten that the site of the Acropolis is
very uneven, with considerable differences of level that were used to constitute imposing
plinths for the buildings. The slightly canted angles produced rich and subtly effective
views; the asymmetrical massing of the buildings creates an intense rhythm. The spectacle
is massive, elastic, charged, devastating in its acuity, dominating.

The plan is the generator.

Without a plan, there is disorder, arbitrariness.

The plan carries within it the essence of the sensation.

The great problems of tomorrow, dictated by collective needs, pose the question of the plan anew.

Modern life demands, awaits a new plan for the house and for the city.

Architecture has nothing to do with the "styles."

It appeals to the most elevated of the faculties through its very abstraction. Architectural abstraction has the distinctive and magnificent quality that, while being rooted in brute fact, it spiritualizes it. Brute fact is amenable to ideas only through the order that is projected onto it.

Volume and surface are the elements through which architecture manifests itself. Volume and surface are determined by the plan. It is the plan that is the generator. So much the worse for those who lack imagination!

THIRD REMINDER: PLAN

The plan is the generator.

The eye of the spectator moves through a site made up of streets and houses. It receives the impact of the volumes that rise up around it. If these volumes are distinct and not debased by

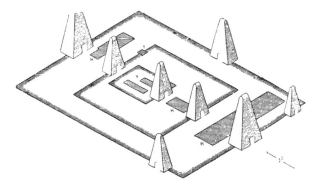

TYPE OF THE HINDU TEMPLE. The towers create a rhythm in space.

untimely modifications, if the ordonnance that groups them expresses a clear rhythm and not an incoherent agglomeration, if the volumetric and spatial relationships are rightly proportioned, the eye transmits coordinated sensations to the brain and the mind derives from them satisfactions of a high order: it is architecture.

The eye observes, in the large hall, the multiple surfaces of the walls and vaults: the domes determine the spaces; the vaults deploy the surfaces; the piers and walls fit together with intelligible logic. The entire structure rises from the base and develops according to a rule that is written on the ground in the plan: beautiful forms, variety of forms, unity of geometric principle. A profound transmission of harmony: it is architecture.

HAGIA SOFIA IN CONSTANTINOPLE. The plan is active throughout the structure: its geometric laws and their modular combinations unfold through all its parts.

The plan is the basis. Without a plan, there is neither grandeur of intention and expression nor rhythm, nor volume, nor coherence. Without a plan there's that sensation, unbearable to man, of formlessness, of something mean, disordered, arbitrary.

A plan demands the most active imagination. It also demands the most severe discipline. The plan determines everything; it is the decisive moment. A plan is not something that's nice to draw

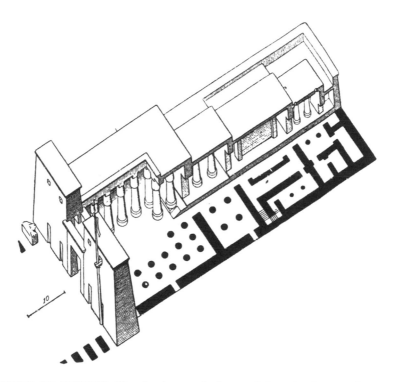

TEMPLE OF THEBES. The plan is organized around the axis of approach: avenue of sphinxes, pylons, peristyle court, sanctuary.

like the face of a Madonna; it is an austere abstraction; it is just an algebrization that's dry to the eye. All the same, the work of the mathematician remains one of the highest activities of the human mind.

Ordonnance is a perceptible rhythm that acts upon every human being, in the same way.

The plan carries within it a determined primary rhythm: the building develops in extent and height according to its prescriptions, with consequences extending from the simplest to the most complex on the same law. Unity of law is the law of the good plan: a simple law that is infinitely modulable.

Rhythm is a state of equilibrium arising from simple or complex symmetries or from skillful compensations. Rhythm is an equation: equalization (symmetry, repetition; *Egyptian and Hindu temples*); compensation (play of contraries; *Acropolis in Athens*); modulation (development of an initial plastic invention; *Hagia Sophia*). So many fundamentally different reactions on the individual, despite the unity of aim that is the rhythm, that is a state of equilibrium. Hence the astonishing diversity of the great periods, a diversity that comes from their architectural principle and not from their ornamental modalities.

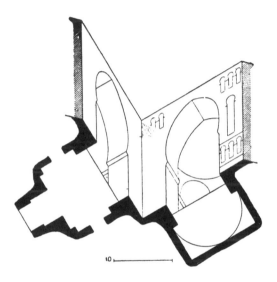

PALACE IN AMMAN (Syria).

The plan carries within it the very essence of the sensation.

But we lost the sense of the plan a hundred years ago. The great problems of tomorrow, dictated by collective needs, based on statistics, and solved with calculations, pose the question of the plan anew. When we have understood the indispensable grandeur of view that must be brought to city plans, we will head into a period such as no era has yet known. Cities should be conceived and planned throughout like the temples of the East and like the Invalides and Versailles of Louis XIV.

The technological capacities of this era — financing techniques and construction techniques — are ready to carry out this task.

Tony Garnier, backed by Herriot in Lyon, has laid out an

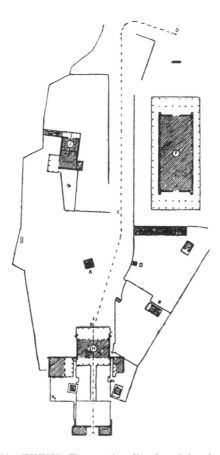

THE ACROPOLIS IN ATHENS. The seeming disorder of the plan will fool only the pro-
fane. The equilibrium is not small-minded. It is determined by the famous landscape that
extends from Peiraeus to Mount Pentelikon. The plan is conceived for distant views: the
axes line up with the valley and the slightly canted angles are the skilled interventions of a
great stage director. The Acropolis on its rock and its supporting walls is seen from afar, as
one block. Its buildings are massed together through the incidence of their multiple planes.

"Industrial City." It is an attempt to instill order and a conjugation
of utilitarian solutions with plastic solutions. A unitary code distributes the same set of essential volumes through all parts of the
city and determines the spaces in ways consistent with needs of a
practical order and with the promptings of a poetic sense that is the
architect's own. Reserving all judgment about the coordination of
the zones of this industrial city, we are here subject to the beneficial

consequences of order. Where order reigns, well-being is born. Through the happy invention of a system of lot division, even the quarters of workers' housing take on high architectural significance. Such are the consequences of a plan.

In the present waiting state (for modern urbanism is not yet born) the most beautiful quarters of our cities should be the factory

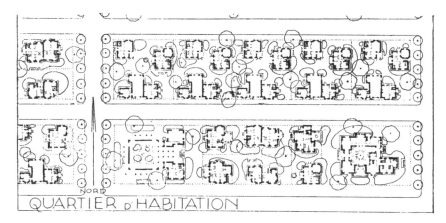

TONY GARNIER. Residential quarter taken from *Une Cité industrielle*. In his remarkable study of an industrial city, Tony Garnier presupposed certain advances in the social order that would facilitate the *normal expansion* of cities: society would be free to dispose of the land as it saw fit. A house for every family; half of the surface area occupied by buildings, the other half public property, it is planted with trees; there are no fences. It is now possible to traverse the city in any direction, independently of the streets, which the pedestrian no longer need follow. And the surface of the city is like a large park. (One can criticize Garnier for one thing: placing such low-density quarters in the heart of the city.)

quarters, where the cause of grandeur and style — geometry — results from the problem itself. A plan has been lacking, is lacking still. An admirable order indeed reigns within the halls and workshops, has dictated the structure of the machines and guides their movements, conditions every gesture of their crews. But filth pollutes the surroundings and incoherence ran rampant when string and T squares fixed the placement of the buildings, rendering their expansion pointless, expensive, and dangerous.

A plan would have sufficed. A plan will suffice. The excess of evils will lead to one.

One day Auguste Perret coined the phrase "Tower-Cities." A sparkling epithet that struck the poet in us. A word that rang out

TONY GARNIER. Walkways between various residences in a residential quarter.

TONY GARNIER. Street in a residential quarter.

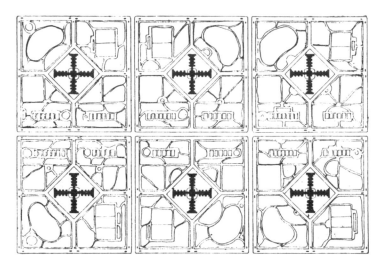

L.-C. 1920. TOWER-CITIES. Land subdivision proposal. Sixty floors, height 220 meters; distance between the towers 250 to 300 m (equivalent to the width of the Tuileries Gardens). Width of the towers, 150 to 200 meters. Despite the large area of the parks, normal urban density is increased 5 to 10 times. It seems that such constructions should be devoted exclusively to business (offices) and thus erected in the center of large cities whose arteries would be relieved of congestion; family life would not adapt well to the astounding machinery of elevators. The figures are stunning and pitiless, magnificent: if every employee were allotted a surface of 10 m², a skyscraper 200 m wide would accommodate 40,000 people. Haussmann, instead of making narrow thoroughfares in Paris, would have demolished entire neighborhoods and condensed them vertically; then he would have planted parks more beautiful than those of the Grand Roy.

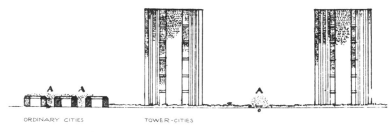

ORDINARY CITIES   TOWER-CITIES

A- DUST ZONES

TOWER-CITIES. This cross section shows at left the suffocating dust, stench, and noise of present-day cities. The towers, on the other hand, are far apart, in healthy air, among greenery. The whole city is covered with greenery.

none too soon because the fact is imminent! Unknown to us, the "great city" incubates a plan. This plan can be gigantic because the

L.-C. 1920. TOWER-CITIES. The towers are amidst gardens and playing fields (sports, tennis, soccer). The main arteries, with their elevated highway, distribute circulation into slow, fast, super-fast.

great city is a rising tide. It is time to repudiate the present layout of our cities in which apartment buildings pile up, all crammed together, and narrow streets interweave, full of noise, gasoline stench, and dust, and where the floors are completely open to inhaling this filth. Large cities have become too dense for the safety of their inhabitants and yet they are not dense enough to answer to the new realities of "business."

Starting from the crucial constructional event that is the American skyscraper, it will suffice to bring this great density of population together at a few isolated points and to raise there immense structures 60 stories high. Reinforced concrete and steel make such boldness possible and lend themselves above all to a particular development of the facade thanks to which all the windows will give onto open sky; in this way, courtyards will henceforth be eliminated. Beginning with the fourteenth floor, there is absolute calm, there is pure air.

In these towers, which will house the work previously smothered in dense neighborhoods and congested streets, all services, in accordance with the happy American experience, will be gathered together, bringing efficiency, time and energy savings, and thereby an indispensable calm. These towers, rising up at great distances one from another, provide vertically what has until now been spread over the ground; they leave vast open spaces that cast the axial streets, full of noise and faster-flowing traffic, far away from them. At the foot of the towers, parks unroll; greenery extends over the entire city. The towers are aligned in imposing avenues; this is truly an architecture worthy of the times.

Auguste Perret formulated the principle of the Tower-City; he did not design it (1). On the other hand, he gave an interview to a reporter from *L'Intransigeant* and let himself be carried away, extending his conception beyond reasonable limits. Thus did he throw a veil of dangerous futurism over a sound idea. The reporter noted that immense bridges link the towers to one another; for what purpose? The traffic arteries are far from the houses, and the population taking its pleasure in the parks, under the trees arrayed in quincunxes on the lawns and playing fields, wouldn't have cared less about crossing vertiginous pedestrian bridges where there was nothing at all to do. The reporter also maintained that this city would be built on countless pilotis of reinforced concrete support-ing, at a height of 20 meters (six floors, if you please), the level of the streets and linking the towers to one another. These pilotis would have left an immense area underneath the city that could quite comfortably accommodate water, gas, and drain pipes, the viscera of the city. A plan had not been drawn up and the idea went no further without a plan.

I put forward this pilotis conception to Auguste Perret long ago; it was a conception of an order much less magnificent, but one that might answer a real need. It applied to the current city, such as the Paris of today. Instead of excavating deep foundations with heavy walls, instead of eternally digging and redigging the road-ways in order to lay pipes (a Sisyphean task) for water and gas, for sewers and underground transit and repairing them endlessly, we could build new neighborhoods at ground level whose foundations would be replaced by a logical number of concrete posts; the latter

(1) Making these sketches in 1920, I thought I was transcribing the ideas of Auguste Perret. But the publication of his own designs in the August 1922 issue of *L'Illustration* revealed a different conception.

would support the ground floors of the apartment buildings and, on corbel supports, the slabs of sidewalks and roadways.

In the space thus gained, 4 to 6 meters high, heavy trucks, the metros replacing cumbersome streetcars, etc. would circulate, with direct access to the basements of the apartment buildings. A complete circulation network, independent of that of the streets meant for pedestrians and rapid vehicular traffic, would be gained, having its own geography independent of the overcrowding of the residential buildings: an ordered forest of pillars within which the city

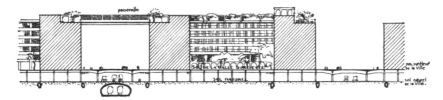

L.-C. 1915. PILOTIS-CITIES. The ground level of the city is raised 4 to 5 meters on pilotis, which serve as foundations for the houses. The city floor is a kind of foundation grid, the streets and their sidewalks bridges of a kind. Under this slab and directly accessible are all the organs that up to now have been buried in the ground and inaccessible: water, gas, electricity, telephone, pneumatic tubes, sewers, neighborhood heating, etc.(1).

could trade its commodities, provision itself, tend to all the slow and cumbersome tasks that now jam circulation.

Cafés, places of relaxation, etc. were no longer a fungus eating into the sidewalk: they were shifted onto roof terraces along with luxury shops (isn't it wholly illogical for a large part of the city's surface to be left unused and reserved for face-to-face encounters between slate roofs and the stars?). Short pedestrian bridges over conventional streets established the circulation of these new recuperated quarters devoted to rest amidst flower beds and greenery.

This conception did nothing less than triple the circulation areas of the city; it was realizable, *corresponded to a need, cost less,*

(1) *L'Intransigeant,* 25 November 1924: boulevard Haussmann extended. And there's nothing but the metro and the double row of ponderous apartment buildings, there are those galleries in the English manner that are to be buried under each sidewalk to accommodate pipes of all kinds. They will be sufficiently high and wide for employees of the electric, compressed air, postal companies, etc. to circulate comfortably, and the ones containing pipes for gas lighting will be covered with removable slabs, such that the smallest problem, leak, or break in the vascular or nervous system of this privileged quarter will not necessarily entail those gigantic laparotomies that occasion half the roadway's being blocked for eight days with the entrails of the sidewalk. J.L.

L.-C. 1920. STREETS WITH INDENTS. Vast spaces with sun and air onto which all apartments open. Gardens and playgrounds at the foot of the houses. Smooth facades with immense openings. A play of shadow is produced by the successive projections of the plan. Richness is provided by the breadth of the layout and by the play of vegetation over the geometric canvas of the facades. It goes without saying that what is in question here, as with the tower-cities, are companies with sufficient financial backing to build entire neighborhoods. Similar small-scale consortiums already existed before the war. A single architect would lay out an entire street: unity, grandeur, dignity, economy.

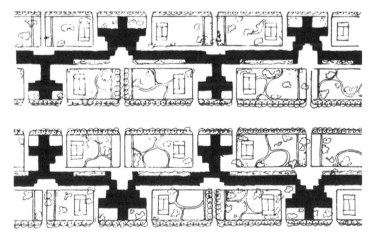

L.-C. 1920. Streets with indents.

and was sounder than the aberrations of today. It was sound within the present framework of our cities, just as the conception of tower-cities will be sound in the cities of tomorrow.

Here again, a layout of streets entailing a complete renewal of the terms of lot division and anticipating a radical reform of the rental house; this imminent reform motivated by the transformation of domestic use calls for new housing plans, and an entirely new organization of the services answering to life in the big city. Here again, the plan is the generator, without which it's the reign of meanness, disorder, arbitrariness (1).

Instead of laying out cities in large quadrangular blocks with narrow channels of streets constricted by seven-story apartment buildings that drop right down to the pavement and wrap around the unhealthy wells of airless and sunless courtyards, we will lay out (in the same surface area and with the same population density) apartment blocks with successive indents snaking along axial avenues. No more courtyards, but apartments opening on every side to air and light, and overlooking not the sickly trees of today's boulevards but lawns, playgrounds, and luxuriant vegetation.

The prows of these blocks would punctuate the long avenues at regular intervals. The indents would occasion a play of shadow favorable to architectural expression.

Construction with reinforced concrete has caused a revolution in the aesthetics of building. By eliminating the pitched roof and replacing it with terraces, reinforced concrete leads to a new, hitherto unknown aesthetic of the plan. The indents and recessions that are henceforth possible bring about plays of half-light and shadow moving no longer from top to bottom but laterally, from left to right.

This is a crucial change in the aesthetic of the plan; it has yet to make itself felt; it will be useful to think about it now in projects to expand cities (2).

*
* *

We are in a period of construction and of readjustment to new social and economic conditions. We are rounding a cape and the

(1) See below: "Mass-Production Housing."
(2) This question will be studied in a book in preparation: *Urbanisme.*

new horizons will recover the great line of traditions only through the complete revision of means that is underway, only through the determination of new constructional foundations based on logic.

In architecture, the old constructional foundations are dead. There will be no rediscovery of the truths of architecture until new foundations have become the logical support for all architectural manifestations. The next twenty years will be taken up with creating these foundations. A period of great problems, a period of analysis and experimentation, also a period of great aesthetic upheavals, a period of the elaboration of a new aesthetic.

It is the *plan* that must be studied, the key to this evolution.

L.-C. and PIERRE JEANNERET. Garden on the roof terrace of a private house in Auteuil.

Illustration nos. 1, 2, 3, 4, 5, 6 in this chapter are from Choisy, *Histoire de l'architecture,* Baranger, publisher. Nos. 7, 8, 9 are taken from: *Une cité industrielle* by Tony Garnier, Vincent, publisher.

PORTE SAINT-DENIS (Blondel).

REGULATING LINES

Of the fateful birth of architecture.

The obligation to order. The regulating line is a guarantee against arbitrariness. It brings satisfaction to the mind.

The regulating line is a means; it is not a formula. Its choices and its expressive modalities are integral parts of architectural creation.

Primitive man has drawn up his wagon, he decides that here will be his ground. He chooses a clearing, he cuts down the trees that are too close, he levels the surrounding terrain; he opens a path that will connect him to the river or to the members of his tribe, which he has just left; he drives the stakes that will hold down his tent. He surrounds this with a palisade in which he sets up a gate. The path is as straight as his tools, his arms, and his time allow. The stakes of his tent describe a rectangle, a hexagon, or an octagon. The palisade forms a rectangle whose four corners are equal, are right angles. The door of the hut opens on the axis of the enclosure and the door of the enclosure is directly opposite the door of the hut.

The men of the tribe have decided to shelter their god. They place it within a duly arranged space; they shelter it under a solid hut and drive the stakes of the hut, in a square, a hexagon, an octagon. They protect the hut with a sturdy palisade and drive stakes where the ropes of the high posts of the barrier will be secured. They decide on an area to be reserved for the priests and set up an altar and sacrificial vases. They open a gate in the palisade and place it on axis with the door of the sanctuary.

In an archaeology book, take a look at a diagram of this hut, a diagram of this sanctuary: it is the plan of a house, it is the plan of a temple. It is this same spirit that we find again in the houses at Pompeii. It is the same spirit of the temple at Luxor.

There is no primitive man; there are primitive means. The idea is a constant, potential from the start.

Notice in these plans how a primary mathematics governs them. There are measurements here. In order to build well and distribute the labor properly, so as to assure the solidity and utility of the work, *measurements* condition the whole. The builder has taken as his measure what was easiest for him, most consistent, the tool that he was least likely to lose: his pace, his foot, his forearm, his finger.

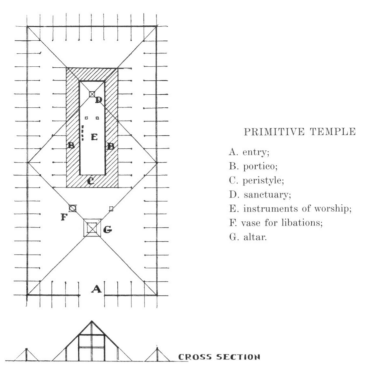

PRIMITIVE TEMPLE

A. entry;
B. portico;
C. peristyle;
D. sanctuary;
E. instruments of worship;
F. vase for libations;
G. altar.

CROSS SECTION

To build well and distribute his labor, to guarantee the solidity and utility of the work, he took measurements, he introduced a module, *he regulated his labor,* he introduced order. For all around him the forest is in disorder, its vines, bushes, and tree trunks obstruct him and forestall his efforts.

He established order by measuring. In order to measure he took his pace, his foot, his forearm, or his finger. By imposing the order of his foot or his arm, he created a module that regulates the entire work; and this work is to his scale, for his convenience, for his comfort, *to his measure.* It is to the human *scale.* It harmonizes with him: that's the main thing.

But when deciding on the shape of the enclosure, on the shape of the hut, on the placement of the altar and its accessories, he went instinctively for right angles, axes, rectangles, circles. For otherwise he couldn't create anything that would give him the impression that he created. For axes, circles, right angles are geometric truths and are effects that our eye measures and recognizes;

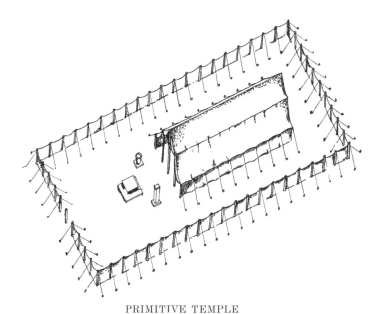

PRIMITIVE TEMPLE

while it would otherwise be chance, anomaly, arbitrariness. Geometry is the language of man.

But when determining the respective distances of objects, he invented rhythms, rhythms sensible to the eye, clear in their relationships. And these rhythms are at the root of human activity. They resound in man through an organic inevitability, the same inevitability that inscribes the golden section in children, in the elderly, in savages, in the educated.

A module measures and unifies; a regulating line constructs and satisfies.

Haven't most architects today forgotten that great architecture is at the very origins of humanity and that it is a direct function of human instincts?

When we see the little houses in the suburbs of Paris, the villas in the dunes of Normandy, modern boulevards, and international expositions, aren't we convinced that architects are inhuman beings, outside of order, far from our own being and who perhaps do their work for another planet?

That is because they have been taught a bizarre craft that consists in making others — masons, carpenters, and joiners — achieve miracles of perseverance, care, and skill by erecting and sticking together elements (roofs, walls, windows, doors, etc.) that no longer have anything in common with one another and no longer have as their real goal, their real result, the serving of some useful purpose.

*_**

For now, there is unanimity in seeing dangerous writers, idlers, incompetents, dullards, and stuffed-shirts in the few individuals who, having understood the lesson of primitive man in his clearing, maintain that regulating lines exist: "With your regulating lines, you will kill the imagination, you will enthrone formula."
"But all previous eras have used this necessary tool.
— That's not true, it's you who invented it, for you are an intellectual maniac!
— But the past has left us proof: iconographic documents, steles, slabs, incised stones, parchments, manuscripts, printed matter."

*_**

Architecture is the first manifestation of man creating his universe, creating it in the image of nature, subscribing to the laws of nature, to the laws that govern our nature, our universe. The laws of gravity, statics, and dynamics impose themselves through a *reductio ad absurdum:* stand up or fall down.
A sovereign determinism clarifies natural creation for our eyes and gives us the certainty of something balanced and reasonably made, of something infinitely modulated, evolving, varied, and unitary.
The primordial physical laws are simple and few. The laws of morality are simple and few.

*_**

The man of today planes a board to perfection with a planer, in a few seconds. The man of yesterday planed a board rather well with a hand plane. Very primitive man did a poor job of squaring a board with a flint or a knife. Very primitive man used a module and regulating lines to make his task easier. The Greeks, the Egyptians, Michelangelo, and Blondel used regulating lines for correctness in their buildings and the satisfaction of their artistic sense and their mathematical thought. The man of today uses nothing at all and makes the boulevard Raspail. But he proclaims that he is a liberated poet and that his instincts suffice; but these express themselves only through the artificial means learned in the schools. A lyric poet set loose with shackles round his neck, someone who knows things, but things that he has neither invented nor even mastered, who in the course of his education has lost that candid and essential energy of the child who keeps asking: "Why?"

***

A regulating line is a guarantee against arbitrariness: it is the verifying operation that ratifies all work created with enthusiasm: the schoolboy's casting out nines, the mathematician's QED.

The regulating line is a satisfaction of a spiritual order that leads to a search for ingenious relationships and for harmonious relationships. It imbues the work with eurythmy.

The regulating line brings forth the sensory mathematics that produces a beneficent perception of order. The choice of a regulating line fixes the fundamental geometry of the work; it determines one of the fundamental impressions. The choice of a regulating line is one of the decisive moments of inspiration, it is one of the crucial operations of architecture.

***

Here are some regulating lines that served to make some very beautiful things and are the cause whereby these things are very beautiful:

COPY OF A MARBLE SLAB FROM PEIRAEUS:

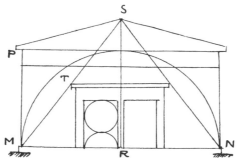

Facade of the Arsenal in Peiraeus.

The facade of the Arsenal in Peiraeus was determined by several simple divisions that make the base proportional to the height, that determine the position and dimensions of the door in close coordination with the proportions of the facade.

EXTRACT FROM A BOOK BY DIEULAFOY:

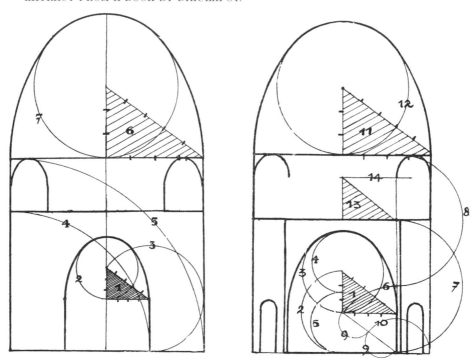

Schematic drawings of Achaemenid domes.

The great Achaemenid domes are among the subtlest applications of geometry. Once the conception of the dome had been established according to the lyrical needs of this race and this era and according to the given statics of the applied building principles, a regulating line was used to rectify, to correct, to perfect, to make all the parts resonate with a single unifying principle, that of a 3-4-5 triangle, which develops its effects from the portal to the summit of the vault.

Notre-Dame de Paris.

MEASURED ON NOTRE-DAME DE PARIS:

The determining surface of the cathedral is regulated by the square and the circle (1).

———————

DRAWN ON A PHOTOGRAPH OF THE CAPITOL:

The right angle helped Michelangelo to hone his intentions, making the same principle that determines the large divisions of the pavilions and the central block control the detailing of the pavilions, the slope of the stairways, the position of the windows, the height of the basement, etc.

The work, conceived in its site, and whose enveloping mass has

(1) Regarding Notre-Dame and the Porte Saint-Denis, be wary of changes in ground level introduced later by the city magistrates.

The Capitol in Rome.

been coordinated with the surrounding volume and space, collects, concentrates, and unifies itself, expresses the same law throughout, becomes compact.

The principal mass is fixed, the opening of the arch is sketched in. Imperative regulating lines, on a module of 3, divide the whole of the gate, divide the parts of the work vertically and horizontally, regulate everything according to the same unifying number.

THE PETIT TRIANON

The Petit Trianon, Versailles.

Placement of the right angle.

CONSTRUCTION OF A VILLA (1916):

The main block of the facades, front as well as back, is governed by the same angle (A) that determines a diagonal whose many parallels and perpendiculars will provide corrective measurements for the secondary elements, doors, windows, panels, etc., down to the smallest details.

This villa of small dimensions, in the midst of other buildings

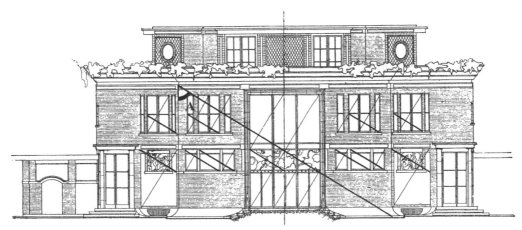

L. C. 1916 VILLA. Facade.

erected without such regulation, seems more monumental, of another order (1).

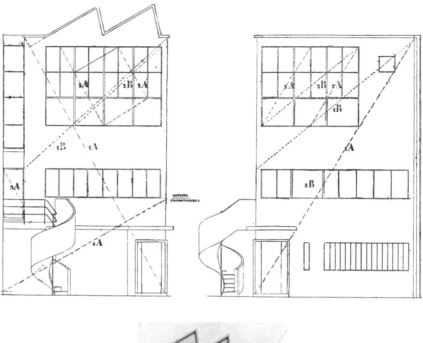

Le Corbusier and Pierre Jeanneret, 1923. House of M. Ozenfant.

(1) I apologize for citing examples by myself here: but despite my investigations, I have not yet had the pleasure of encountering contemporary architects who have concerned themselves with this matter; re this subject, I have only prompted astonishment or encountered opposition and skepticism.

L. C. 1916. VILLA. Rear facade.

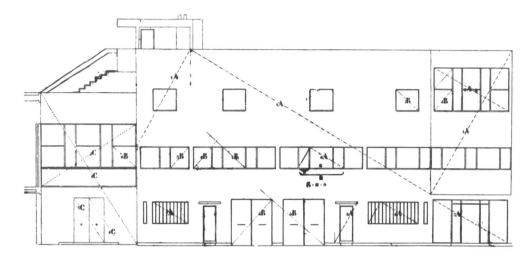

L. C. and P. J. 1924.
Two private mansions in Auteuil.

The liner *Flandre*. Cie Transatlantique.

EYES THAT DO NOT SEE...

I

LINERS

A great era has just begun.

There exists a new spirit.

There exists a host of works in this new spirit, they are encountered above all in industrial production.

Architecture suffocates in routine.

The "styles" are a lie.

Style is a unity of principle that animates all the works of an era and that results from a distinctive state of mind.

Our era fixes its style every day.

Our eyes, unfortunately, are not yet able to discern it.

There is a new spirit: it is a spirit of construction and synthesis guided by a clear conception.

Whatever one makes of this, it animates today the greater part of human activity.

A GREAT ERA HAS JUST BEGUN

Program of L'Esprit nouveau, *no. 1, October 1920.*

No one today denies the aesthetic that is emerging from the creations of modern industry. More and more, constructions and machines arise with proportions, with a play of volumes and materials, such that many among them are true works of art, for they entail number, which is to say order. Now the elite individuals who make up the world of industry and business and who live, consequently, in this virile atmosphere in which undeniably beautiful works are created, imagine themselves to be far indeed from all aesthetic activity. They are wrong, *for they are among the most active creators of the contemporary aesthetic.* Neither the artists nor the industrialists are aware of this. It is in general production that the style of an era is found and not, as is too often thought, in a few productions whose end is ornamental, mere redundancies coming to encumber a mental system that alone provides the elements of a style. Rocaille is not Louis XV style, the lotus is not Egyptian style, etc., etc.

Leaflet issued by *L'Esprit nouveau.*

The "decorative arts" flourish! After thirty years of silent labor they are at their height. Enthusiastic commentators talk of *a regeneration of French art!* Let us retain from this adventure (which will end badly) that something other than a regeneration of decor was born: a new era is replacing an era that is dying. Mechanization, a new fact in human history, has called forth a new spirit. An era creates its own architecture, which is the clear image of a system of thought. In the confusion of this period of crisis, preceding the advent of a new age with ideas that are worked out, lucid, resolutely clear, the decorative arts were like reeds we thought we could grab onto while the storm raged. Illusory salvation. Let us retain from the adventure that the decorative arts were an opportune occasion to drive out the past and try to feel our way toward the spirit of architecture. The spirit of architecture can result only from a state of things and from a state of mind. It would seem that events have followed one another with sufficient speed

PAUL VÉRA: tailpiece (La Renaissance).

for the era's state of mind to assert itself and for a spirit of architecture to formulate itself. If the decorative arts are at that perilous height preceding a fall, we can say that minds, uplifted by them, took cognizance of what they aspired to. We can think that architecture's time has come.

The Greeks, the Romans, the Grand Siècle, Pascal and Descartes, mistakenly called to testify in favor of the decorative arts, have enlightened our judgment, and now we find ourselves in architecture, architecture that is everything, but that is not the decorative arts.

Tailpieces, lamps, and garlands, exquisite ovals where triangular doves kiss and kiss again, boudoirs decorated with "pumpkin" cushions in black and gold velvet are no longer anything but the insufferable witnesses to a dead spirit. These sanctums smothered in coke and soppy "peasant" idiocies are offensive to us.

We have developed a taste for free air and bright light.

* *
*

Anonymous engineers, greasy mechanics in workshops and forges have conceived and built those formidable things that are

The liner *Aquitania,* Cunard Line, carries 3,600 persons.

ocean liners. The rest of us landsmen, we lack the means of appreciation, and it would be a good thing if, to teach us to tip our hats to these works of "regeneration," we had occasion to take the kilometers-long walk that's involved in a visit to a liner.

**

Architects live within the narrow confines of what they learned in school, in ignorance of the new rules of building, and they readily let their conceptions stop at kissing doves. But the builders of liners, bold and masterful, realize palaces beside which cathedrals are tiny things: and they cast them onto the waters!

Architecture suffocates in routine.

Use of the thick walls that were once a necessity has persisted, even though thin membranes of glass or brick can enclose a ground floor surmounted by fifty stories.

In a city like Prague, for example, an obsolete regulation imposes a wall thickness of 45 centimeters at the top of the "house" and 15 additional centimeters for each lower story, which leads to walls as thick as 1 m 50 on the ground floor. Today, the composition of facades using large blocks of soft stone has the paradoxical result that windows meant to introduce light are contained within deep embrasures that categorically thwart the intention.

On the valuable ground of large cities, we still see enormous piles of masonry spring forth from building foundations, even

The *Aquitania*. Cunard Line.

though simple concrete piles would be just as efficient. Roofs, wretched roofs, continue to reign, an inexcusable paradox. Basements remain damp and cluttered, and the service mains of cities are still buried under stone slabs like dead organs, even though a logical conception that is now viable would provide a solution.

The "styles" — for one must do *something* — intervene as the great contribution of the architect. They intervene in the decoration of facades and of salons; they are corruptions of the styles, remnants of a past age; they are a respectful and servile call to "Attention!" before the past: an unnerving timidity. A lie, for in the great days facades were smooth, pierced at regular intervals, and of fine human proportions. Walls were as thin as possible. Palaces? They were fine for the grand dukes back then. Does the well-bred gentleman copy today's grand dukes? Compiègne, Chantilly, Versailles are just fine from a certain point of view, but... there's much to be said about this.

Houses like tabernacles, tabernacles like houses, furniture like palaces (with pediments, statues, columns spiral and not spiral),

The *Lamoricière*. Cie Transatlantique.
To architects: a beauty more technical. Oh Gare d'Orsay!
An aesthetic closer to its real causes!

ewers as house-furniture, and dishes by Bernard Palissy that won't
hold three hazelnuts!

The "styles" are still with us!

* *
*

A house is a machine for living in. Baths, sun, hot water, cold
water, controlled temperature, food conservation, hygiene, beauty
through proportion. An armchair is a machine for sitting in, etc.:
Maple has shown the way. Ewers are machines for washing oneself:
Twyford has created them.

Our modern life, that of all our activities except taking chamomile or linden tea, has created objects: its suits, its pens, its
Eversharp pencils, its typewriters, its telephones, its admirable
office furniture, Saint-Gobain mirrors and "Innovation" trunks,
the Gillette razor and the English pipe, the bowler hat and the limousine, the liner and the airplane.

The *Aquitania*. Cunard Line.
The same aesthetic as that of your English pipe, your office furniture, your limousine.

The *Aquitania*. Cunard Line.
For architects: a wall that's all windows, a room flooded with light. What a contrast with the windows of our houses, which pierce the wall and create patches of shadow on either side, rendering the room drab and making the light so bright that curtains are indispensable to filter and soften it.

The liner *France* built by the Saint-Nazaire yards.

Of proportions. — Look at these and dream of the palaces in Vichy, Zermatt, or Biaritz, and also of the new streets in Passy.

The *Aquitania*. Cunard Line.

To Architects: A villa on the dunes of Normandy conceived like these liners would be more apt than the large "Norman roofs" that are so old, so old! But it might be claimed that this isn't the maritime style at all!

The *Aquitania*. Cunard Line.

To architects: The value of a long promenade, a volume that's satisfying and interesting; unity of materials, beautiful arrangement of the structural elements, soundly set out and combined into a unity.

The *Lamoricière*. Cie Transatlantique.

To architects: New architectural forms, elements on a human scale that are vast and intimate, liberation from the suffocating styles, contrast between solids and voids, between strong masses and slender elements.

Empress of France. Canadian Pacific.
An architecture that is pure, crisp, clear, clean, sound. — Contrast the carpets, cushions, canopies, damasked wallpaper, gilded and carved furniture, musty and Ballets Russes colors: the dreary dullness of our Western bazaar.

Our era fixes its style every day. It is right before our eyes.
Eyes that do not see.

* *

There's a misunderstanding that must be cleared up: we are rotten from art confused with respect for decor. Displacement of the feeling for art, coupled with a trivial-mindedness reprehensible in all things, in favor of the theories and campaigns led by decorators who don't know their era.

Art is an austere thing that has its sacred hours. They are profaned. Frivolous, art winces at a world that needs organization, tools, means; that strains painfully toward the stabilization of a new order. A society lives first of all on food, on sun, on necessary comforts. Everything remains to be done! An immense task! And it is so pressing, so urgent, that the whole world is absorbed in this imperious necessity. Machines will lead to a new order of labor and

Empress of Asia. Canadian Pacific.
"Architecture is the masterful, correct, and magnificent play of volumes brought together in light."

rest. Whole cities must be built or rebuilt in view of a minimum of comfort, the prolonged lack of which might unsettle the social equilibrium. Society is unstable, cracking under a state of things upended by fifty years of advances that have changed the face of the world more than the six preceding centuries.

It is time for construction, not for idle talk.

The art of our era is in its rightful place when it addresses itself to elites. Art is not a popular thing, still less a deluxe whore. Art is a necessary foodstuff only for elites that must reflect so as to be able to lead. Art is in its essence elevated.

In the painful childbirth of this era in formation, a need for harmony asserts itself.

May our eyes see: this harmony is there, a function of labor governed by *economy* and conditioned by the inevitability of physics. This harmony has reasons; it is not at all the effect of caprice but that of construction that is logical and congruous with the ambient world. In the bold transposition of human labors, nature is present, and all the more rigorously insofar as the problem was difficult. The creations of machine technology are organisms tending toward purity and subject to the same evolutionary rules as are natural objects that arouse our admiration. There is harmony in the works that come from the workshop and the factory. This is not Art, this is not the Sistine Chapel, nor the Erechtheum; these are the everyday works of a whole universe that labors with awareness, intelligence, and precision, with imagination, daring, and rigor.

*
* *

If we forget for a moment that a liner is a transport tool and look at it with new eyes, we will sense that we stand before an important manifestation of temerity, discipline, and harmony, a beauty that is calm, vigorous, and strong.

A serious architect who looks as an architect (a creator of organisms) will find in the liner a liberation from cursed enslavement to the past.

To an indolent respect for tradition, he will prefer respect for the forces of nature; to the pettiness of middling conceptions, the majesty of solutions following from a problem well posed, and required by this century of great endeavors that has just taken a giant step forward.

The land-dweller's house is the expression of an outdated world of small dimensions. The liner is the first stage in the realization of a world organized in accordance with the new spirit.

Photo Draeger.

EYES THAT DO NOT SEE...

II

AIRPLANES

The airplane is a product of high selection.

The lesson of the airplane is in the logic that governed the statement of the problem and its realization.

The problem of the house has not been posed.

Current architectural things do not answer to our needs.

Yet there are standards for the dwelling.

The mechanical carries within it the economic factor that selects.

The house is a machine for living in.

There is a new spirit: it is a spirit of construction and of synthesis guided by a clear conception.

Whatever one makes of this, it animates today the greater part of human activity.

A GREAT ERA HAS JUST BEGUN

Program of L'Esprit nouveau, *no. 1, October 1920.*

There is one trade and one only, architecture, where progress is not obligatory, where indolence reigns, where the point of reference is yesterday.

Everywhere else, worry about tomorrow leads to a solution: if you don't move forward, you go bankrupt.

But in architecture, no one ever goes bankrupt. A privileged trade. Alas!

**
* **

In modern industry, the airplane is certainly one of the products of highest selection.

The War was the insatiable client, never satisfied, always demanding better. The orders were to succeed and death implacably followed error. So we can say that the airplane mobilized invention, intelligence, and daring: *imagination* and *cool reason.* The same spirit built the Parthenon.

**
* **

I look at things from the point of view of architecture, in the state of mind of the inventor of airplanes.

The lesson of the airplane is not so much in the forms created, and one must first of all learn not to see in an airplane a bird or a dragonfly, but a machine for flying; the lesson of the airplane is in the logic that governed the statement of the problem and that led to the success of its realization. When a problem is posed to our era, it inevitably finds the solution.

The problem of the house has not been posed.

A commonplace among architects (the young ones): *It is necessary to emphasize construction.*

Another commonplace among them: *When something answers a need, it is beautiful.*

Sorry! Emphasizing construction is fine for students at the Arts et métiers who want to show what they're worth. The good Lord indeed emphasized wrists and ankles, but then there's all the rest.

When something answers a need, it is not beautiful, it satisfies one whole part of our minds, the first part, that without which no later satisfactions are possible. Let us reestablish this chronology.

Architecture has another sense and other ends than emphasizing construction and answering needs (needs understood in the sense, implicit here, of utility, of comfort, of practical design). ARCHITECTURE is the art par excellence, one that attains a

"Air Express."

"FARMAN."

state of Platonic grandeur, mathematical order, speculation, perception of harmony through stirring formal relationships. These are
the ENDS of architecture.

But let's get back to chronology.

If we feel the need for another architecture, an organism that
is clear and purified, that is because in the current state of affairs,
sensations of a mathematical order cannot reach us because *the
things do not answer a need,* because there is no longer any construction in architecture. An extreme confusion reigns: current architecture is no longer solving the modern question of the dwelling and

BLÉRIOT SPAD 33, passenger plane. Herbemont, engineer.

does not understand the structure of things. It does not fulfill the primordial conditions and it is not possible for the higher factor of harmony and beauty to intervene.

The architecture of today does not satisfy the necessary and sufficient conditions of the problem.

That is because the problem has not been posed for architecture. There has been no useful war as was the case for the airplane.

Yes indeed, peace sets the problem now: to rebuild the north. But that's just it: we are totally disarmed, we do not know how to build modern — materials, structural systems, CONCEPTION OF THE DWELLING. Engineers have been busy with dams, bridges, transatlantic liners, mines, railroads. Architects have been asleep.

The north has not been rebuilt in the last two years. Only recently, in the large companies, have engineers taken up the problem of the house, the structural part (materials and structural systems) (1). IT REMAINS TO DEFINE THE CONCEPTION OF THE DWELLING.

(1) 1924. But the engineers were blackballed. Public opinion was against them. Their solutions weren't wanted. Routine prevailed. They built as before, nothing was changed. The North did not want to be the wondrous revelation of the postwar moment.

CAPRONI Tricellular Hydroplane, 3,000 horsepower, carries 100 passengers.

The airplane shows us that when a problem is well posed its solution is found. Wanting to fly like a bird, that was to pose the problem badly, and Ader's "Bat" did not get off the ground. To invent a machine for flying without paying the slightest attention to what's alien to pure mechanics, in other words, to look for a way of achieving lift and a means of propulsion, that was to pose the problem well: in less than ten years the whole world could fly.

LET US POSE THE PROBLEM.

Let us close our eyes to what exists.

A house: a shelter against heat, cold, rain, thieves, the inquisitive. A receptacle for light and sun. A certain number of compartments intended for cooking, for work, for private life.

A room: an area for moving about freely, a bed for reclining, a chair for relaxing and working, a table for working, storage units for keeping everything in the "right place."

Caproni Triplane, 2,000 horsepower, carries 30 passengers.

How many rooms: one for cooking and one for eating. One for working, one for washing oneself, and one for sleeping.

Such are the standards for the dwelling.

Why then, on the pretty villas all around, these big useless roofs? Why these scant windows with small panes, why these large houses with so many locked rooms? Why the mirrored armoires, the washstands, the chests of drawers? And why these bookcases decorated with acanthus, these consoles, these vitrines, these china cabinets, these dressers, these sideboards? Why these enormous chandeliers? Why these mantelpieces? Why these draped curtains? Why this wallpaper full of colors, of damask, of motley vignettes?

There's no light in your houses. Your windows are hard to open. There are no ventilators like those in any dining car. Your chandeliers hurt my eyes. Your stuccos and your colored wallpaper are as impudent as valets, and I'll take home the picture by Picasso that I came to give you, for no one will see it in the bazaar of your interior.

"AIR EXPRESS," Paris-London in two hours.

And all that cost you 50,000 francs.

Why don't you require of your landlord:

1° Storage units for underwear and clothing in your bedroom, all the same depth, at the height of a human being and as practical as an "Innovation" trunk.

2° In your dining room, storage units for dishes, silver, and glassware that close properly and have enough drawers to make for a handy "cleanup," with everything built in so that you have room to circulate easily around your table and chairs and you have a feeling of space that brings the calm needed for good digestion.

3° In your big room, *storage units to protect your books from dust as well as your collection of paintings and works of art,* and in such fashion that the walls of your room are bare. Then you could take out of the picture cabinet and hang on the wall the Ingres (or a photo of it if you're poor) that a column in the evening paper reminded you about.

Your china cabinets, your mirrored armoires, your silver cabinets, you'll sell those to somebody from one of these young nations that's just appeared on the map and where, precisely, *Progress* reigns supreme and where they're forsaking the traditional house (with its storage units, etc.) to live in progressive "European" houses with stuccos and mantelpieces.

Photo Branger.   The FARMAN *Moustique.*

Let us repeat the fundamental axioms:

a) *Chairs are made for sitting in.* There are church chairs with rush seats for 5 francs, Maple armchairs for 1,000 francs, and adjustable Morris reclining chairs with portable reading trays, coffee trays, foot extensions, adjustable backs with handles for setting the most perfect positions from napping to working, hygienically, comfortably, and correctly. Your Louis XV *bergères* and love seats with Aubusson upholstery, your Salon d'Automne pieces with "pumpkin" pillows, are they machines for sitting in? Between us, you are more comfortable at your club, your bank, or your office.

b) *Electricity provides light.* There is concealed lighting, and there are also diffusers and projectors. You see as clearly as in bright daylight and never have sore eyes.

A 100-candlepower bulb weighs 50 grams, but you have 100-kilogram chandeliers with curlicues on them, made of bronze or wood and so big that they take up the whole center of the room and whose maintenance is awful because of the flies that make caca on them. They're also very bad for your eyes in the evening.

c) *Windows are for admitting light — a little, a lot, or none at all — and for looking outside.* There are the windows in sleeping cars that close hermetically or open at will; there are the great windows of modern cafés that close hermetically but can be opened completely thanks to a crank that lowers them into the ground; there are the windows of dining cars that have small glass louvers that open to

Blériot Spad xiii: Bechneau, engineer.

ventilate a little, a lot, or not at all; there's the Saint-Gobain plate glass that has replaced bottle bottoms and stained glass; there are

"Air Express," two hundred kilometers per hour.

FARMAN Goliath, for bombing.

roll shutters that can be lowered gradually and block the light as one likes depending on the opening between their slats. But architects only use windows from Versailles or Compiègne, Louis X, Y, or Z that shut badly, have tiny little panes, are difficult to open, and have external shutters; if it rains at night, you get drenched closing them.

d) *Paintings are made for meditation.* Raphaels and Ingres and Picassos are made for meditation. If Raphael, Ingres, and Picasso cost too much, photographic reproductions are cheap. In order to meditate in front of a painting, it must be presented in the right place and in a calm atmosphere. The real collector organizes his paintings in a storage unit and hangs up the painting he wants to look at; but your walls are like stamp collections with lots of worthless stamps.

e) *A house is made to be lived in.* — Not possible! — But yes! — You are a utopian!

To tell the truth, the modern man is bored to death at home; he goes to his club. The modern woman is bored outside her boudoir; she goes to five o'clock tea. The modern man and woman are bored at home; they go dancing. But humbler folk who have no club settle down in the evenings under the ceiling lamp and are afraid to move

"AIR EXPRESS," the Farman Goliath.

about in the warren of their furniture, which takes up all the space and is all their fortune and all their pride.

The plans of houses cast man out and are devised for furniture storage. This conception is favorable to commerce on the Faubourg Saint-Antoine but harmful to society. It kills the spirit of the family, of the hearth; there's no hearth here, no family and no children, since it makes for living that's too uncomfortable.

The temperance societies and the league for repopulation should make an urgent appeal to architects; they should print a HOUSING MANUAL, distribute it to mothers of families, and demand the resignation of the professors at the École des Beaux-Arts.

HOUSING MANUAL

Demand a bathroom in full sunlight, one of the largest rooms in the apartment, the old drawing room for example. One wall that's all windows, opening if possible onto a terrace for sunbathing; porcelain sinks, bathtub, shower, exercise equipment.

Adjoining room: walk-in closet where you will dress and undress. Don't undress in your bedroom. It's untidy and creates a tiresome disorder. In the walk-in closet (1), require cabinets for linen and clothing, not more than 1 m 50 in height, with drawers, hangers, etc.

Demand one large room instead of all those drawing rooms.

Demand bare walls in your bedroom, in your large room, in your dining room. Built-in storage units will replace furniture that's expensive, consumes space, and has to be maintained.

Demand the elimination of the stuccos and the doors with beveled panels that involve a dishonest style.

If you can, put the kitchen directly under the roof to avoid smells.

To compensate for the stuccos and tapestries, demand that your landlord install electric lighting that's concealed or diffused.

Demand a vacuum cleaner.

Buy only practical furniture and never decorative furniture. If you want to see the bad taste of the great kings, go to old châteaus.

Put only a few paintings on the walls and only works of quality. Lacking paintings, buy photographs of these paintings.

Put your collections in drawers or in storage units. Have deep respect for true works of art.

The gramophone or the Pianola will give you accurate interpretations of Bach fugues and will spare you the concert hall, and colds, and the frenzies of virtuosos.

Demand ventilating panes in the windows of all your rooms.

Teach your children that a house is habitable only when there's abundant light, only when the floors and walls are clean. To keep your wooden floors in good repair, do without furniture and oriental carpets.

Demand of your landlord one car, bicycle, or motorcycle garage per apartment.

Demand a maid's room on the main floor. Don't cram your servants under the eaves.

Rent an apartment half the size of the one to which your parents accustomed you. Think about the economy of your gestures, your orders, and your thoughts.

(1) I don't know why in modern French a toilet is called a closet; the days of the clyster pipe are long gone.

The FARMAN Goliath. Paris-Prague in six hours, Paris-Warsaw in nine hours.

THE PROBLEM BADLY POSED:

EYES THAT HAVE NOT SEEN...

Farman.

Conclusion. Every modern man has a mechanical side: a feeling for the mechanical spurred by everyday activity. This feeling for the mechanical is one of respect, of gratitude, of esteem.

The mechanical carries within it the economic factor that selects. In the feeling for the mechanical, there is something of moral feeling.

The man who is intelligent, coolheaded, and calm has acquired wings.

Men who are intelligent, coolheaded, and calm: they are what's needed to build the house, to plan the city.

Mss. Loucheur and Bonnevay have introduced a law whose object is the construction over 10 years (1921 to 1930) of 500,000 economical and healthy housing units.

The financial projections are based on an anticipated cost of 15,000 francs (1) per house.

Presently, the smallest houses, built according to the givens of traditionalist architects, cost no less than 25,000 to 30,000 francs.

To realize the Loucheur program, we must completely transform the current routine of architects, sift the past and all its memories through the mesh of reason, pose the problem as the aviation engineers posed it for themselves, and build mass-production machines for living in.

(1) 1921. Today it would be as high as 28 or 40,000 francs.

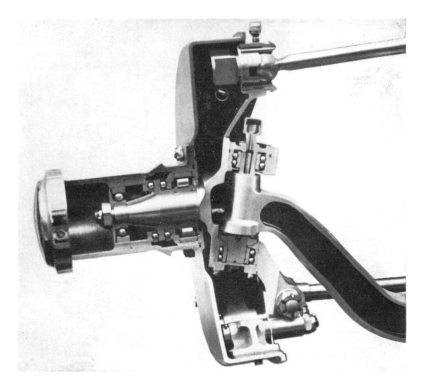

DELAGE FRONT-WHEEL BRAKE.
This precision, this clarity of execution, does not just gratify a newborn feeling for the mechanical. Pheidias felt this way; the entablature of the Parthenon bears witness. Likewise the Egyptians when they polished the Pyramids. This was in an age when Euclid and Pythagoras dictated the conduct of their contemporaries.

EYES THAT DO NOT SEE...

III

AUTOMOBILES

We must see to the establishment of standards so we can face up to the problem of perfection.

The Parthenon is a product of selection applied to a standard.

Architecture works on standards.

Standards are a matter of logic, of analysis, of scrupulous study; they are based on a problem well posed. Experimentation definitively fixes the standard.

DELAGE, 1921.

If the problem of housing, of the apartment, were studied like a chassis, we would see our houses rapidly transformed and improved. If houses were built industrially, mass produced like chassis, we would soon see forms emerge that, while unexpected, were sound, tenable, and an aesthetic would be formulated with surprising precision.

There is a new spirit: it is a spirit of construction and of synthesis guided by a clear conception.

Program of L'Esprit nouveau, *no. 1, October 1920.*

We must see to the establishment of *standards* so we can face up to the problem of *perfection*.

PAESTUM, 600–550 B.C.

The Parthenon is a product of selection applied to an established standard. Already for a century, the Greek temple had been organized in all its elements.

When a standard has been established, direct and fierce competition comes into play. It's a "match"; to win, you must do better

Photo from *La Vie automobile*.   HUMBERT, 1907.

Photo Albert Morancé.   PARTHENON, 447–434 B.C.

than your adversary *in all the parts,* in the general lines and in all the details. Then there is intense study of the parts. Progress.

The standard is a necessity for order brought to bear on human labor.

The standard is established on sure foundations, not arbitrarily,

DELAGE Grand-Sport, 1921.

HISPANO-SUIZA, 1911. Ozenfant coachwork.

but with the certainty of justified things and of a logic controlled by analysis and experimentation.

All men have the same organism, the same functions.

All men have the same needs.

The social contract that evolves through the ages determines standard classes, functions, and needs yielding products for standard uses.

The house is a product necessary to man.

The painting is a product necessary to man in order to answer to needs of a spiritual order, determined by standards of emotion.

All great works are based on a few great standards of the heart: *Oedipus, Phaedra,* the *Prodigal Son,* Madonnas, *Paul and Virginia, Philemon and Baucis, The Poor Fisherman,* the *Marseillaise, "Madelon vient nous verser à boire"...*.

To establish a standard is to exhaust all practical and reasonable possibilities, to deduce a recognized type consistent with function, maximal return, and minimum expenditure of means, manpower, and materials, words, forms, colors, sounds.

The automobile is an object with a simple function (to run) and complex ends (comfort, resistance, looks) that has placed major industry under an imperious necessity to standardize. All automobiles are essentially organized the same way. Through the relentless

BIGNAN-SPORT, 1921.

competition of the countless firms that build them, each has found itself under obligation to dominate the competition, and, on top of the standard for realized practical things, there has intervened a search for perfection and harmony outside of brute practical fact, a manifestation not only of perfection and harmony, but of beauty.

Thence is born style, which is to say the unanimously acknowledged acquisition of a unanimously felt state of perfection.

The establishment of a standard proceeds from the organization of rational elements according to a line of conduct that is likewise rational. The enveloping mass is not preconceived, *it results;* it can look strange at first. Ader making a "Bat" that didn't fly; Wright and Farman making airfoils that were odd and disconcerting, but that flew. The standard was fixed. Then came the fine-tuning.

The first automobiles were built and shaped the old way. This was contrary to the conditions of a body's motion and rapid penetration. Study of the laws of penetration fixed the standard, a standard that evolves between two different ends: speed, large mass in front (racing cars); comfort, large volume to the rear (limousine). In both cases, there's no longer anything in common with the old slow-moving carriage.

Civilizations advance. They leave behind the age of the peasant, the warrior, and the priest to attain what is rightly called

Photo Albert Morancé.   THE PARTHENON.

Little by little, the temple is formulated, passes from construction to architecture.
A hundred years later the Parthenon will fix the culminating point of the ascent.

culture. Culture is the outcome of an effort of selection. Selection means discarding, pruning, cleansing; making the Essential stand out anew stripped and clear.

From the primitivism of the Romanesque chapel, we have moved on to Notre-Dame de Paris, to the Invalides, to the Concorde. We have purified, refined the sensation, set aside decoration, and conquered proportion and measure; we have advanced; we have passed from primary satisfactions (decor) to higher satisfactions (mathematics).

If there are still Breton cupboards in Brittany, that is because the Bretons have stayed in Brittany, quite remote, quite stable, still occupied with fishing and animal husbandry. It is unbecoming for gentlemen of good standing to sleep in Breton beds in their Parisian townhouses; it is unbecoming for gentlemen who own limousines to sleep in Breton beds, etc. One need only take stock and draw the logical conclusions. To own a limousine and a Breton bed is, alas, a frequent occurrence.

Photo Albert Morancé.   THE PARTHENON.

Each part is decisive, scores the maximum in precision and expression; proportion here
reads as categorical.

Everyone exclaims with conviction and enthusiasm: "The limousine sets the style of our era!" while Breton beds are still sold and still made for "antique" dealers.

So let us put the Parthenon and the automobile on show to make it clear that it's a question here, in different domains, of two products of selection, the one having reached its outcome, the other still progressing. This ennobles the automobile. And then? Well, it remains to compare our houses and our palaces with automobiles. Here's where we get stuck, where everything gets stuck. Here's where we don't have our Parthenons.

The standard for the house is of a practical order, a structural order. I tried to articulate it in the preceding chapter on airplanes.

The Loucheur program, which calls for 500,000 housing units to be built over ten years, will doubtless fix one for worker's housing.

Caproni Tricellular Hydroplane.
This image shows how plastic organisms are created at the sole instigation
of a problem well posed.

The standard for furniture is well along the way of experiment at the manufacturers of office furniture and trunks, clockmakers, etc. We must continue down that path: the engineer's task. And all the nonsense about the unique object, about art furniture, rings false and shows a regrettable incomprehension of the needs of the present hour: a chair is by no means a work of art; a chair has no soul; it is a tool for sitting.

Art, in a land of high culture, finds its means of expression in true works of art, concentrated and rid of all utilitarian ends: paintings, books, music.

All human manifestations require a certain quantum of interest, and especially in the aesthetic domain; this interest is of a sensory order and an intellectual order. Decoration is of a sensory and primary order like color, and it suits simple peoples, peasants, and savages. Harmony and proportion appeal to the intellect and make the cultivated man take notice. The peasant likes ornament and

CAPRONI-EXPLORATION.

Poetry is not only of the word. Stronger still is the poetry of facts. Objects that signify
something and are arranged with tact and talent create a poetic fact.

paints frescoes. The civilized man wears English suits and owns
easel paintings and books.

Decoration is the necessary superfluity or quantum of the
peasant, and proportion is the necessary superfluity or quantum of
the cultivated man.

In architecture, the quantum of interest is achieved through
the grouping and proportion of rooms and furniture: the architect's
task. And beauty? That is an imponderable that can act only
through the formal presence of primordial foundations: rational
satisfaction of the mind (utility, economy); then cubes, spheres,
cylinders, cones, etc. (sensory). Then... the imponderable, relationships that create the imponderable: that's genius, inventive
genius, plastic genius, mathematical genius, the capacity to make

BELLANGER Sedan.

us measure order and unity, to organize according to clear laws all those things that excite and fully satisfy our visual senses.

Then there arise the diverse sensations — evocative of everything that a man of high culture has seen, felt, loved — that trigger, through implacable means, those shivers already experienced in the drama of life: nature, men, the world.

In this period of science, struggle, and drama, when the individual is always being violently shaken up, the Parthenon seems to us a living work, full of grand sonorities. The mass of its infallible elements gives the measure of what man, absorbed in a problem definitively posed, can attain in the way of perfection. The perfection here is so outside the norm that, at the present time, a view of the Parthenon can strike a chord only with a very limited set of our sensations — surprisingly enough, only with mechanical sensations, with those great impressive machines that we have seen and that seemed to us the most perfect results of present activity, the only achieved products of our civilization.

Voisin. Torpédo-Sport, 1921.

One can pass judgment on a truly elegant man more conclusively than on a truly elegant woman, because male dress is standardized. The presence of Pheidias beside Iktinos and Kallikrates is indisputable, and also his dominant role, because the temples of the era were all of the same type and the Parthenon surpasses them all beyond measure.

Pheidias would have loved to live in this era of standards. He would have assumed the possibility, the certainty of success. His eyes would have seen our era and the probative results of its labor. Before long, he would have repeated the experience of the Parthenon.

Architecture works on standards. Standards are things of logic, of analysis, of scrupulous study. Standards are based on a problem well posed. Architecture is plastic invention, is intellectual speculation, is higher mathematics. Architecture is an art of great dignity.

The standard, imposed by the law of selection, is an economic and social necessity. Harmony is a state of accord with the norms of our universe. Beauty dominates; it is a purely human creation; it is a necessary superfluity only for those with elevated souls.

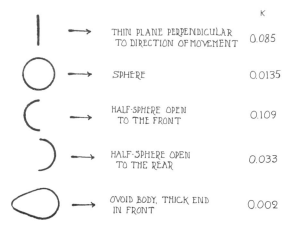

		K
	THIN PLANE PERPENDICULAR TO DIRECTION OF MOVEMENT	0.085
	SPHERE	0.0135
	HALF-SPHERE OPEN TO THE FRONT	0.109
	HALF-SPHERE OPEN TO THE REAR	0.033
	OVOID BODY, THICK END IN FRONT	0.002

The cone of maximum penetration determined through experiment and calculation bears out natural creations: fish, birds, etc. Experimental applications: the dirigible, the racing car.

But we must first see to the establishment of standards so we can face up to the problem of perfection.

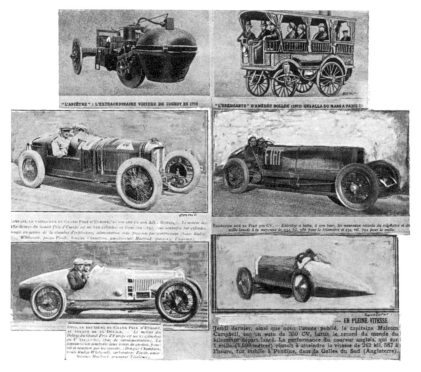

In search of a standard.

Photo Albert Morancé.   THE PARTHENON.

Pheidias, in building the Parthenon, did not do the work of a builder, an engineer, a drafter
of plans. All the elements existed. He made a work of perfection, of high spirituality.

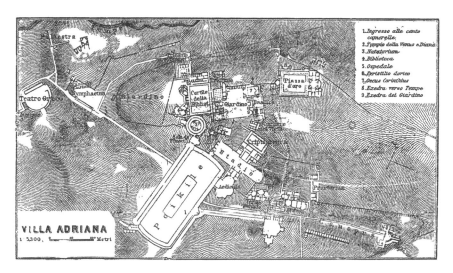

1. Ingresso alle cento
   camerelle.
2. Tempio della Venus o Diana
3. Natatorium
4. Biblioteca
5. Ospedale
6. Peristilio dorico
7. Oecus Corinthius
8. Esedra verso Tempe
9. Esedra del Giardino

VILLA ADRIANA
1 : 5,300,

HADRIAN'S VILLA, near Tivoli, A.D. 130.

ARCHITECTURE

I

THE LESSON OF ROME

Architecture is the use of raw materials to establish stirring relationships.

Architecture goes beyond utilitarian things.

Architecture is a plastic thing.

Spirit of order, unity of intention, a sense of relationships; architecture organizes quantities.

Passion can make drama out of inert stone.

You work with stone, with wood, with concrete; you make them into houses and palaces; this is construction. Ingenuity is at work.

But suddenly you touch my heart, you do me good, I am happy, I say: "It is beautiful." This is architecture. Art is present.

My house is practical. Thank you, as I thank the engineers of the railroad and the telephone company. You have not touched my heart.

But the walls rise against the sky in an order such that I am moved. I sense your intentions. You were gentle, brutal, charming, or dignified. Your stones tell me so. You rivet me to this spot and my eyes look. My eyes look at something that states a thought. A thought that clarifies itself without words or sounds, but only through prisms that have relationships with one another. These prisms are such that the light reveals them clearly. These relationships don't necessarily have anything to do with what is practical or descriptive. They are a mathematical creation of your mind. They are the language of architecture. With inert materials, based on a more or less utilitarian program that you *go beyond,* you have established relationships that moved me. It is architecture.

Rome is a picturesque landscape. The light there is so beautiful that it ratifies everything. Rome is a bazaar where everything is sold. All the implements of the life of a people have remained there, children's toys, warriors' arms, old altar rags, the Borgias' bidets, and adventurers' panaches. In Rome, monstrosities are legion.

If we consider the Greeks, we think the Romans had bad taste: the Roman-romans, Julius II and Victor-Emmanuel.

Ancient Rome was squeezed inside walls that were always too tight; a city that is crammed together is not beautiful. Renaissance Rome had a pompous fervor, disseminated to the four corners of the city. The Rome of Victor-Emmanuel collects, labels, preserves, and installs its modern life in the corridors of this museum, and proclaims itself "Roman" through the monument commemorating Victor-Emmanuel I, in the center of the city, between the Capitol and the forum... forty years' work, something bigger than everything else, and in white marble!

Without a doubt, everything is too crammed together in Rome.

THE PYRAMID OF CESTIUS, 12 B.C.

I

ANCIENT ROME

Rome kept itself busy conquering the universe and administering it.

Strategy, provisioning, legislation: a spirit of order. To manage a large business firm, one adopts principles that are basic, simple, indisputable. Roman order is an order that is simple, categorical. If it is brutal, so much the better or so much the worse.

They had an immense desire for domination and organization. In architectural Rome, there was nothing to be done, the city walls were too tight, the houses stacked their floors ten levels up, old skyscrapers. The Forum must have been ugly, a bit like the hodgepodge of the sacred city of Delphi. Urbanism, grand plans? Nothing to be done.

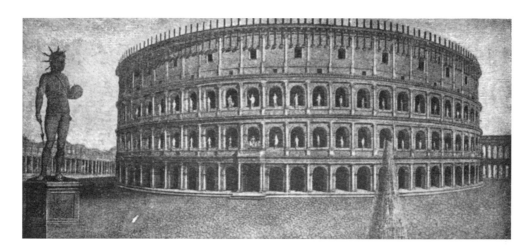

THE COLOSSEUM, A.D. 80.

ARCH OF CONSTANTINE, A.D. 12.

INTERIOR OF THE PANTHEON, A.D. 120.

One must go and see Pompeii, which is moving in its rectitude. They had conquered Greece and, like good barbarians, they found the Corinthian more beautiful than the Doric, because more florid. Bring on the acanthus capitals, the entablatures decorated without much moderation or taste! But underneath was something Roman that we're going to take a look at. In sum, they built superb chassis but designed dreadful coachwork like the landaus of Louis XIV. Outside of Rome, where there was air, they built Hadrian's Villa. There you meditate on Roman grandeur. There they imposed order. It is the first grand ordonnance of the West. If you measure Greece against this gauge, you say: "The Greek was a sculptor, nothing more." But careful, architecture is not just ordonnance. Ordonnance is one of the fundamental prerogatives of architecture. To

THE PANTHEON, A.D. 120.

walk about Hadrian's Villa and say to oneself that the modern power of organization that is "Roman" has yet to do anything: what torment for a man who feels himself party and accomplice to this confounding mess!

The problem here was not devastated regions but fitting out conquered lands: much the same thing. So they invented construction methods and used them to make impressive "Roman" things. The word means something. Unity of method, strength of intention, classification of elements. The immense domes, the drums that support them, the imposing barrel vaults, all this holds together with Roman cement and remains an object of admiration. These were great entrepreneurs.

Strength of intention and classification of elements, that is proof of a turn of mind: strategy, legislation. The architecture is responsive to these intentions, *it renders*. The light caresses the pure forms: *it renders*. The simple volumes unfold vast surfaces that express themselves with a characteristic variety depending on their being domes, barrel vaults, cylinders, rectangular prisms, or pyramids. The surface decoration (openings) is of the same geometric class. The Pantheon, the Colosseum, the aqueducts, the Pyramid of Cestius, triumphal arches, the Basilica of Constantine, the Baths of Caracalla.

No verbosity; ordonnance, a single idea, boldness and unity of construction, the use of elementary forms. Sound morality.

Let us retain from the Romans the bricks and Roman cement and travertine stone, and let's sell Roman marble to the millionaires. The Romans knew nothing about marble.

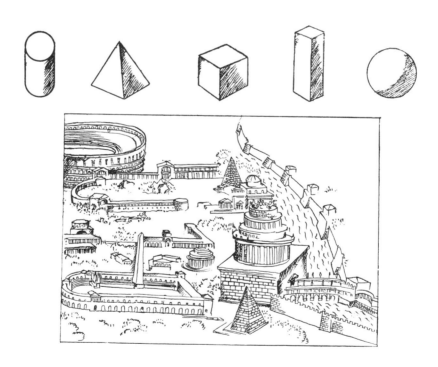

INTERIOR OF SANTA MARIA IN COSMEDIN

II

BYZANTINE ROME

Another jolt from Greece, by way of Byzantium. This time, it's not a simpleton's amazement before a florid tangle of acanthus: native Greeks came to build Santa Maria in Cosmedin. A Greece far removed from Pheidias but having retained its seed, which is to say the sense of relationships, the mathematics thanks to which perfection becomes attainable. This tiny little church of Santa Maria, a church for poor people, proclaims, in loudly luxurious Rome, the signal splendor of mathematics, the unbeatable power of proportion, the sovereign eloquence of relationships. The theme is just a basilica, which is to say the architectural form from which barns and hangars are made. The walls are of rough lime plaster. There is but one color, white: a force that is certain because it is absolute. This minuscule church transfixes you with respect. "Oh!" you gasp, you who came from Saint Peter's or from the Palatine or from the Colosseum. Artistic sensualists and artistic hedonists will be made

uncomfortable by Santa Maria in Cosmedin. To think that this church existed in Rome when the great Renaissance reigned supreme with its gilded palaces and its horrors!

Greece by way of Byzantium, a pure creation of the mind. Architecture is not just ordonnance and beautiful forms in light. It is a thing that ravishes us, it is measure. To measure. To divide up into quantities that are rhythmic, animated by a like breath, to imbue everything with unifying and subtle relationships, to balance, *to solve the equation.* For if this expression is forced when one talks painting, it suits architecture, which doesn't concern itself

with figuration, with any elements pertaining to the face of man, this architecture that organizes *quantities*. These quantities are piles of materials ready to be put to work; measured, plugged into the equation, they create rhythms, they speak of numbers, they speak of relationships, they speak of mind.

In the silent equilibrium of Santa Maria in Cosmedin, the oblique handrail of a pulpit rises, the stone book of a lectern inclines in silent conjugation like a gesture of assent. These two humble obliques conjugated in the perfect movement of a spiritual mechanism: this is the pure and simple beauty of architecture.

THE APSES OF SAINT PETER'S

III

MICHELANGELO

Intelligence and passion. There is no art without emotion, no
emotion without passion. Stones in quarries are inert, dormant, but
the apses of Saint Peter's make drama. Drama is all around the
decisive works of humanity. Architectural drama = man of the universe and in the universe. The Parthenon is poignant; the Egyptian
pyramids, their granite formerly polished and gleaming like steel,

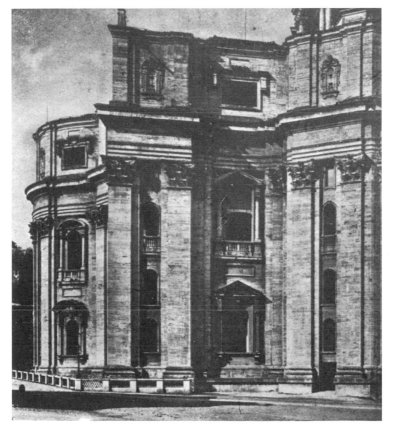

THE APSES OF SAINT PETER'S

were poignant. To give off emanations, storms, gentle breezes on plain and sea, to raise up lofty alps with stones like those in the walls of a man's house: that is to make successful concerted relationships.

Like man, like drama, like architecture. Not to assert with too much confidence that the masses give rise to their man. A *man* is an exceptional phenomenon that repeats at lengthy intervals, perhaps by chance, perhaps according to a cosmographic rhythm yet to be determined.

Michelangelo is the man of our last thousand years as Pheidias was the man of the preceding millennium. The Renaissance did not make Michelangelo, it made a fine bunch of fellows who had talent.

The work of Michelangelo is a *creation*, not a revival, a creation that towers over stylistic categories. The apses of Saint Peter's are in the Corinthian style. Imagine! See them and think of the Madeleine. The Colosseum was seen by him and its felicitous measure-

ENTABLATURE OF THE APSES OF SAINT PETER'S (executed by Michelangelo).

ments retained; the Baths of Caracalla and the Basilica of
Constantine showed him what limits it might be well to surpass
through recourse to an elevated intention. Thence the domes, the

Plan of Saint Peter's, present state, the nave was extended throughout the hatched area. Michelangelo wanted to say something, it was all wrecked.

PORTA PIA BY MICHELANGELO

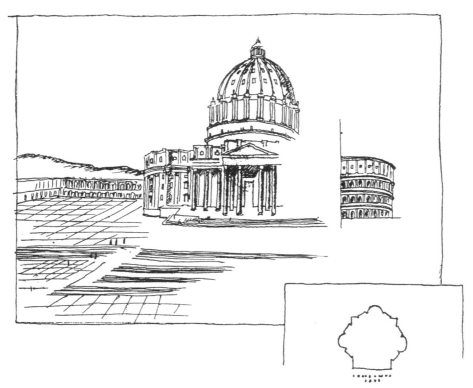

Saint Peter's. Design by Michelangelo (1547 1564). The dimensions are considerable. Building such a dome of stone was a tour de force that few dared risk. Saint Peter's covers 15,000 m² and Notre-Dame de Paris, 5,955; Hagia Sophia in Constantinople 6,900 m². The dome is 132 m high, the diameter at the crossing 150 m. The ordonnance of the apses and of the attic is related to that of the Colosseum; the heights are the same. The design had total unity; it grouped together the most beautiful and most opulent elements: the portico, the cylinders, the square forms, the drum, the dome. The use of moldings is as **passionate** as can be, fierce and full of pathos. Everything rose as a block, single and whole. The eye grasped it at once. Michelangelo completed the apses and the drum of the dome. Then the rest fell into barbaric hands, everything was annihilated. Humanity lost one of the crucial works of intelligence. If you think about Michelangelo sensing the disaster, a terrifying drama comes to light.

Saint Peter's Square, present state; empty verbosity, misplaced words. The colonnade by Bernini is beautiful in itself. The facade is beautiful in itself but has nothing to do with the dome. The whole point was the dome; it was hidden! The dome went with the apses; they were hidden! The portico was highly volumetric; it was made into facade cladding.

setbacks, the canted walls, the drum of the dome, the hypostyle portico, a gigantic geometry of concordant relationships. Then a renewal of the rhythms through stylobates, pilasters, entablatures with profiles that are completely new. Then windows and niches that take up the rhythm yet again. The whole mass makes for a gripping novelty in the dictionary of architecture; it is good to pause and reflect for a moment on this post-quattrocento coup de théâtre.

Finally, there was to have been an interior that would have been the monumental climax of a Santa Maria in Cosmedin; the

WINDOW IN THE APSES OF SAINT PETER'S

Medici Chapel, in Florence, allows us to gauge what this work, so carefully worked out in advance, might have been. But rash and thoughtless popes dismissed Michelangelo; wretches ruined Saint Peter's inside and out; it stupidly became the Saint Peter's of today, that of a very rich and enterprising cardinal, without... *everything.* An immense loss. A passion, an intelligence beyond norms, it was an affirmation; it has very sadly become a "perhaps," an "apparently," an "it might be," an "I doubt it." A miserable failure.

Since this chapter is entitled *Architecture,* it was permissible to talk here about one man's passion.

IV

ROME AND US

Rome is a picturesque open-air bazaar. It has all the horrors

THE ROME OF HORRORS

1. Renaissance Rome, Castel Sant'Angelo.   1. Modern Rome. Palace of Justice.
2. Renaissance Rome, Colonna Gallery.   2. Renaissance Rome, Barberini Palace.

(see the four grouped reproductions) and bad taste of the Roman Renaissance. We judge this Renaissance with our modern taste, which separates us from it by four great centuries of effort: the 17th, the 18th, the 19th, the 20th.

We reap the benefits of this effort, we judge harshly, but with a justified clear-sightedness. This is lacking in Rome, asleep these four centuries after Michelangelo. Setting foot in Paris again, we regain consciousness of the gauge.

The lesson of Rome is for the wise, for those who know and can appreciate, for those who can resist, who can verify. Rome is the perdition of those who don't know much. To put architecture students in Rome is to wound them for life. The Prix de Rome and the Villa Medici are the cancer of French architecture.

Plan of the city of Karlsruhe.

ARCHITECTURE

II

THE ILLUSION OF THE PLAN

The plan proceeds from the inside out; the exterior is the result of an interior.

The elements of architecture are light and shadow, walls and space.

Ordonnance is the hierarchy of goals, the classification of intentions.

Man sees architectural things with eyes that are 1 m 70 from the ground. We can reckon only with goals accessible to the eye, with intentions that take the elements of architecture into account. If we reckon with intentions that do not belong to the language of architecture, we end up with an illusory plan, we break the rules of the plan through faulty conception or through a penchant for vain things.

You work with stone, with wood, with concrete; you make them into houses and palaces; this is construction. Ingenuity is at work.

But suddenly you touch my heart, you do me good, I am happy, I say: "It is beautiful." This is architecture. Art is present.

My house is practical. Thank you, as I thank the engineers of the railroad and the telephone company. You have not touched my heart.

But the walls rise against the sky in an order such that I am moved. I sense your intentions. You were gentle, brutal, charming, or dignified. Your stones tell me so. You rivet me to this spot and my eyes look. My eyes look at something that states a thought. A thought that clarifies itself without words or sounds, but only through prisms that have relationships with one another. These prisms are such that the light reveals them clearly. These relationships don't necessarily have anything to do with what is practical or descriptive. They are a mathematical creation of your mind. They are the language of architecture. With inert materials, based on a more or less utilitarian program that you go beyond, you have established relationships that moved me. It is architecture.

———

To make a plan is to clarify, to fix ideas.

It is to have had ideas.

It is ordering these ideas such that they become intelligible, feasible, and transmissible. So it is necessary to manifest a clear intention, to have had ideas that made it possible to set oneself an intention. A plan is in some sense a concentrate like an analytic table of contents. In a form so concentrated that it seems like a crystal, like a geometric blueprint, it contains an enormous quantity of ideas and a driving intention.

In a great public institution, the École des Beaux-Arts, the principles of the good plan have been studied, then, over the years, dogmas, formulas, and tricks have become fixed. An education that was useful at first has become a perilous practice. The inner idea has been made into a few hallowed exterior signs and appearances. The plan, a cluster of ideas and an intention integral to that cluster of ideas, has become a sheet of paper on which black marks that are walls and lines that are axes play at being mosaics and decorative panels, make diagrams with dazzling stars, create optical illusions. The most beautiful star becomes the Prix de Rome. But the plan is the generator, "the plan determines everything; it is an austere abstraction, an algebrization dry to the eye." It is a plan of battle. The battle ensues, and that is the great moment. The battle consists of the clash of volumes in space and the morale of the troops is the bundle of preexisting ideas and the driving intention. Without a good plan nothing exists, everything is fragile and does not last, everything is poor even under a clutter of opulence.

From the outset, the plan implies the methods of construction; the architect is first of all an engineer. But let us confine ourselves to the question of architecture, this thing that endures over time. Looking at things from this point of view exclusively, I will begin by drawing attention to this crucial fact: a plan proceeds *from the inside out,* for a house or a palace is an organism similar to any living creature. I will speak of the architectural *elements* of the interior. I will then turn to *ordonnance.* Considering the impact of a work of architecture on its site, I will show that here again the *outside* is always an *inside.* With a few basic statements clarified by illustrations, I will be able to show the *illusion of the plan,* this illusion that kills architecture, leads minds astray, and creates dishonesty in architecture through the transgression of irrefutable truths, the consequence of false conceptions or the fruit of vanity.

A PLAN PROCEEDS FROM THE INSIDE OUT

A building is like a soap bubble. This bubble is perfect and harmonious if the air is evenly distributed and properly ordered from the inside. The exterior is the result of an interior.

In Bursa in Asia Minor, at the GREEN MOSQUE, you enter through a small doorway to human scale; a very small vestibule works on you the change of scale that's necessary to appreciate, after the dimensions of the street and the place you've just come from, the dimensions that are meant to impress you. Then you experience the grandeur of the mosque and your eyes take its measure. You are in a large space white with marble, inundated with

Fig. 1. — Great Mosque of Sulemaniye in Istanbul.

FIG. 2. — Plan of the Green Mosque in Bursa.

light. Beyond is a second space that is similar and of like dimensions, filled with half-light and raised several steps (a repeat in the minor key); on either side, two smaller spaces still in half-light; you turn around, two very small spaces in shadow. From bright light to shadow: a rhythm. Tiny doors and immense openings. You are captivated, you have lost all sense of usual scale. You are overcome by a sensory rhythm (light and volume) and by skilled measurements, in a world unto itself that tells you what it meant to tell you. What emotion! What faith! There, that's the driving intention. The bundle of ideas is the means that has been used (fig. 2). Consequences: in Bursa, as in Hagia Sophia in Constantinople and in the Great Mosque of Suleiman in Istanbul, an exterior results (figs. 1 and 2a).

FIG. 2a. — Hagia Sophia in Constantinople.

FIG. 3. — Case del Noce, the Cavaedium, Pompeii.

CASA DEL NOCE, in Pompeii. Again a small vestibule that clears the street from your mind. And suddenly you are in the cavaedium (atrium); four columns in the center (four *cylinders*) rise in one go toward the shadow of the roof, a sensation of strength and

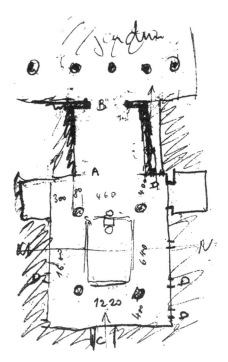

FIG. 4. — Casa del Noce.

witness to potent means; but to the rear, the sparkle of a garden seen through a peristyle that spreads this light with a grand gesture, distributes it and draws attention to it, stretching it far to left and right, creating a large space. Between the two, a tablium narrowing this vision like the viewfinder of a camera. Right and left, two spaces that are shadowy, small. From the bustling street, a whole world of picturesque accident open to all, you have entered the house of a *Roman*. Magisterial grandeur, order, magnificent breadth: you are in the house of a *Roman*. How were these rooms used? That is beside the point. After twenty centuries, without historical allusions, you feel the architecture, and all this in what is really a very small house (figs. 3 and 4).

ARCHITECTURAL ELEMENTS OF THE INTERIOR

At our disposition are straight walls, a floor that extends, holes that are passages for man or for light: doors and windows. The holes brighten or darken: make cheerful or sad. The walls are sparkling with light or in half-light or shadow: make cheerful,

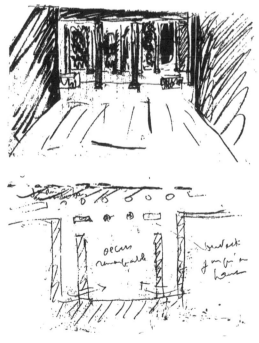

Fig. 5. — Hadrian's Villa, Rome.

serene, or sad. Your symphony is prepared. Architecture has as its goal to make us cheerful or serene. Have respect for walls. The Pompeian does not put holes in his walls; he has devotion for walls, a love for light. Light is intense if it is between walls that reflect it. The man of antiquity made walls, walls that extend and join together to make for still larger walls. Thus did he create volumes, the foundation of architectural sensation, of sensory sensation. The light explodes with definite intent at one end and illuminates the walls. The *impression* of light extends beyond through cylinders (I

FIG. 6. — Hadrian's Villa, Rome.

don't like to say *columns,* the word has been spoiled), peristyles, or pillars. The floor extends wherever it can, uniform, without irregularities. Sometimes, to add another impression, the floor rises a step. There are no other architectural elements of the interior: light and the walls that reflect it in great sheets and the floor that is a horizontal wall. To make well-lit walls is to constitute the architectural elements of the interior. There remains proportion (figs. 5, 6, and 7).

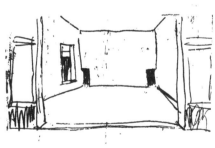

FIG. 7. — Pompeii.

ORDONNANCE

The axis is perhaps the first human manifestation; it is the means of every human act. The toddling infant tends toward an axis, the man struggling through life's tempest describes an axis. The axis is architecture's order-maker. To make order is to begin a work. Architecture is based on axes. The axes of the École des Beaux-Arts are the calamity of architecture. The axis is a line of conduct toward a goal. In architecture, an axis must have a goal. At the École this has been forgotten and axes crisscross to make stars, all leading toward infinity, the undefined, the unknown, nothingness: without a goal. The axis of the École is a formula, a trick (1).

Ordonnance is the hierarchy of axes, thus the hierarchy of goals and the classification of intentions.

So the architect assigns goals to his axes. These goals are a wall (a solid; sensory sensation) or light and space (sensory sensation).

In reality, axes are not perceived in the bird's-eye views shown in plans on the drawing board, but from the ground, by a man standing erect and looking before him. The eye sees far and, an imperturbable lens, sees all, even beyond what was intended and willed. The axis of the Acropolis goes from Peiraeus to Pentelikon, from sea to mountain. From the Propylaea perpendicular to the axis to the far horizon, to the sea: a horizontal perpendicular to the direction that the architecture has imprinted on you where you stand, an orthogonal perception that tells. From the Propylaea facing the other direction, the colossal statue of Athena on axis and Mount Pentelikon in the distance. That tells. And because they are outside this driving axis, the Parthenon at right and the Erechtheum at left, *you have the good fortune to see them in three-quarter view,* in their whole physiognomy. Don't put all architectural things on axis, for they will be like so many people talking at once (fig. 8).

(1) So much a trick is it that they're drawn on paper so as to make stars, as a peacock spreads its tail.

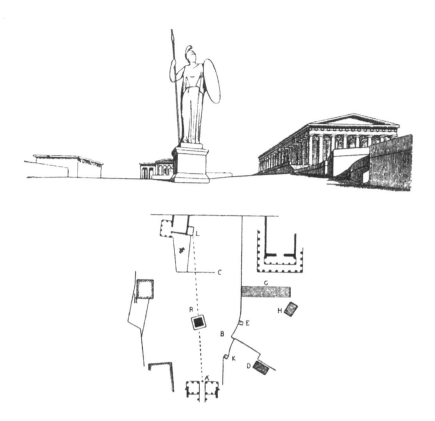

FIG. 8. — The Acropolis in Athens.

FORUM IN POMPEII: Ordonnance is the hierarchy of goals,
the classification of intentions. The plan of the Forum contains

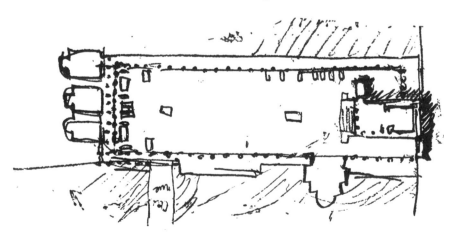

FIG. 9. — Forum in Pompeii.

many axes, but it would never win third prize at the Beaux-Arts; it would be rejected, it doesn't make a star! It brings joy to the mind to look at such a plan, to walk through the forum (fig. 9).

And here IN THE HOUSE OF THE TRAGIC POET the subtleties of a consummate art. Everything relates to an axis but

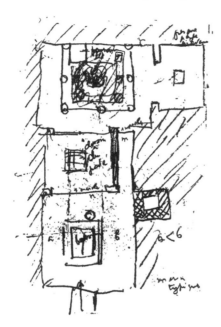

Fɪɢ. 10. — House of the Tragic Poet, Pompeii.

you'd have a hard time drawing a straight line through it. The axis is in the intentions, and the splendor given by the axis extends to the humble things that the latter affects with a skillful gesture (the corridors, the main passage, etc.), through optical illusions. The axis here is not a dry theoretical thing; it links the crucial volumes yet spells them out and differentiates them from one another. When you visit the House of the Tragic Poet, you see that everything is in order. But the sensation is rich. Then you observe some artful shifts from the axis that give the volumes intensity: the central motif in the paving is pushed back behind the room's center; the well at the entrance is to the side of the pool. The fountain to the rear is in the corner of the garden. An object placed in the center of a room often ruins the room since it prevents your placing yourself in the center of the room and having the axial view; a monument in the center of a square often ruins the square and the buildings around it — often, but not always; every such case has its own logic.

Ordonnance is the hierarchy of axes, thus the hierarchy of goals and the classification of intentions (fig. 10).

THE OUTSIDE IS ALWAYS AN INSIDE

When, at the École, they draw axes that make stars, they imagine that the spectator arriving in front of the building senses only this building and that his eye goes to it infallibly and stays riveted solely to the center of gravity that these axes have determined. The human eye, in its investigations, is always turning and man also turns to the right, to the left, clear round. He takes in everything and is drawn toward the center of gravity of the site as a whole. Suddenly the problem spreads to the surroundings. The neighboring houses, the near or distant mountain, the low or high horizon are formidable masses whose cubic volumes make a powerful effect. The apparent cubic volume and the real cubic volume are gauged instantaneously, anticipated by the intelligence. The cubic sensation is immediate, primordial; your building cubes 100,000 cubic meters, but what is around it cubes millions of cubic meters, which tells. Then comes the density sensation: a boulder, a tree, a hill are less strong, of lesser density than a geometric arrangement of forms. Marble is denser to the eye and the mind than wood and so forth. Always hierarchy.

To sum things up, in architectural spectacles, the elements of the site intervene by virtue of their cubic volume, their density, the quality of their materials, the bearers of sensations that are quite distinct and quite different (wood, marble, tree, lawn, blue horizons, near or distant sea, sky). The elements of the site rise up like walls rigged out to the power of their "cubic" coefficient, stratification, material, etc., like the walls of a large room. Walls and light, shadow and light, sad, cheerful, or serene, etc. It is necessary to compose with these elements:

On the ACROPOLIS IN ATHENS, the temples that incline toward one another to shape a bosom that the eye readily embraces

FIG. 11. — Propylaea and Temple of the Wingless Victory.

(fig. 11). The sea that makes a composition with the architraves (fig. 12), etc. This is to compose with the infinite resources of an art full of perilous riches that produce beauty only when they are brought into order:

FIG. 12. — The Propylaea.

Fig. 13. — Hadrian's Villa, Rome.

At HADRIAN'S VILLA: the floors set at levels concordant with the Roman plain (fig. 13); the mountains that close off the composition, which indeed is based on them (fig. 14).

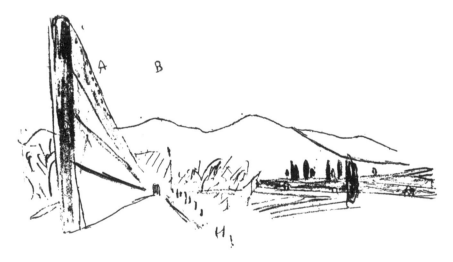

Fig. 14. — Hadrian's Villa, Rome.

FIG. 15. — Forum at Pompeii.

At the FORUM IN POMPEII: views from every building onto the complex as a whole, onto various details, onto groupings that constantly renew their interest (figs. 9 and 15).

Etc. Etc.

TRANSGRESSION

In the examples I now offer, they did not take into account that a plan works from the inside out, they did not compose with volumes animated by a single well-regulated breath, in conformity with a goal that was the driving intention of the work, a goal that anyone can then observe with his own eyes. They did not reckon with the architectural elements of the interior that are the surfaces that come together to receive light and to emphasize volumes. They did not think in spatial terms but made stars on paper, drew axes that crisscrossed. They reckoned with intentions that do not belong to the language of architecture. They transgressed the rules of the plan through an error in conception or through a tendency toward vain things.

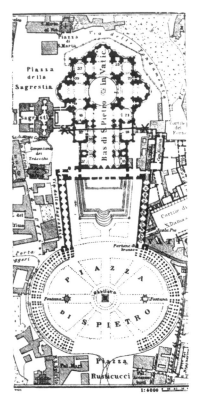

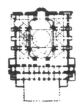

Hagia Sophia
in Constantinople.

FIG. 16. Saint Peter's in Rome.
The line through the third bay of the basilica indicates where Michelangelo planned his
facade (see Michelangelo's conception in the preceding chapter).

SAINT PETER'S IN ROME: Michelangelo made an enormous dome surpassing everything that had previously been seen;
having crossed the portico, you were under the immense dome. But
the popes added three bays in front and a large vestibule. The idea
is destroyed. One must now pass through a tunnel 100 meters long
before reaching the dome; two equivalent volumes fight it out; the
benefit of architecture is lost (the initial error is disproportionately
magnified by a decor of coarse vanity, and Saint Peter's remains an
enigma for architects). Hagia Sophia in Constantinople triumphs
with a surface area of 7,000 square meters, while Saint Peter's
encloses 15,000 (fig. 16).

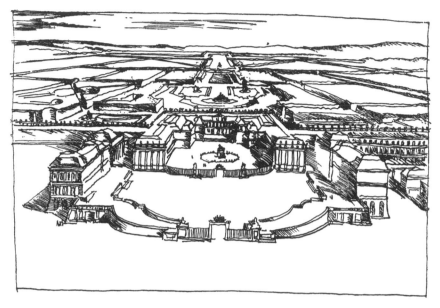

FIG. 17. — Versailles, after a drawing from the period.

VERSAILLES: Louis XIV is no longer just the successor of Louis XIII. He is the SUN KING. Immense vanity. At the foot of the throne, his architects bring him bird's-eye plans that seem like an astral chart; immense axes, stars. The Sun King swells with pride; the gigantic works are carried out. But a man has only two eyes that are 1 meter 70 from the ground, and that fix on just one point at a time. The arms of the stars are visible only one after another and are straight lines under foliage. A straight line is not a star; the stars fall apart. And so does everything else: the large pool, the embroidery parterres that are external to a vision of the whole, the buildings that can be seen only in fragments and by moving about. It's trickery, illusion. Louis XIV deceived himself at his own instigation. He transgressed the truths of architecture because he did not proceed with the objective elements of architecture (fig. 17).

And the little prince of a grand duchy, one who, like so many others, paid court to the Sun King's glory, laid out the city of KARLSRUHE, which is the most lamentable failure of an intention, a perfect "knockout." The star remains stuck on paper: slight consolation. An illusion. The illusion of the beautiful plan. From every corner of the city only three windows of the château are visible and they always seem to be the same ones; the humblest apartment building would be just as effective. From the château, it's always the same street you're going down, and all the streets in any little town make a similar effect. Vanity of vanities. We must not forget, when laying out a plan, that it is the human eye that observes its effects (see fig. at the head of this chapter).

When we pass from construction to architecture it is because we have an elevated intention. We must shun vanity. Vanity is what causes the vanities of architecture.

PARTHENON.

ARCHITECTURE

III

PURE CREATION OF THE MIND

Contour modulation is the touchstone of the architect. The latter reveals himself as artist or mere engineer.

Contour modulation is free of all constraint.

It is no longer a question of routine, nor of traditions, nor of construction methods, nor of adaptation to utilitarian needs.

Contour modulation is a pure creation of the mind; it calls for the plastic artist.

You work with stone, with wood, with concrete; you make them into houses and palaces; this is construction. Ingenuity is at work.

But suddenly you touch my heart, you do me good, I am happy, I say: "It is beautiful." This is architecture. Art is present.

My house is practical. Thank you, as I thank the engineers of the railroad and the telephone company. You have not touched my heart.

But the walls rise against the sky in an order such that I am moved. I sense your intentions. You were gentle, brutal, charming, or dignified. Your stones tell me so. You rivet me to this spot and my eyes look. My eyes look at something that states a thought. A thought that clarifies itself without words or sounds, but only through prisms that have relationships with one another. These prisms are such that the light details them clearly. These relationships don't necessarily have anything to do with what is practical or descriptive. They are a mathematical creation of your mind. They are the language of architecture. With inert materials, based on a more or less utilitarian program that you *go beyond,* you have established relationships that moved me. It is architecture.

What distinguishes a beautiful face is the quality of the features and the quite distinctive value of their unifying relationships. Every individual has a facial type: nose, mouth, forehead, etc., as well as a proportional mean among these elements. There are millions of faces built on these essential types, yet all are different: there is variation in the quality of the features and variation in their unifying relationships. We say that a face is beautiful when the precision of the modeling and the disposition of the features reveal proportions that *we sense as harmonious* because at our core, beyond our senses, they give rise to a resonance, to a kind of sounding board that is set vibrating. The trace of an indefinable absolute preexisting at the core of our being.

This sounding board that vibrates within us is our criterion of harmony. This must be the axis along which man is organized, in perfect accord with nature and, probably, with the universe: an axis of organization that must be the same as the one along which all phenomena and all objects of nature align. This axis leads us to suppose a unifying management in the universe, to assume a single

PARTHENON. — Temples were raised on the Acropolis that are of one mind and that swept up the desolate landscape and made it serve the composition. So from all along the horizon's rim, the thought is one. That is why no other works of architecture with this grandeur exist. We can speak of "Doric" when man, having raised his sights and completely sacrificed the accidental, has attained the uppermost region of the mind: austerity.

Inner porch of the Propylaea. The plastic system declares itself in unity.

PROPYLAEA. — Where does the emotion come from? From a certain relationship between categorical elements: cylinders, polished floor, polished walls. From an accord with the things of the site. From a plastic system whose effects encompass every element of the composition. From a unity of idea extending from unity of materials to unity of contour modulation.

PROPYLAEA. — The emotion comes from a unity of intention. From an unbending determination that dressed the marble with a will to the purest, the clearest, the most economical. They sacrificed and stripped away until the moment when it was imperative to remove nothing more, to leave only those concise and violent things, sounding clear and tragic like bronze trumpets.

ERECHTHEUM. — There was a moment of compassion and the Ionic was born; but the Parthenon dictated the forms of the Caryatids.

PARTHENON. — Poet-exegetes have declared that the Doric column was inspired by a tree
that shot up from the ground without a base, etc. etc., proof that all beautiful artistic
forms are drawn from nature. This is utterly false, because trees with straight trunks are
unknown in Greece, where only stunted pines and twisted olives grow. *The Greeks created
a plastic system that activates our senses directly and powerfully:* columns, column fluting,
entablatures complicated and heavy with intention, steps that contrast and join with the
horizon. They implemented the most learned distortions, impeccably adapting the contour
modulation to the laws of optics.

will at the origin. The laws of physics would follow from this axis,
and if we acknowledge (and love) science and its works, that is
because the one and the other leave us to assume that they were
prescribed by this first will. If the results of calculations seem to us
satisfying and harmonious, that is because they come from the axis.
If, through calculations, the airplane takes on the appearance of a
fish, of a natural object, that is because it recovers the axis. If the
dugout canoe, the musical instrument, and the turbine, the results
of experiment and calculation, seem to us like "organized" phenomena, which is to say as though imbued with a certain life, that

PARTHENON. — We must get it into our heads that Doric did not spring up in the fields with the asphodels, and that it is a pure creation of the mind. Its plastic system is so pure that one has the sensation of something natural. But careful, it is a complete work of man, one that gives us full perception of a profound harmony. Its forms are so distinct from the look of nature (and how superior to the Egyptian and the Gothic), they are so alert to the logic of light and materials, that they seem linked to the sky, linked to the ground, naturally. This creates a fact as natural to our understanding as the fact "sea" or the fact "mountain." What works of man have attained this level?

is because they are aligned with the axis. Hence a possible definition of harmony: a moment of accord with the axis that lies within man, and thus with the laws of the universe — a return to the general order. This would provide an explanation for our satisfaction on seeing certain objects, a satisfaction that commands at every moment an effective unanimity.

If we stop in front of the Parthenon, that is because the sight of it makes the inner chord sound; the axis is touched. We do not

PARTHENON. — Plastic system.

PARTHENON. — A machine for stirring emotion. We enter into the implacability of the mechanical. There are no symbols attached to these forms; these forms give rise to categorical sensations; no longer any need for a key to understand. Brutality, intensity, great gentleness, extreme delicacy, extreme strength. And who hit upon the composition of these elements? An inventor of genius. These stones were inert in the quarries of Pentelikon, unformed. To group them in this way, one did not have to be an engineer; one had to be a great sculptor.

PROPYLAEA. — Things become more precise, the moldings tighten, relationships are established between the annulets of the capital, the abacus, and the bands of the architrave.

stop in front of pediments (the same primary elements), because beyond raw sensation, the Madeleine is not going to touch our axis; we do not feel the profound harmony, we are not riveted to the spot by this recognition.

Natural objects and works based on calculations are clearly formed; their organization is without ambiguity. It is because *we see well* that we can read, know, and feel the accord. I repeat: the work of art must be *clearly formulated.*

If the objects of nature *live,* and if works based on calculations *turn* and provide jobs, that is because a unity of driving intention animates them. I repeat: the work of art must have a driving unity.

If natural objects and works of mathematical calculation command our attention and stir our interest, that is because they have,

PARTHENON. — Fractions of a millimeter come into play. The curve of the echinus is as rational as that of a large artillery shell. The annulets are fifteen meters from the ground, but they tell much more than the baskets of acanthus of the Corinthian order. The Corinthian state of mind or the Doric state of mind. two different things. A moral event creates an abyss between them.

one and all, a fundamental attitude that is characteristic of them. I repeat: the work of art must have a character of its own.

To formulate the work clearly and animate it with unity, to give it a basic attitude or character: pure creation of the mind.

This is generally accepted when it comes to painting and music, but architecture is reduced to its utilitarian causes: boudoirs, water closets, radiators, reinforced concrete, barrel vaults or pointed arches, etc. etc. These pertain to construction, which is not architecture. Architecture is when there is poetic emotion. Architecture is a plastic thing. Plasticity is what we see and what we measure with our eyes. It goes without saying that if the roof leaked, if the heating didn't work, if the walls cracked, the joys of architecture would be greatly hindered, like a gentleman listening to a symphony while sitting on a pincushion or in a draft blowing through the door.

Almost all periods of architecture have been linked to structural

This is a magnificent full-scale cast in the École des Beaux-Arts. The influence of the teachers is such, on the quai Voltaire, that the students prefer the Grand Palais.

investigations. The conclusion has often been drawn: architecture is construction. Architects may well have largely channeled their efforts into the constructional problems of the day, but this is no reason to confuse the two. It is clear that the architect ought to have mastered his construction at least as precisely as the thinker has mastered his grammar. But construction being, in other respects, a science more difficult and complex than grammar, the

PARTHENON. — Fractions of a millimeter come into play. There are many molding elements, but everything is organized to benefit strength. Astonishing manipulations: string courses curve inward or tilt forward the better to present themselves to the eye. Incised lines underscore background shadows that otherwise would be indecisive.

efforts of the architect long remain tied up with it; he ought not to be brought to a standstill by it.

The plan of the house, its cubic volume, and its surfaces have been determined partly by the utilitarian givens of the problem and partly by imagination and plastic creation. Already in his plan, and

consequently in everything that rises in the space, the architect has
been a plastic artist; he has disciplined utilitarian demands in
virtue of a plastic goal that he pursued; *he has made a composition.*

Then came the moment when the *lines of the face* had to be
incised. He made plays of light and shadow that reinforce what he

PARTHENON. — The whole of this plastic mechanics is realized in marble with the rigor that
we have learned to apply in machines. The impression is one of cut and polished steel.

wanted to say. Contour modulation intervened. And contour modulation is free of all constraint; it is a total invention that makes a
face radiant or withers it. With contour modulation, one acknowl-
edges the plastic artist; the engineer steps aside and the sculptor
works. Contour modulation is the touchstone of the architect; it
puts him up against the wall: to be or not to be a plastic artist.
Architecture is the masterful, correct, and magnificent play of
volumes in light; contour modulation is still and exclusively the

masterful, correct, and magnificent play of volumes in light. Contour modulation leaves the practical man, the bold man, the ingenious man behind; it calls for the plastic artist.

Greece, and in Greece the Parthenon, marked the pinnacle of this pure creation of the mind: contour modulation.

PARTHENON. — Austere profiles. Doric morality.

We sense that it is no longer a question of routine, nor of traditions, nor of construction methods. It is a question of pure invention, so personal that we can speak of a man; Pheidias made the Parthenon, for Iktinos and Kallikrates, the official architects of the Parthenon, built other Doric temples that seem to us cold and of middling interest. Passion, generosity, grandeur of soul: so many virtues that are inscribed in the geometries of the contour modulation, quantities manipulated into precise relationships. It is Pheidias who made the Parthenon, Pheidias the great sculptor.

There is nothing like it in the architecture of all the world and all time. It is the moment of utmost acuity when a man, moved by

PARTHENON. — The courage of squared moldings.

the noblest thoughts, crystallized them in a plastique of light and shadow. The contour modulation of the Parthenon is infallible, implacable. Its rigor surpasses our habits and the normal possibilities of man. Here we find fixed the purest witness to the physiology of sensations and to the mathematical speculation that can be tied to this; our senses are riveted, our minds are ravished; we touch the axis of harmony. There is no question of religious dogma, of symbolic description, of natural figuration: these are pure forms in precise relationships, to the exclusion of all else.

For two thousand years, those who have seen the Parthenon have felt: this was a decisive moment for architecture.

We stand before a decisive moment. At the present time when the arts are feeling their way and when painting, for example, finding little by little the formulas for a robust expression, jars the spectator so violently, the Parthenon brings certainties: superior emotion, mathematical order. Art is poetry: emotion of the senses, the joy of a mind that measures and appreciates, the recognition of an axial principle that affects the core of our being. Art is this pure

PARTHENON. — The courage of squared moldings, austerity, elevated mind.

creation of the mind that shows us, at certain heights, the height of *creation* to which man can attain. And man experiences great happiness *on feeling himself create.*

NOTA. — The photographs that illustrate this chapter come from the book *Le Parthénon* by Collignon, published by Éditions Albert Morancé, 30 and 32 rue de Fleurus, Paris, and from the book *L'Acropole* available now from the same publisher. These two magnificent books, genuinely accurate documents of the Parthenon and the Acropolis, were made possible thanks to the skill of the photographer Frédéric Boissonnas, whose perseverance, enterprise, and qualities as a plastic artist have revealed to us the most important Greek works of the great period.

The Acropolis in Athens (site).

PARTHENON. — The tympanum of the pediment is bare. The profile of the cornice is taut like the line of an engineer.

Photo Hostache.

MASS-PRODUCTION HOUSING

A great era has just begun.

There exists a new spirit.

Industry, invading like a river that rolls to its destiny, brings us new tools adapted to this new era animated by a new spirit.

The law of Economy necessarily governs our actions; only through it are our conceptions viable.

The problem of the house is a problem of the era. Social equilibrium depends on it today. The first obligation of architecture, in an era of renewal, is to bring about a revision of values, a revision of the constitutive elements of the house.

Mass production is based on analysis and experimentation.

Heavy industry should turn its attention to building and standardize the elements of the house.

We must create a mass-production state of mind:

A state of mind for building mass-production housing,

A state of mind for living in mass-production housing,

A state of mind for conceiving mass-production housing.

If we wrest from our hearts and minds static conceptions of the house and consider the question from a critical and objective point of view, we will come to the house-tool, the mass-production house that is healthy (morally, too) and beautiful from the aesthetic of the work tools that accompany our existence.

Beautiful too from all the life that the artistic sense can bring to these strict and pure organs.

The program has just been established. MM. Loucheur and Bonnevay ask the Chamber for a law decreeing the construction of 500,000 low-cost housing units. This is an exceptional opportunity in the annals of construction, an opportunity that requires equally exceptional means.

But everything remains to be done; nothing is ready for the realization of this immense program. *The state of mind does not exist.*

The state of mind for building mass-production housing, the state of mind for living in mass-production housing, the state of mind for conceiving mass-production housing.

Everything remains to be done; nothing is ready. Specialization has scarcely been broached in the realm of building. Neither the factories nor the specialized technicians exist.

But in the blink of an eye, if a mass-production state of mind came into being, everything would soon be underway. In effect, in all the branches of building, industry, as powerful as a natural force, invading like a river that rolls to its destiny, tends more and more to transform raw natural materials and to produce what are called "new materials." These are legion: cements and limes, steel beams, ceramics, insulating materials, pipes, hardware, waterproofing compositions, etc. etc. For the moment, all this arrives at buildings under construction in bulk, is fitted together haphazardly, entails enormous costs in labor, provides hybrid solutions. That is because the various objects of construction have not been mass produced. That is because the state of mind being absent, no one has undertaken a rational study of the objects, much less a rational study of construction itself; the mass-production state of mind is hateful to architects and to inhabitants (through contagion and persuasion). Imagine: we've just gotten as far, all breathless, as r-e-g-i-o-n-a-l-i-s-m! Phew! And the funniest thing is the devastation of the invaded lands along the way. Faced with the immense task of rebuilding everything, people go to their little bags, take out

L. C., 1915. Cluster of mass-production houses with "Domino" frames. In 1915, the price of steel and cement made possible the significant use of reinforced concrete. Formed frames were delivered by a contractor onto six blocks previously set up on a level surface, above ground. The walls and partitions were only light in-fill construction and could be built, without specialized labor, out of adobe, bricks, or cinder blocks. The height between two slabs was coordinated with that of the doors and imposts, cup-

L. C., 1920. Houses made of poured concrete. They are poured from above, as one would fill a bottle, with liquid cement. The house is built in three days. It emerges from the formwork like a piece of cast metal. But people revolt in the face of such "offhand"

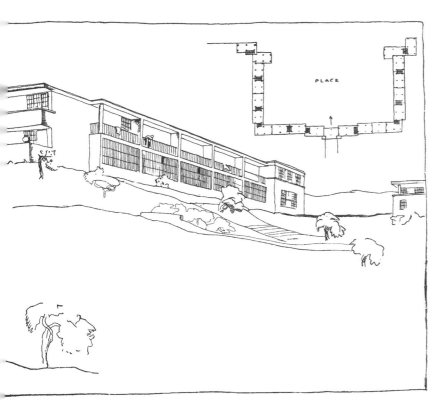

PLACE

boards, and windows, all of which were to the same module. Contrary to normal practice, the factory-produced woodwork was installed before the walls, automatically dictating the alignment of the latter as well as of the interior partitions; the walls and partitions were built up round the woodwork and the house could be erected in its entirety by a single corps of craftsmen: masons. That left only the pipes to be installed. (One day soon, we will be able to use windows that are much more refined than the ones presently available to us.)

methods; people don't believe in houses built in three days; a year is necessary, and pitched roofs, and dormers, and mansards.

their pipes of Pan, and play them: play them in committees and commissions. Then they vote resolutions. This one, for example, which is worth mentioning: to put pressure on the Compagnie des Chemins de fer du Nord to build thirty stations in different styles along the Paris-Dieppe line, because each of the thirty stations bypassed by express trains has a hill and such and such an apple tree that sets it apart and are its character, its soul etc. Fateful pipes of Pan!

The first effects of the industrial evolution in "building" manifest themselves in this primordial stage: the replacement of natural materials by artificial materials, of heterogenous and unreliable materials by materials that are homogenous and laboratory tested and produced with standardized elements. Standardized materials should replace natural materials, which are infinitely variable.

Furthermore, the law of Economy comes into its own: steel beams and, more recently, reinforced concrete are pure manifestations of calculations, of using materials completely and precisely; whereas the old timber beam perhaps harbors some traitorous knot and its squaring off leads to a considerable loss of material.

Finally, in certain domains the technicians have spoken. Water and lighting utilities are evolving rapidly; central heating has taken into account the structure of walls and windows — cooling surfaces — and consequently stone, the good natural stone in walls a meter thick has been outdone by light double skins made of cinder block, and so forth. Some entities, virtual demigods, have fallen: the roofs that no longer need be pitched to repel water, the big and so beautiful window embrasures that irritate us because they immure and deprive us of light; the massive pieces of wood that are as thick as can be, solid for eternity, but no, that pop and split in front of a radiator, whereas plywood 3 millimeters thick remains intact, etc.

In the good old days (and they continue, alas) you saw big horses bring enormous stones to construction sites, and lots of men for unloading them, cutting them, dressing them, lifting them onto scaffolding, and fitting them by verifying their six faces carefully, measure in hand; it took two years to build a house like that; today we build apartment buildings in a few months; the Paris-Orléans Railway has just completed its immense cold storage building at Tolbiac. Only sand granules and clinkers, no bigger than hazelnuts, were brought to the construction site; the walls are as thin as

membranes; there are huge loads in this building. Thin walls to
protect against temperature differences and partitions 11 centimeters thick despite the huge loads. Things certainly have changed!

The transport crisis was at its height; people noticed that
houses represented a considerable tonnage. What if we reduced this
tonnage by four-fifths? Now there's a modern state of mind.

The war shook us up; there was talk of Taylorism; it was implemented. Contractors bought machines that were ingenious, stead-
fast, and agile. Will construction sites soon be factories? There is
talk of houses that are poured from above with liquid concrete in a
single day, as one might fill a bottle.

And one thing leads to another. After having manufactured so
many canons, airplanes, trucks, and railway cars, we ask ourselves:
"Can we not manufacture houses?" Now there's a state of mind
wholly of our era. Nothing is ready, but everything can be done.
Within twenty years, industry will have bulk standardized materials like those of metallurgy. Technical advances will take heating,
lighting, and rational construction methods far beyond anything we
know. Construction sites will no longer be places of erratic birth
throes where all problems are complicated by their being crammed
together. Financial and social organization will successfully address
the housing problem through concerted and powerful methods, and
construction sites will be immense, managed and operated like
administrative bodies. Urban and suburban site plans will be vast
and orthogonal and no longer horribly misshapen; they will allow
for the use of mass-produced parts and the industrialization of the
construction site. Perhaps we will finally stop building "to measure." An inevitable social evolution will have transformed the relationship between tenant and landlord, will have changed our
conception of housing, and cities will be ordered instead of chaotic.
The house will no longer be a squat thing that pretends to defy the
centuries and that is an opulent object manifesting wealth; it will
be a tool like the automobile is becoming a tool. The house will no
longer be an archaic entity heavily rooted in the ground by deep
foundations, built "solid," and to which the cult of family, bloodline
etc. has so long been devoted.

If we wrest from our hearts and minds static conceptions of the
house and consider the question from a critical and objective point
of view, we will come to the house-tool, the mass-production house

L. C., 1915. "Domino" house. The construction method is here applied to a mansion realized at the same rate per cubic meter as a simple worker's dwelling. The architectural resources of the construction method permit arrangements that are gener-

accessible to all, healthy, incomparably more so than the old one (morally too) and beautiful from the aesthetic of the work tools that accompany our existence.

ous and rhythmic and make it possible to produce true architecture. It is here that the principle of the mass-production house shows its moral value: a definite connection between housing for the rich and that for the poor, decency in housing for the rich.

It will be beautiful too from all the animation that an artistic sense can bring to its strict and pure organs.

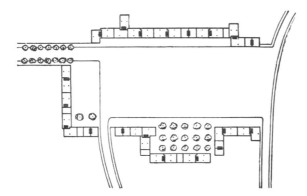

"Domino" housing development.

But we must create the state of mind for living in mass-production housing.

Everyone rightly dreams of the safety and security of a home of his own. Since this is impossible in our present state, this dream, considered unrealizable, induces a veritable sentimental hysteria; building one's house is a bit like making one's will.... When I build my house ... I will put my statue in the foyer and my little dog Ketty will have his sitting room. When I have a roof over my head, etc. A

"Domino" house. Residence and workshop. No bearing walls; the windows go right round the house.

L. C., 1915. Interior of a "Domino" house. Mass-produced windows, mass-produced doors, mass-produced cabinets; combinations of two, four, twelve window elements; one door with one impost, or two doors with two imposts, or two doors without imposts, etc., cupboards with glazed upper portions and lower ones with drawers, serving as bookshelves, chests of drawers, service buffets, etc. All these elements, which are to be provided by major industry, are to a common module; they fit together perfectly. The frame of the house having been cast, they are placed side by side in the empty shell and provisionally secured with battens: the voids are filled in with plaster, bricks, or lath work. Things are done counter to routine methods and months are gained. Also gained is an architectural unity of crucial importance and, with the module, proportion enters into the house of itself.

subject for the neurological specialist. When the time for building this house has come, it is not the hour of the mason or of the technician, it is the hour when every man fashions at least one poem in his life. So we have, for the last forty years, in the cities and their periphery, not houses but poems, poems of Indian summer, for a house is the crowning moment of a career ... the precise moment when one is so old and worn out by existence as to be prone to rheumatism and death ... and wacky ideas.

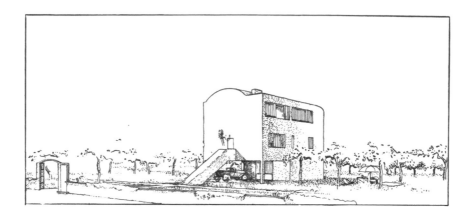

L. C., 1922. House of an artist; reinforced concrete frame and cavity "cement-gun" walls, each skin 4 centimeters thick. Formulating the problem clearly; determining the typical needs of a dwelling; resolving the question as railroad cars, tools, etc. are resolved.

L. C., 1919. Houses made of coarse concrete. The terrain consisted of gravel beds. A quarry was opened on the site; lime and gravel were mixed and poured to make a platform 40 centimeters thick; reinforced concrete floors. A special aesthetic is born directly from the

L. C., 1922. Mass-production workers' housing. A well-designed housing development, the same house presents itself from various angles. Four concrete posts; "cement-gun" walls. Is it aesthetic? Architecture is a matter of plastique, not of romanticism.

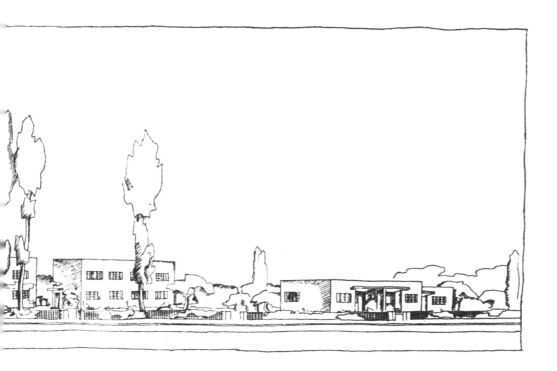

process. The sound economic management of modern building sites requires the exclusive use of straight lines, the straight line is the grand acquisition of modern architecture, and it is a good thing. We must clear our minds of romantic cobwebs.

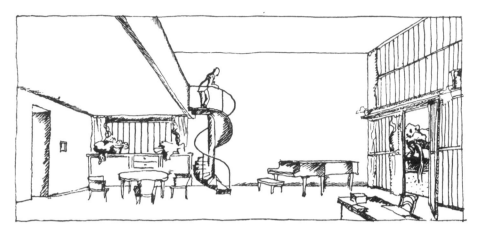

L.C., 1921. "Citrohan" (not to say Citroën) mass-production house. In other words, a house like an automobile, conceived and built like a bus or a ship's cabin. Present housing necessities can be identified and require solutions. We must work against the old house that misused space. We must (present necessity: low net cost) look upon the house as a machine for living in or as a tool. When you create an industry, you buy the equipment; when you set up house, at present you rent a stupid apartment. Until now we made houses into barely coherent groupings of many large rooms; in the rooms there was always too much space and not enough space. Today, fortunately, we no longer have enough money to perpetuate this routine and since we don't want to consider the problem in its true light (machines for living in) we cannot build in the cities and a disastrous crisis is the result; with budgets, we could build apartment buildings that are admirably laid out, on the condition, of course, that tenants change their mindset; besides, they will conform anyway under pressure of necessity. Windows and doors should have their dimensions rectified; railway cars and limousines have proven to us that man can pass through small openings and that we can calculate space to the square centimeter; it is criminal to build four-square-meter bathrooms. Building costs having quadrupled, we must reduce old architectural pretensions by half and the square footage of houses by at least half; this is henceforth a problem for the technician; we call upon the discoveries of industry; we com-

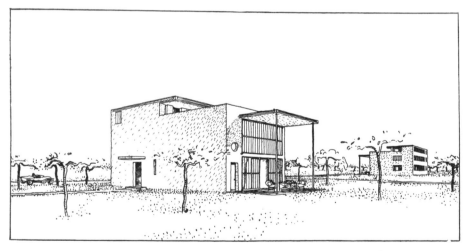

L. C., 1922. Mass-production villa, 72 m². Concrete and cement-gun frame. One large room, 9 x 5 m; kitchen and maid's room; bedroom with bathroom and boudoir; two bedrooms and a solarium.

pletely change our state of mind. Beauty? It is always present when the intention and the means *that are proportion* exist; proportion doesn't cost the owner anything, just the architect. The heart will be touched only if reason is satisfied and it can be when things are calculated. We must not be ashamed to live in houses without pitched roofs, to own walls as thin as sheet metal and windows similar to factory chassis. But what we can be proud of is having a house as practical as our typewriter.

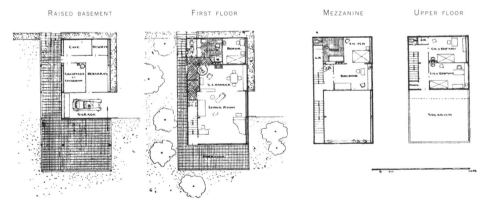

RAISED BASEMENT   FIRST FLOOR   MEZZANINE   UPPER FLOOR

L.C., 1921. A "Citrohan" house. Frame on concrete supports poured on-site and raised with winches. Cavity walls with 20-centimeter voids enclosed by 3-centimeter skins made of cement sprayed onto stretched sheet metal; floor slabs to the same module; strips of factory window frames with practical openings to the same module. Spatial arrangements consistent with domestic use; abundant light consistent with the purpose of the rooms; hygienic needs met and servants treated with respect.

L. C., 1919. "Monol" House. Transport crisis: the ordinary house weighs too much: bricks, woodwork, concrete, flooring, tiles, and wood frames mean formidable convoys of railroad cars rolling through the French countryside.

The problem of the factory-produced house is posed. Construction principle: asbestos cement blocks with walls 7 millimeters thick that form foundations 1 meter high filled with rough materials found on-site (rocks, gravel, rubble etc.), bound together loosely with lime but leaving gaps that give the walls a significant insu-

L. C., "Monol" House. When we talk about mass-production houses, we talk about entire housing developments. Unity of structural elements is a guarantee of beauty. The variety that an architectural ensemble must have is provided by housing developments that foster the grand ordonnances, the veritable rhythms of architecture. A town that is well laid out and built with mass-produced elements

lation ratio; the ceilings and floors are of arched corrugated sheet metal (very shallow arch) made of asbestos cement that forms a shutter supporting a concrete screed several centimeters thick. The arched sheet metal remains in place and forms a permanent insulation barrier. Woodwork, windows, and doors are fitted at the same time as the asbestos cement blocks. The house is completed by a single professional corps of craftsmen and the only transport needed is that of a double skin of asbestos cement 7 millimeters thick.

will seem calm, ordered, and neat; it will inevitably impose discipline on the inhabitants: America offers us the example of eliminating garden walls thanks to the new state of mind created over there of respect for the property of others; this would give suburbs a more spacious aspect, for the disappearance of enclosing walls means a net gain in sun and light for everyone.

L. C., 1921. Seaside villa built with mass-produced elements: reinforced concrete posts at an equal spacing of five meters in each direction; floors of slightly arched reinforced concrete. Within this frame, similar to those found in all industrial buildings, the plan is easily taken care of with light partitions. The net construction cost is among the lowest in building. There is an aesthetic gain in modular unity of the first importance. The savings realized over complicated construction methods make it possible to enclose more floor space and more volume. The light partitions can be shifted afterward and the plan can easily be changed.

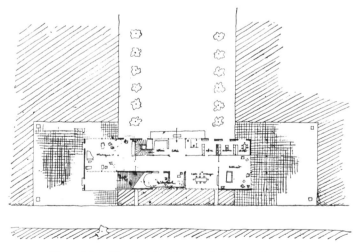

Plan of the villa, showing the regularly spaced supports.

Salon of the seaside villa. The supports of uniform section, the ceilings with shallow arches, the standardized window units, the solids and voids make up the architectural elements of the construction.

L. C., Interior of a "Monol" House adapted for comfortable living. If cultivated people knew that perfectly harmonious dwellings costing much less than their city apartments could be built using mass-produced elements, they would pressure the national railroad to put a stop to the shameful spectacle of the suburban trains in Gare Saint-Lazare; they would do like the Berliners, and that would be ideal. Then we could make use of those vast areas on the periphery. The mass-production house would enable precisely those solutions that are most practical and of a *pure aesthetic*. But we must wait for the awakening of the railroad companies and the stirring of major industry, which must provide the mass-produced elements.

"Villa apartments":
120 stacked villas.

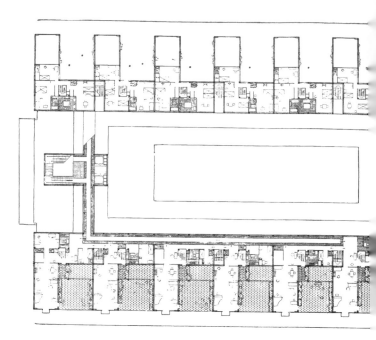

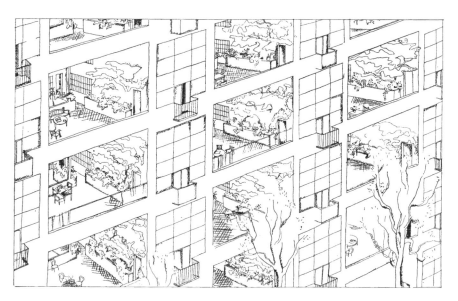

"Villa apartments": fragment of the facade. Every garden completely independent of the neighboring ones.

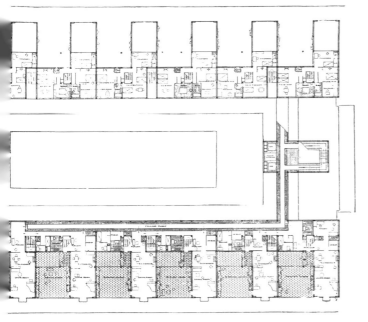

Floor plan of the villas.

At street level, a large entrance hall; on the upper floors, large staircase and main corridor.

Ground-floor plan of the villas: shading indicates the hanging gardens.

L. C., 1922. Large rental apartment building. The drawings that follow show a proposal for a group of a hundred stacked villas on five levels, each two-story villa having its own garden. A hotel management agency administers the communal building services and provides the solution to the servant crisis (a crisis that is just beginning and is an ineluctable social fact). Modern technics applied to so large an enterprise substitute the machine and organization

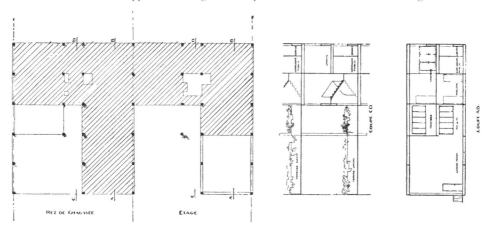

REZ DE CHAUSSÉE   ÉTAGE

"Villa apartments": mass-production construction using posts and slabs. Cavity walls.

"Villa apartments": one of the hanging gardens.

for human fatigue: hot water, central heating, refrigeration, vacuum cleaners, purified water, etc. Servants are no longer attached to particular households; they arrive here, as at a factory, to put in their eight hours, and an alert staff is available day and night. Raw and cooked foods are provided by a purchasing service, which leads to quality and economy. A

"Villa apartments": view of a villa dining room (through window at right, the hanging garden).

"Villa apartments": general view (120 stacked villas).

vast kitchen provides meals for either the villas or a communal restaurant, as preferred. Every villa has a sports room, but on the roof there's a large communal sports facility and a 300-meter track. Likewise on the roof, a recreation hall for use by the residents. The usual mean entry to the house with the inevitable concierge's lodge is replaced by a vast hall; a doorman receives visitors here day and night and directs them to the elevators. In the large open courtyard and on the roof of the underground garage, tennis courts. Trees, flowers all around the courtyard, and all around the street in the gardens of the villas. On all floors, ivy and flowers in hanging gardens. Here the "Standard" comes into its own. The villas represent the type of rational and sensible design, shorn of all pomposity but adequate and practical. With the rental-purchase system, old and outmoded ownership systems no longer exist.

You pay no rent; you own stock that is paid off in twenty years and the interest on which represents a very low rent.

More than anywhere else, *mass production* imposes itself on the large residential block: *low rent*. And the *mass-production spirit* brings benefits that are many and unexpected in a period of social crisis: *domestic economy*.

"Villa apartments" entry hall.

L. C

Let us analyze the 400 m² of terrain allocated to each inhabitant of a garden city: house
and dependencies, 50 to 100 m²; 300 m² are allocated to lawns, orchards, vegetable
gardens, planted parterres, vacant land. Maintenance that is difficult, costly, taxing;
yield: a few boxes of carrots and a basket of pears. There are no playgrounds; children, men, and women cannot play, cannot do sports. Sports should be an option
every hour of every day, and they should be possible right outside the house and not
at stadium grounds where only professionals and the idle go. Let us pose the problem more logically: house 50 m²; pleasure garden 50 m² (this garden and this house
are situated on the ground floor or 6 or 12 meters above the ground, in so-called honeycomb clusters. Right outside the houses, vast playing fields (soccer, tennis, etc.) at
a rate of 150 m² per house. In front of the houses (at a rate of 150 m² per house)
land for industrialized farming, intensive farming with substantial yield (irrigation by

1 small garden

3 houses and
2 small gardens

2 houses and
3 small gardens

3 houses

New Frugès quarter in Bordeaux.
A first group under construction.

eret, 1925.

pipes, cultivation by a farmer, carts for fertilizer and transport of soil and crops, etc.). A farmer sees to surveillance and administration for each group. Sheds protect the harvested crops. Agricultural labor abandons the countryside; with the eight-hour shift, the worker here becomes a farmer and produces a significant portion of the things he consumes. Architecture, urbanism? Logical study of the cell and its functions relative to the ensemble provide a solution rich in consequences.

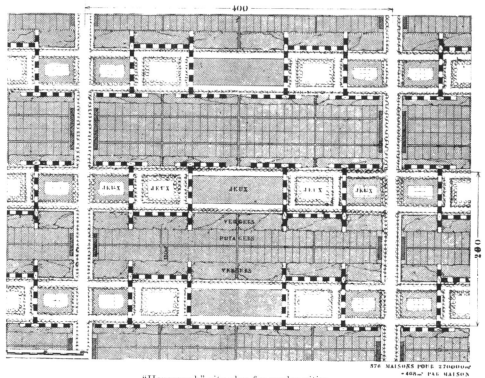

"Honeycomb" site plan for garden cities.

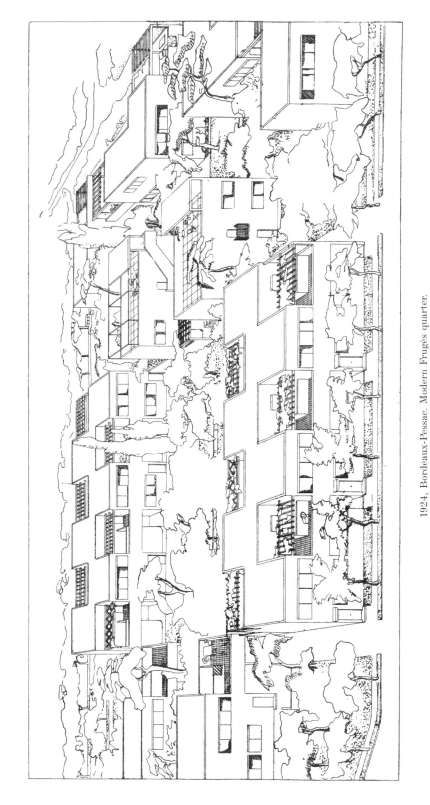

1924, Bordeaux-Pessac. Modern Frugès quarter.

Fragment of a large residential development built with cement guns. A typical housing unit was meticulously established, and it is repeated in the most varied combinations. It is a veritable industrialization of the construction site.

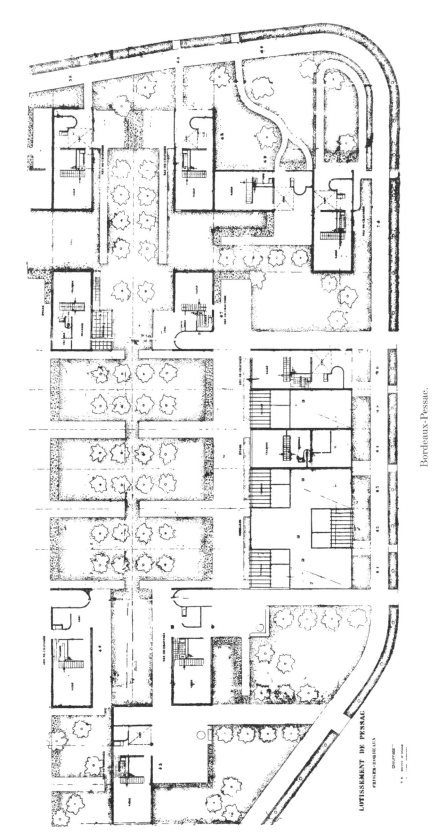

Bordeaux-Pessac.

The first edition of this book deeply touched a major industrialist in Bordeaux. A decision was taken to wipe clear the slate of habit and routine. An elevated conception of industrial things and of architecture's destiny prompted this industrialist to take the most courageous of initiatives. Perhaps for the first time in France, thanks to him, the present architectural problem is resolved in a spirit consistent with the era. Economy, sociology, aesthetics: it's a new realization with new means.

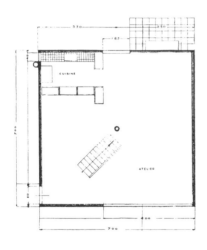

GROUND FLOOR

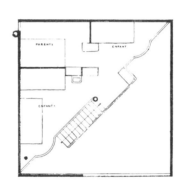

MEZZANINE

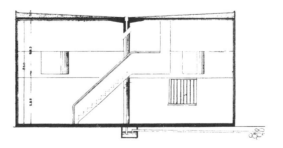

DIAGONAL CROSS SECTION

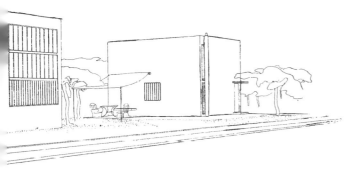

L. C. and P. J., 1924.

Mass-production housing for craftsmen. The problem: to house craftsmen in a large workshop (open space 7 x 4.5 m 50) with good light. To reduce costs by doing away with partitions and doors, by reducing, through the play of architecture, the usual floor areas and room heights. The house is supported by a single hollow column of reinforced concrete. Thermally insulating walls of "solomite" (compressed straw) coated on the exterior with 5 centimeters of concrete applied with a cement gun, plaster on the interior. In the whole house, two doors. The mezzanine on the diagonal allows the ceiling to develop to its full extent (7 m x 7 m); the wall also displays its full dimensions and, in addition, the diagonal of the mezzanine creates *an unexpected dimension:* this little 7-meter house impresses the eye with a major element that is 10 meters long.

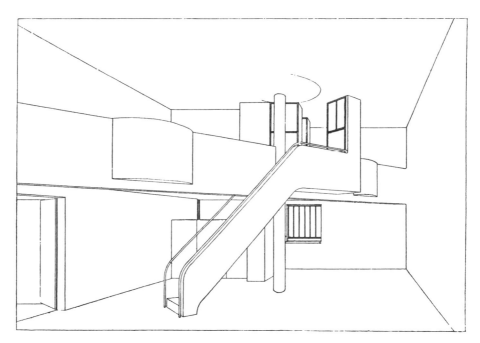

Interior view.
(The walls of the kitchen and part of the mezzanine consist of mass-produced elements — fittings — from the U.P. series; see page 283.)

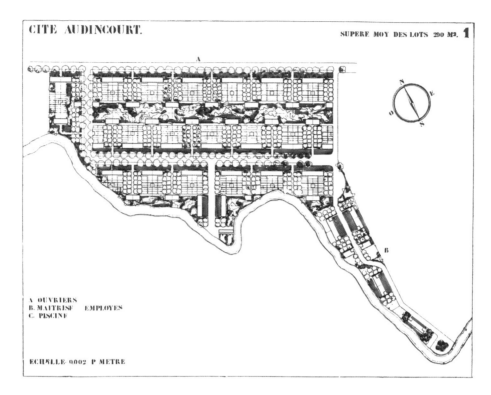

1924. L. C. and P. J. Orthogonal lot division.

All the houses are built with standardized elements that make up the typical cell. The plots are of equal size; the ordonnance is regular. Architecture has full scope here to express itself with precision and ease.

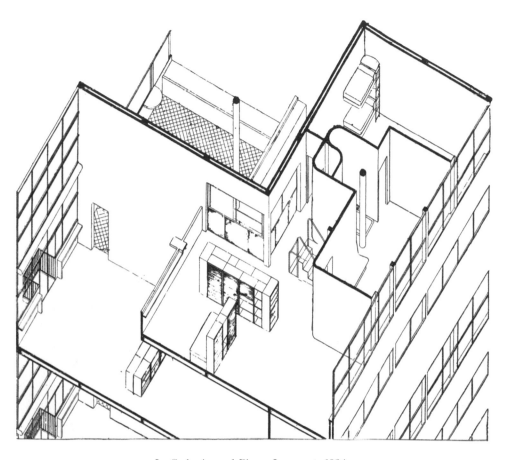

Le Corbusier and Pierre Jeanneret, 1924.

This is one cell in the "villa apartments" (see above). It is also the Pavillon de l'Esprit Nouveau at the International Exposition of Decorative Arts in Paris 1925. A mass-production house *for the man of today,* standardized architectural elements, fully industrialized construction.

Masonry executed by G. Summer, masonry contractor, using the Ingersoll-Rand cement gun applied to Solomite (compressed straw); floors and terraces idem. The floor armatures as well as the mass-produced windows by Raoul Decourt, construction engineer. Joinery is completely eliminated; *carpenters no longer set foot in the building:* the UNITED U P BUSINESSES of Czechoslovakia have produced standardized fittings that are suitable for every bedroom and can be assembled like office filing cabinets. Glazing and painting: RUHLMAN and LAURENT.

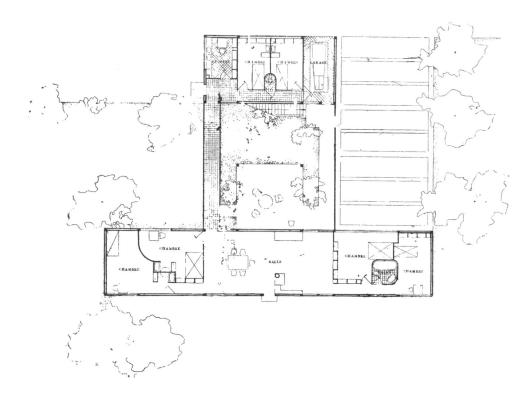

L. C. and P. J., 1925. Villa in Bordeaux.

Built with mass-production elements using the same machinery as the houses in the garden
    city of Pessac (pp. 276–78).

Mass production is not an obstacle to architecture. On the contrary, it brings unity and per-
    fection to details and offers variety in ensembles.

Axonometric perspective of the villa.

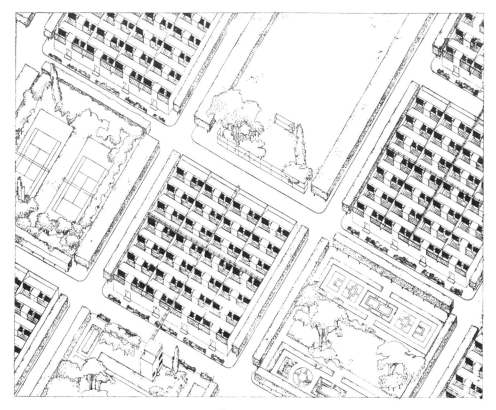

General view.

1925. L. C. and P. J. University residential complex. We build student housing complexes at
great expense by committing ourselves to revive the poetry of the old buildings at Oxford.
A poetry that costs us dear, disastrously so. The student belongs to an age of protest
against old Oxford; old Oxford is a fantasy of the donor-patrons of university housing complexes. What the student wants is a monk's cell, well lit and well heated, with a corner to
gaze at the stars. He wants to be able to find ready-to-hand whatever he needs to play
sports with his fellows. His cell should be as self-contained as possible.

Plan and cross sections.

Every student has a right to the same cell; it would be cruel if the cells of poor students were
different from the cells of rich ones. So the problem is posed: university housing as cara-
vansary; each cell has its vestibule, its kitchen, its bathroom, its living room, its sleeping
loft, and its roof garden. Walls afford privacy to all. Everyone assembles on the adjacent
playing fields or in the common rooms of shared service facilities. To classify, to establish
the type, to fix the cell and its elements. Economy. Efficiency. And architecture? Always,
when the problem is clear.

The university housing complex is conceived here in terms of the "shed," a mode of construction that permits of indefinite expansion as it ensures ideal lighting and eliminates
masses that are *load bearing* (expensive). The walls are no longer anything but light, insulating in-fill materials.

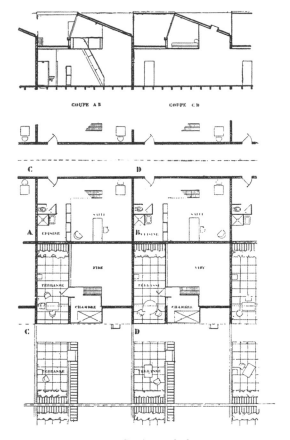

COUPE AB   COUPE CD

Section and plan

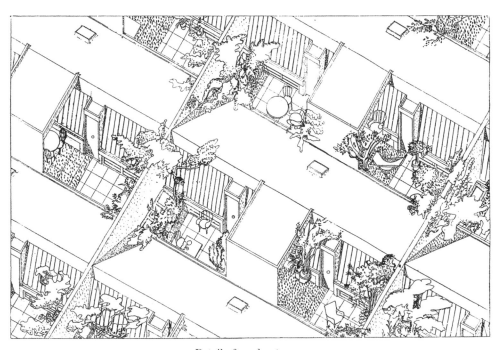

Detail of garden terraces.

L. C. and P. J. A painter's atelier (see p. 142). (see p. 142)

A question in the new spirit:
I am 40 years old, why not buy myself a house; for I need this tool; a house like the Ford I bought (or my Citroën, if I'm a dandy).

Committed collaborators: major industry, specialized factories.
Desirable collaborators: suburban railroads, financial organizations, a transformed École des Beaux-Arts.

The goal: mass-production housing.

Coalition: architects and aesthetes, the immortal cult of the home.

Implementers: business enterprise and true architects.
Casting out nines: 1° the Salon of Aviation; 2° celebrated cities of art (the Procurator's Offices, the rue de Rivoli, the place des Vosges, the place de La Carrière, the palace of Versailles, etc.: *repetition*). For mass-production housing automatically implies layouts that have breadth and grandeur. For mass-production housing entails a close study of all household objects and the search for a standard, a type. When a type is created, we are at the portals of beauty (the automobile, the liner, the railway car, the airplane). For mass-production housing will impose a unity of elements: windows, doors, construction methods, materials. *Unity of details and grand overall plans,* that is what, in the century of Louis XIV, in a composite, congested, inextricable, uninhabitable Paris, was called for by a very intelligent priest, Laugier, who dabbled in town planning: *uniformity in the details, tumult in the whole* (the contrary of what we do: a mad variety of details and a drab uniformity in the planning of streets and cities).

Conclusion: What is in question is a problem of the era. More than that: *the* problem of the era. Social equilibrium is a question of building. We conclude with this defensible dilemma: *Architecture or Revolution.*

Low-pressure ventilator (Société Rateau. Mass production).

40,000-kilowatt electric turbine in Gennevilliers.

ARCHITECTURE
OR REVOLUTION

In every domain of industry, new problems have been posed, tools capable of solving them have been created. If we set this fact against the past, there is revolution.

In building, the factory production of standardized parts has begun; on the basis of new economic needs, part elements and ensemble elements have been created; conclusive realizations have been achieved in parts and in ensembles. If we set ourselves against the past, there is revolution in the methods and the magnitude of enterprises.

Whereas the history of architecture evolves slowly over the centuries in terms of structure and decor, in the last fifty years iron and concrete have brought gains that are the index of a great power to build and the index of an architecture whose code is in upheaval. If we set ourselves against the past, we determine that the "styles" no longer exist for us, that the style of an era has been elaborated; there has been a revolution.

———————

Consciously or unconsciously, minds have become aware of these events; consciously or unconsciously, needs are born.

The social mechanism, deeply disturbed, *oscillates between improvements of historical importance and catastrophe.*

It is a primal instinct of every living being to ensure a shelter. The various working classes of society no longer have suitable homes, *neither laborers nor intellectuals.*

It is a question of building that is key to the equilibrium upset today: architecture or revolution.

In every domain of industry, new problems have been posed and new equipment created to solve them. We underestimate the extent of the break between our era and earlier periods; it is agreed that this era has brought great transformations, but what would be useful would be to compare its intellectual, social, economic, and industrial activity not only with the period prior to the start of the nineteenth century, but with the history of civilizations in general. We would soon see that human tools, the automatic inducers of social needs, hitherto subject only to slowly evolving changes, have just been transformed with a fabulous speed. Human tools were always *in the hand of man:* today, completely renewed and formidable, they momentarily elude our grasp. The human beast remains breathless and panting before this tool that he cannot get a grip on; progress seems as hateful to him as it is laudable; all is confusion in his mind; he feels enslaved to a forcibly imposed order of things and has no sense of liberation, of relief, of improvement. A period of great crisis and above all of moral crisis. To put the crisis behind us, we must create a state of mind for understanding what is happening, we must teach the human beast to use his tools. When the human beast is put back in his new harness and knows what sort of effort is expected of him, he will recognize that things have changed: that they have been *improved.*

Another word on the subject of the past. Our era, with just these last fifty years, sets itself against ten centuries past. During these ten previous centuries man ordered his life after systems qualified as "natural": he did his own work and saw it through to the end, being the sole initiator of his little enterprise; he rose with the sun, went to bed at nightfall; he put down his tools thinking about the project underway and the things he would undertake

Equitable Building, New York.

tomorrow. He worked at home in a small shop and his family
was around him. He lived like a snail in its shell, in a home made
to his exact measure; nothing prompted him to change this state of
things, which overall was harmonious enough. Family life ran its
normal course. The father kept watch over his children in the
cradle, then in the shop; efforts and gains succeeded one another
smoothly within the familial order; things worked out well for the
family. Now when things work out well for the family, the society is
stable and likely to last. This applies to ten centuries of work
organized on the family module; this holds just as well for all past
centuries up to the middle of the nineteenth century.

Built by the Steel Corporation.

But let's take a look at the mechanism of the family today. Industry has led to mass-produced parts; man and machine work in close collaboration; intelligence selection proceeds with an imperturbable certainty: unskilled laborers, skilled workers, foremen, engineers, directors, and administrators are all in their rightful place; and anyone who has the stuff of an administrator will not long remain in unskilled labor; every position is accessible to all. Specialization ties a man to his machine; everyone is held to an implacable standard of precision, for a part that passes into the hands of the next worker cannot be "put right" by him, corrected and adjusted; it must be precise to continue in its role as a precision component, required to fit automatically into a whole. The father no longer teaches his son the myriad secrets of his craft; an unfamiliar foreman strictly controls the rigorous performance of a limited and circumscribed task. The worker makes a very small

America. A 250-horsepower racing car capable of 263 km per hour.

part, the same one for months, perhaps years, perhaps his whole life. He sees the outcome of his labor only in the finished work: in that moment when, shiny, polished, and pure, it passes into the factory yard on its way to the delivery trucks. The workshop spirit no longer exists, but a more collective spirit certainly does. If the worker is intelligent, he will understand the fate of his labor and he will develop a well-deserved pride. When *Auto* magazine publishes a car that has just gone 260 km an hour, the workers will gather and say to one another: "It's our car that did that." This is a morale factor that matters.

The eight-hour day! Three eight-hour shifts in the factory! The shifts work in relays. This one begins at 10 p.m. and ends at 6 in the morning; another completed its work at 2 in the afternoon. What were legislators thinking when they authorized the eight-hour day? What's a man who's free from 6 a.m. until 10 p.m., from 2 p.m. until after midnight going to do? Until now only "bistros" have taken appropriate measures. What becomes of the family in these conditions? The home is there to take in the human beast and welcome him, and the worker is cultivated enough to know how to put so many free hours to good use. But no, that's just it: the home

New York.

is hideous, and the mind has not been educated for so many free hours. So we can indeed write: Architecture or demoralization, demoralization and revolution.

Let's look at something else:

The incredible industrial activity of today, necessarily of great concern to us, puts before our eyes every hour, either directly or through newspapers and magazines, objects of arresting novelty whose whys and wherefores interest, delight, and disconcert us. All these objects of modern life end up creating a certain modern state of mind. We shift our attention with alarm to the old rotten things that are our snail shells, our dwellings, which hold us in their putrid and useless grip every day and offer nothing in return. Everywhere we see machines that serve to produce something and that produce it admirably, with purity. The machine we live in is an old crate of a plane riddled with tuberculosis. We don't bridge the gap between our daily activities at the factory, at the office, at the bank, healthy, useful, and productive, and our familial activity that's handicapped at every contour. Everywhere, the family is ruined and minds are demoralized by being tied like slaves to anachronistic things.

Demag crane.

The mind of every man, shaped by his daily collaboration with the modern event, has consciously or unconsciously formulated his desires; these desires are inevitably connected to the family, the fundamental instinct of society. Every man knows today that he must have sun, heat, clean air, and clean floors; he has been taught to wear a bright white collar, and women like underclothing that is white and delicate. Man senses today that he must have the intellectual diversion, bodily relaxation, and physical exercise necessary to recover from the muscular or mental tensions of work, of "hard labor." This bundle of desires constitutes a summa of demands.

But our social organization has nothing ready in the way of a response.

Another thing: What are intellectuals to conclude in the face of the present realities of modern life?

The splendid industrial explosion of our era has created a special class of intellectuals so large that it constitutes the active social stratum.

In the factory, in technical firms, in analysts' offices, in banks, in department stores, in newspapers and magazines, there are engineers, department heads, submanagers, secretaries, editors, and accountants who design, on commission, the formidable things that are our concern: those who design the bridges, the liners, the airplanes, who create the motors, the turbines, those who manage

Ships' coalers on the Rhine.

construction sites, those who distribute capital and see to the accounting, those who buy from the colonies or from factories, those who edit so many articles about everything beautiful and horrible that is produced, who keep track of the fever curve of a humanity in labor, in constant childbirth, in crisis, sometimes delirious. All human material passes through their hands. **They of course end up observing, and drawing conclusions. These people have their eyes fixed on the display windows of the department stores of humanity.** The modern era lies before them, sparkling and radiant... on the other side of the barricades. Back home, in precarious comfort, their salaries not really related to the quality of their work, they again find their dirty old snail shells and they cannot dream of starting a family. If they start a family, they begin the slow martyrdom that we know. These people too claim their right to a machine for living in that is plain and simply humane.

Laborers and intellectuals are prevented from following the profound injunctions of the family; they use, every day, the brilliant and actively efficient tools of the era, but they do not have the option of putting them to work for themselves. Nothing is more discouraging, more maddening. Nothing is ready. Well might we write: Architecture or Revolution.

Modern society does not pay intellectuals judiciously, but it still tolerates old patterns of ownership at odds with the transformation of the city and the house. Old ownership is based on inheritance and thinks only of inertia, of changing nothing, of perpetuating the *status quo*. While all other human enterprises are subjected to the tough ethic of competition, the owner sitting on his properties escapes the common law like a prince; he reigns. Under the current principle of ownership, it is impossible to establish a budget that will hold up. So no one builds. But if the patterns of ownership were to change, and they are changing (the Ribot law for workers, the construction of blocks of apartments

Disk for a 40,000-kilowatt turbine. Le Creusot factories.

for individual sale, etc., and many other even bolder private or state initiatives that might intervene) we would be able to build, we would be enthusiastic about building, and we would avoid revolution.

The advent of a new age intervenes only when earlier work has quietly prepared the way.

Industry has created its tools;

Enterprise has changed its ways;

Construction has found its means;

Architecture finds itself faced with an amended code.

Industry has created new tools; the accompanying illustrations offer moving proof of this. Such tools are made for improving human welfare and lightening human labor. If we set this renewal against the past, there is revolution.

Enterprise has altered its routines; it is now encumbered by heavy responsibilities: cost, time frame, solidity of the work.

Rateau ventilators, hourly capacity: 59,000 m³.

A Bugatti engine.

Numerous engineers fill its offices, make their calculations, in-
tently apply the law of economy, and try to bring into accord two
divergent factors: low price and high quality. Intelligence is at the

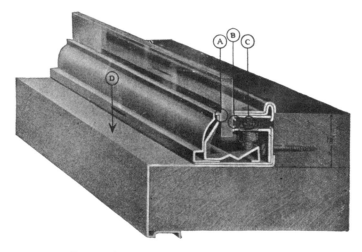

Chicago. Construction of a window: industrialization.

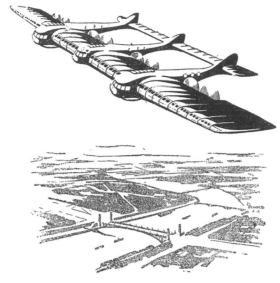

Forecast: the airplane of tomorrow (Bréguet).

root of every initiative, bold innovations are wanted. Entrepreneurial morality has been transformed; large-scale industry is today a
sound and moral organism. If we set this new fact against the past,
there is revolution in the methods and magnitude of enterprises.

Construction has found its means, means that, in themselves,
amount to a liberation that previous millennia sought in vain.
Everything is possible with calculation and invention when you
have tools of sufficient perfection, and these tools exist. Concrete

Limousin et Freyssinet factory.

and steel have completely transformed the organization of building as hitherto known, and the exactness with which these materials adapt to theory and calculations gives us each day results that are encouraging, first because of their success, then because of their look, which recalls natural phenomena and is constantly catching up with experiments carried out in nature. If we set ourselves against the past, we see that new formulas have been found that need only be exploited and that, if we can break with routine, will bring real liberation from the constraints hitherto endured. There has been a revolution in construction methods.

Architecture finds itself faced with an amended code. Constructional innovations are such that the old styles, with which we are obsessed, can no longer accommodate them; the materials now being used evade the designs of decorators. There is such novelty in the forms and rhythms produced by the construction methods, such novelty in their ordonnance and in the new industrial, rental, and urban programs, that we finally understand in a flash the true and profound laws of architecture based on volume, rhythm, and proportion; the styles no longer exist, the styles are outside of us; if they still assail us, it is as parasites. If we set ourselves against the past, we see that the old codification of architecture, weighed down by forty centuries' worth of rules and regulations, ceases to interest

Conception and construction by Freyssinet et Limousin.
Width 80 meters, height 50 meters, length 300 meters.
The nave of Notre-Dame de Paris is 12 meters wide and 35 meters high.

us; it is no longer our concern; there has been a revision of values; there has been revolution in the conception of architecture.

———

Disturbed by the reactions that act on him from every quarter, the man of today senses, on the one hand, a world that is elaborating itself regularly, logically, clearly, that produces with purity

Freyssinet et Limousin. Contractors. Large dirigible hangar at Orly.
Width 80 m, height 56 m, length 300 m.

Fiat factory in Turin with autodrome on the roof.

things that are useful and usable; and on the other hand, he finds himself still disconcerted, still inside the old hostile framework. This framework is his home; his city, his street, his house, his apartment rise up against him and, unusable, prevent his tranquil pursuit of the same spiritual path that he took in his work, prevent his tranquil pursuit of the organic development of his existence, which is to start a family and, like all the animals of the earth and like all men of all times, to live an organized family life. Thus is society witness to the destruction of the family, and it senses with terror that this will be its ruin.

A great disaccord reigns between a modern state of mind that is an injunction and the suffocating stock of centuries-old detritus.

This is a problem of adaptation where the objective things of our lives are at issue.

Society has a passionate desire for something that it will obtain or that it will not obtain. Everything is there; everything will depend on the effort made and on the attention paid to these alarming symptoms.

Architecture or revolution.

Revolution can be avoided.

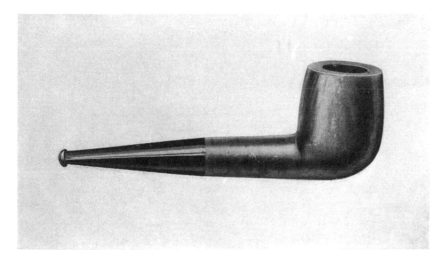

"La Pipe" Cooperative.

Editor's and Translator's Notes

These notes have been researched and written primarily by Jean-Louis Cohen with the help of Sylvie Young, who identified some American sources. Notes provided by John Goodman are enclosed in brackets. Different type treatments are used to distinguish the three categories of notes: **bold** type for information about illustrations, serif type for background information, and sans-serif type for text changes between the 1923 and 1924 editions.

The present volume includes a translation of the 1928 printing of the 1924 edition of *Vers une architecture*. Significant changes introduced between the first edition of 1923 and the second edition of 1924 are specified. Minor deletions and word substitutions have been omitted. For a complete documentation of the changes introduced compared to the articles published in *L'Esprit nouveau* from 1920 to 1922, see the rigorous information provided in the notes to Le Corbusier, *Vers une architecture*, eds. Giovanni Maria Lupo and Paola Paschetto (Turin: Bottega d'Erasmo, 1983), which are unfortunately extremely difficult to decipher.

Abbreviations used in the notes:
FLC   Fondation Le Corbusier, Paris
GRI   Getty Research Institute, Los Angeles
IFA   Institut français d'architecture, Paris

Cover. Photograph of the liner *Empress of Asia*, built in 1912 for the Canadian Pacific.
Name of the author: "Le Corbusier" replaces 1923 ed.: "Le Corbusier-Saugnier."
False title page. Missing in the 1924 ed.: "To Amédée Ozenfant" (*À Amédée Ozenfant*)
Added in 1924: Introduction to the second ed. The typescript is B2(15)24, FLC.

p. 83. Le Corbusier alludes to the architect François Blondel (1618–86), whose Porte Saint-Denis he discusses in the main text.

["To do architecture": *architecturer,* a neologism.]

p. 85. Added in 1924: "He attains harmony" (*Il atteint l'harmonie*). Added in 1924: "he determines the diverse movements of our minds and our hearts" (*il détermine des mouvements divers de notre esprit et de notre coeur*). "engineers use geometric forms, [...] their works are on the way to great art" (*... les ingénieurs usent de formes géométriques [...] leurs oeuvres sont sur le chemin du grand art*). 1923 ed.: "engineers employ geometric forms [...] their works come close to great art" (*les ingénieurs pratiquent les formes géométriques [...] leurs oeuvres s'approchent du grand art*).

[p. 85 and passim. "ordonnance": *ordonnance*. On the decision to anglicize the French term in this translation, see "From the Translator."]

p. 86. "Architects today are afraid of the geometric constituents of surfaces" (*Les architectes ont, aujourd'hui, peur des constituantes géométriques des surfaces*). 1923 ed.: "Architects today are afraid of the geometry of surfaces" (*Les architectes ont, aujourd'hui, peur de la géométrie des surfaces*).

[p. 86 and passim. "the generators and directing vectors": *les directrices et les génératrices*. Technical terms in geometry (word order reversed by the translator).]

p. 88 "with intentions that take the elements of architecture into account" (*avec des intentions qui font état des éléments de l'architecture*). 1923 ed.: "with intentions that make use of the elements of architecture" (*avec des intentions qui usent des éléments de l'architecture*).

["contour modulation": *la modénature*. See "From the Translator" and the introduction.]

p. 89. Added in 1924: "beautiful too from all the life that the artistic sense can bring to strict and pure organs" (*Belle aussi de toute l'animation que le sens artiste peut apporter à des stricts et purs organes*).

p. 91. Ill.: The Garabit railway bridge over the Truyère River in the Cantal region was built by the engineering firm of Gustave Eiffel and the architect Léon Boyer in 1884. See the sketch in Le Corbusier to Auguste Perret, 20 January 1914, IFA, fig. 2 of the introduction to the present volume. The uncropped original print is kept in the *France ou Allemagne?* file: B1(20)110, FLC.

p. 92. Added in 1924: "He attains harmony" (*Il atteint l'harmonie*). Added in 1924: "He determines the diverse movements of our minds and our hearts" (*Il détermine des mouvements divers de notre esprit et de notre coeur*).

"Plastic emotions": Guillaume Apollinaire celebrates in *The Cubist Painters: Aesthetic Meditations*, trans. Lionel Abel (New York: Wittenborn, 1944); original ed., *Les peintres cubistes: Méditations esthétiques* (Paris: Figuière, 1913), the "plastic virtues" (p. 9). The French term *plastique*, meaning the sculptural quality of an artwork, is derived from the German *Plastik*, denoting "sculpture." On this question, Le Corbusier wrote an important article together with Ozenfant: "Sur la plastique I. Examen des conditions primordiales," *L'Esprit nouveau* 1, no. 1 (1920).

p. 95. Le Corbusier echoes French architect Eugène-Emmanuel Viollet-le-Duc, who observed in 1873 that "architects have played out their role" (*les architectes ont fini leur rôle*) whereas "that of engineers is just beginning" (*celui des ingénieurs commence*); Eugène-Emmanuel Viollet-le-Duc, *Entretiens sur l'architecture*, vol. 2 (Paris: A. Morel, 1872), 445. He likewise mirrors the "toast" that César Daly offered engineers shortly thereafter: César Daly, "Toast aux ingénieurs," *Revue générale de l'architecture et des travaux publics* 34 (1877): 101.

Le Corbusier's frequent contact since 1909 with his friend and engineer-partner Max Du Bois had also convinced him of the virtues of this profession. Du Bois had translated a book on concrete by Emil Mörsch that Jeanneret had read: *Le Béton armé, étude théorique et pratique* (Paris: C. Béranger, 1909); original ed., *Der Eisenbetonbau: seine Theorie und Anwendung* (Stuttgart: Wittwer, 1902).

p. 97. "Aubusson": in the French Creuse region, traditional center of carpet production. "Salon d'automne": refers to the exhibition in 1910 of Munich applied arts at the Salon.

The date of 1921 in Le Corbusier's note refers to the postwar context of the *retour à l'ordre* (return to order).

Deleted in 1924, after "cleansing" (*nettoyage*): "A certain sense of morality pushes us toward it" (*Un certain sens de la moralité nous y pousse*).

p. 98. Ill.: Pisa, 1907; photograph by Charles-Édouard Jeanneret; L4(19)99, FLC.

p. 99. Ill.: Unidentified North American grain elevator.

p. 100. "their works are on the way to great art" (*leurs oeuvres sont sur le chemin du grand art*). 1923 ed.: "their works come close to great art" (*leurs oeuvres s'approchent du grand art*).

p. 101. Ill.: Unidentified North American grain elevator.

In a letter to Charles L'Eplattenier, Jeanneret had already mentioned on 11 January 1911 "volumes brought together in light" (*volumes qui jouent sous la lumière*): Le Corbusier, *Lettres à ses maîtres*, vol. 2, *Lettres à Charles L'Eplattenier*, ed. Marie-Jeanne Dumont (Paris: Éditions du Linteau, 2006), 252.

p. 102. Ill.: Unidentified North American grain elevator.

p. 103. Top ill.: Grand Trunk Pacific elevator, Fort William, Ontario, 1910; published in Walter Gropius, "Die Entwicklung moderner Industriebaukunst," in *Die Kunst in Industrie und Handel. Jahrbuch des deutschen Werkbundes 1913* (Jena: Eugen Diederichs, 1913), n.p. Bottom ill.: Bunge & Born grain silo, Buenos Aires, 1903, demolished in 1998; published in Gropius, "Die Entwicklung moderner Industriebaukunst" (this note), n.p. The pediments of the original have been whitened out. The corresponding page and the ones featuring other images used by Le Corbusier are missing in his copy of the *Jahrbuch* kept at the FLC; personal library of Le Corbusier, B2, FLC.

p. 104. Top ill.: John S. Metcalf Co., grain elevator number 2, harbor of Montreal, 1912, demolished in 1978; published in Gropius, "Die Entwicklung moderner Industriebaukunst" (note for p. 17), n.p., retouched (the cupola of the Bonsecours market has been eliminated on the right). See also *Old and New Montreal* (Montreal: International Press Syndicate, 1913), n.p. Bottom ill: Dakota elevator, Buffalo, New York, circa 1910; published in Gropius, "Die Entwicklung moderner Industriebaukunst" (note for p. 17), n.p.

p. 105. Ill.: Pennsylvania elevator, also known as Canton elevator number 3, built for James Stewart & Co., Baltimore, 1908; published in *Why Build Fireproof?* (Chicago: Portland Cement Association, 1917), p. 20.

"La Gare du quai d'Orsay": alludes to the station built by Victor Laloux in 1900, the same time that the Grand Palais was built by Henri-Adolphe-Auguste Deglane.

"Pochés": *pochés*. In architectural plans, these inked areas denote masonry structures, referring to the use of a particular type of brush called *pinceau à pocher*. *Pochés* allow for the negotiation between complex lot forms and regular or symmetrical room shapes and are considered by Le Corbusier to be typical of the Beaux-Arts design culture.

p. 106. Ill.: Canadian government elevator, Saskatoba, Saskatchewan, 1918. A slightly different view can be found in Charles S. Clark, *Plans of Grain Elevators,* 4th ed. (Chicago: Grain Dealers Journal, 1918), xliv.

"stir in us architectural emotions" (*provoquant* [sic] *en nous des émotions architecturales*). 1923 ed.: "achieve great emotions" (*atteignent aux grandes émotions*).

p. 107. Ill.: Donato Bramante, Raphael, loggia of the Cortile di San Damaso, Rome,

begun in 1508 by Bramante and completed by Raphael after his death in 1514; Alinari photograph 11830.

[p. 108. and passim. "accentuators": *accusatrices*. As used here, a neologism consistent with the two terms from the lexicon of geometry discussed in the note for p. 86.]

p. 109. Ill.: Unidentified American factory.

p. 110. Top and center ills.: Unidentified American factories.

Bottom ill.: Walter Gropius and Adolf Meyer, Fagus factory, Alfeld-an-der-Leine, 1911–14. In 1928, replaced with Albert Kahn and Edward Grey, Ford factory, Highland Park, Michigan, 1908; published in *Factories and Warehouses of Concrete* (Philadelphia: Association of the American Portland Cement Manufacturers, 1911), 49; and Gropius, "Die Entwicklung moderner Industriebaukunst" (note for p. 17), n.p. Le Corbusier retouched the original image by whitening out the superstructures. He states his intention to replace the Gropius image in the handwritten note "Livre; illustrations nouvelles," B2(15)164, FLC.

p. 111. Top ill.: Cass Gilbert, Army Supply Base, Brooklyn, 1917. Bottom ill.: Unidentified American factory; in 1928, replaced with William Higginson, Gair Building, Brooklyn, 1904. In 1922, Le Corbusier had asked the American city planner George B. Ford for a photograph of Bush Terminal and one of "42nd St. New York City"; Le Corbusier, undated note T1(1)652, FLC.

Added in 1924: "the application of a mass-production spirit to construction" (*l'application de l'esprit de série dans l'organisation du chantier*).

p. 112. Ill.: Unidentified American factory.

["to model": *modeler*. The only two instances of this word in the 1924 French text. See the discussion of *modénature* in "From the Translator" and the introduction.]

Mansart: Le Corbusier refers to the architect Jules Hardouin-Mansart (1645–1708).

p. 113. Ill.: James and Merritt Reid, architects, Charles Strobel, engineer, *San Francisco Call* or Claus Spreckels Building, San Francisco, 1898. Photographed after the earthquake of 1906.

p. 115. Ill.: The 1923 and the 1928 eds. feature a perspective and plan of the Acropolis from Auguste Choisy, *Histoire de l'architecture,* 2 vols. (Paris: Gauthier-Villars, 1899), 1:415. Le Corbusier kept an unbound copy of the books with pencil marks for the sizing and cropping of photo reproductions used in *L'Esprit nouveau* and subsequently in *Vers une architecture;* personal library of Le Corbusier, Z99, FLC.

"subtly effective" (*d'un effet subtil*). 1923 ed.: "contorted" (*mouvementées*).

p. 117. Ill.: Type of the Hindu temple; from Choisy, *Histoire de l'architecture* (note for p. 115), 1:175. Choisy underlines the resemblance of this illustration to those in Ram-Raz, *Essay on the architecture of the Hindus* (London: John William Parker, 1834).

p. 118. Ill.: Hagia Sophia; from Choisy, *Histoire de l'architecture* (note for p. 31), 2:49.

p. 119. Ill.: Referred to as Thebes Temple but in fact is the Temple of Khons, at Karnak; from Choisy, *Histoire de l'architecture* (note for p. 115), 1:64.

"consequences extending" (*conséquences s'étendant*). 1923 ed.: "developments extending" (*développements allant*).

"play of contraries" (*mouvement des contraires*). 1923 ed.: "contraries" (*contrastes*).

["algebrization": *algébrisation*, a neologism.]

p. 120. Ill.: Umayyad Qasr, Amman, Jordan, A.D. 720–742; from Choisy, _Histoire de l'architecture_ (note for p. 115), 1:128. Choisy located it in "Transjordanian Syria." Le Corbusier opts for Syria alone.

Added in 1924: "development of an initial plastic invention" (_développement d'une invention plastique initiale_).

Added in 1924: "a diversity that comes from their architectural principle and not from their ornamental modalities" (_diversité qui est dans le principe architectural et non dans des modalités ornementales_).

"The technological capacities of this era—financing techniques and construction techniques—are ready to carry out this task" (_La technicité de cette époque—technique de la finance et technique de la construction—est prête à réaliser cette tâche_). 1923 ed.: "The technological capacities of this era, financial and constructional, are ripe for carrying out this task" (_La technicité de cette époque, financière et constructive, est mûre pour réaliser cette tâche_).

"It is an attempt to instill order" (_C'est une tentative de mise en ordre_). 1923 ed.: "Order reigns." (_L'ordre règne_).

In fact the first version of the _Cité industrielle_ was designed in 1901 and a second, more sophisticated one was created in 1916 and published the following year. Édouard Herriot (1872–1957), the radical-socialist mayor of Lyon from 1905 to his death, had nothing to do with the project, but the later version incorporated drawings of projects built by Garnier for him, such as the Gerland slaughterhouses, transformed into industrial sheds in the version published in 1917.

It is remarkable that Le Corbusier apparently envisioned putting the German architect Heinrich Tessenow, designer of the Hellerau garden-city near Dresden, on the same plan as Garnier; untitled note, A2(15)153, FLC.

p. 121. Ill.: Plan of the Acropolis, Athens, after rebuilding by Cimon and Pericles; from Choisy, _Histoire de l'architecture_ (note for p. 115), 1:412.

Added in 1924 to caption: "The Acropolis on its rock and its supporting walls is seen from afar, as one block. Its buildings are massed together through the incidence of their multiple planes" (_L'Acropole sur son rocher et ses murs de soutènement est vue de loin, d'un bloc. Ses edifices se massent dans l'incidence de leurs plans multiples_).

"A unitary code distributes the same set of essential volumes through all parts of the city and determines the spaces in ways consistent with needs of a practical order and with the promptings of a poetic sense that is the architect's own. Reserving all judgment about the coordination of the zones of this industrial city, we are here subject to the beneficial consequences of order. Where order reigns, well-being is born. Through the happy invention of a system of lot division, even the quarters of workers' housing take on high architectural significance. Such are the consequences of a plan" (_Une règle unitaire distribue dans tous les quartiers de la ville le même choix de volumes essentiels et fixe les espaces suivant des nécessités d'ordre pratique et les injonctions d'un sens poétique propre à l'architecte. Réservant tout jugement sur la coordination des zones de cette cité industrielle, l'on subit les conséquences bienfaisantes de l'ordre. Où l'ordre règne, naît le bien-être. Par la création heureuse d'un système de lotissement, les quartiers d'habitation même ouvrière prennent une haute signification architecturale. Telle est la conséquence d'un plan_). 1923 ed.: "Unitary rules distribute through all the quarters the same set of volumes and spaces in accordance with variations in size and quantity dictated by purpose: the residential complex amidst greenery, the public service complex at the point of maximum civic pride, the industrial quarter alongside its docks and its factories. Where there is order, there is harmony, whatever the source of this esthetic or utilitarian order. Thus, for example, even quarters of workers' housing here have the aspect of real architecture" (*Des règles unitaires distribuent dans tous les quartiers le même choix de volumes et d'espaces suivant des variations de grandeur et de quantité dictées par la destination: la cité de l'habitation au milieu des verdures, la cité des services publics au point fier de la ville, la cité industrielle avec ses docks et ses usines. Où il y a ordre, il y a harmonie, d'où que provienne cet ordre esthétique ou utilitaire. Ainsi, par exemple, les quartiers d'habitation même ouvrière ont ici une véritable tenue architecturale*).

p. 122. **Ill.: Plan of a residential district; from Tony Garnier, *Une cité industrielle, étude pour la construction des villes* (Paris: A. Vincent, 1917), detail of pl. 79.**

"In the present waiting state (for modern urbanism is not yet born)" (*Dans l'état d'attente actuelle [car l'urbanisme moderne n'est pas encore né]*). 1923 ed.: "While waiting for something better" (*En attendant mieux*).

"has dictated the structure of the machines and guides their movements, conditions every gesture of their crews; but filth pollutes the surroundings and incoherence ran rampant when string and T squares fixed the placement of the buildings, rendering their expansion pointless, expensive, and dangerous. A plan would have sufficed. A plan will suffice. The excess of evils will lead to one" (*a dicté la structure des machines et gère leurs mouvements, conditionne chaque geste des équipes; mais la saleté infecte les alentours et l'incohérence sévissait lorsque le cordeau et l'équerre fixèrent l'implantation des bâtiments, rendant leur extension caduque, coûteuse et périlleuse. Il aurait suffi d'un plan. Un plan suffira. Les excès du mal y conduiront*). 1923 ed.: "but incoherence and filth infect the surroundings. A plan would have sufficed. One will come to it" (*mais l'incohérence et la saleté infectent les alentours. Il suffirait d'un plan. On y viendra*).

"One day Auguste Perret coined the phrase 'Tower-Cities.' A sparkling epithet that struck the poet in us. A word that rang out none too soon because the fact is imminent! Unknown to us, the 'great city' incubates a plan. This plan can be gigantic because the great city is a rising tide. It is time to repudiate the present layout of our cities" (*Un jour Auguste Perret créa ce mot: les "Villes-Tours." Epithète étincelante qui en nous secoua le poète. Mot qui sonnait à l'heure parce que le fait est imminent! A notre insu, la "grande ville" incube un plan. Ce plan peut être gigantesque puisque la grande ville est une marée montante. Il est temps de répudier le tracé actuel de nos villes*). 1923 ed.: "Auguste Perret spoke of 'Tower-Cities'; a topic about which it was written: 'Too soon.' Why? Given the limits of possible density in a greater urban region, it is time to reject the solution of cities laid out like Paris" (*Auguste Perret a parlé des "Villes-Tours"; on a écrit à ce sujet: "anticipation." Pourquoi? Etant donné la limite de densité possible d'une agglomération urbaine, il est temps de répudier la solution de villes tracées comme Paris*).

p. 123. **Top ill.: View of a residential district; from Garnier, *Une cité industrielle* (note for p. 122), pl. 84, slightly cropped.**

Bottom ill.: Plan of a residential district; from Garnier, *Une cité industrielle* (note for p. 122), pl. 87, slightly cropped.

p. 124. **Top ill.: Le Corbusier, Tower-Cities, 1920; drawing, B(15)19, FLC.**

Bottom ill.: Le Corbusier, elevation of Tower-Cities.

["Grand Roy": Louis XIV.]

p. 125. Ill.: Le Corbusier, Tower-Cities, 1920; image reproduced in Willi Boesiger and Oscar Storonov, *Le Corbusier et Pierre Jeanneret: Oeuvre complète de 1910–29* (Zurich: Girsberger, 1930), 34.

Added in 1924: "Large cities have become too dense for the safety of their inhabitants and yet they are not dense enough to answer to the new realities of 'business'" (*Les grandes villes sont devenues trop denses pour la sécurité des habitants et pourtant elles ne sont pas assez denses pour répondre au fait neuf des "affaires"*).

"the work previously smothered in dense neighborhoods" (*le travail jusqu'ici étouffé des quartiers compacts*). 1923 ed.: "the population hitherto squashed in massive neighborhoods" (*la population jusqu'ici écrasée dans des quartiers massifs*).

Deleted in 1924: "in the immediate proximity of the apartment buildings, tennis courts and playing fields are available" (*s'offrent à proximité immédiate des immeubles, les tennis et terrains de sports*).

p. 126. Added in 1924: "thereby an indispensable calm" (*et par là un calme indispensable*).

"extending his conception beyond reasonable limits. Thus did he throw a veil of dangerous futurism over a sound idea" (*distendre sa conception au delà des limites raisonnables. Il a jeté ainsi sur une idée saine un voile de futurisme dangereux*). 1923 ed.: "expanding his conception beyond the limits of reason, which is regrettable. For thus did he throw over this sound idea a veil of futurism [that was] quite dangerous and a bit incoherent" (*agrandir sa conception au delà des limites de la raison, ce qui est regrettable. Car il a jeté ainsi sur cette idée saine un voile de futurisme bien dangereux et quelque peu incohérent*).

Added in 1924: "A plan had not been drawn up and the idea went no further without a plan" (*Le plan n'avait pas été tracé et l'idée ne se portait pas sans plan*).

p. 127. Ill.: Le Corbusier, Pilotis-Cities, 1915. This section derives from the "future street" presented by Eugène Hénard in 1910; Eugène Hénard, "Les villes de l'avenir," in *Town-Planning Conference, London, 10–15 October 1910, Transactions* (London: Royal Institute of British Architects, 1911), 345–67.

Added in 1924: "were no longer a fungus eating into the sidewalk" (*n'étaient plus cette moisissure qui ronge les trottoirs*); "along with luxury shops" (*ainsi que le commerce de luxe*); "did nothing less than triple the circulation areas of the city" (*ne faisait rien moins que tripler la surface circulable de la ville*); "entailing a complete renewal of the terms of lot division and anticipating a radical reform of the rental house; this imminent reform motivated by the transformation of domestic use calls for new housing plans, and an entirely new organization of the services answering to life in the big city. Here again, the plan is the generator, without which it's the reign of meanness, disorder, arbitrariness" (*entraînant un renouvellement complet des modes de lotissement et allant au-devant d'une réforme radicale de la maison à loyers; cette réforme imminente motivée par la transformation de l'exploitation domestique réclame des plans neufs de logements, et une organisation entièrement nouvelle des services répondant à la vie dans la grande ville. Ici aussi le plan est le générateur; sans lui règnent l'indigence, le désordre, l'arbitraire*).

Added in 1924: note 1: "See below: 'Mass-Production Housing' (*Voir plus loin: "Maisons en série"*).

p. 128. Top and bottom ill.: Le Corbusier, perspective and plan of the Indent-Cities, 1920; original drawings, B2(15)20, FLC, and B2(15)21, FLC.

p. 129. Note 1 added in 1924.

p. 130. Ill.: Le Corbusier and Pierre Jeanneret, roof of the Jeanneret House, Paris, 1923–24. Added in 1924.

In 1924, the word "constructional" (*constructives*) was added to "the old foundations" (*les bases anciennes*): "In architecture, the old constructional foundations are dead" (*En architecture, les bases constructives anciennes sont mortes*).

p. 131. Ill.: François Blondel, Porte Saint-Denis, Paris, 1671–73. Drawing of the regulating lines by Le Corbusier. This is a simplified version of the drawing published in Choisy, *Histoire de l'architecture* (note for p. 115), 2:746, by which Le Corbusier intends to "translate into a diagram the dimensional relationships that he [Blondel] indicates as having defined the beautiful ordonnance of the Porte Saint-Denis."

Added in 1924, after "Porte Saint-Denis": "(Blondel)."

p. 133. "sacrificial vases" (*vases du sacrifice*). 1923 ed.: "vases for libations" (*vases des libations*).

p. 134. Ill.: "Primitive temple," sketch plan and section by Le Corbusier; tracing of the reconstruction drawing of the *Stiftshütte* (religious building), published by the arch-conservative historian Reinhold Freiherr von Lichtenberg in his *Haus, Dorf, Stadt, eine Entwicklungs-Geschichte des antiken Stadtbildes* (Leipzig: Rudolf Haupt, 1909), 18; drawing, B2(20)9, FLC.

p. 135. Ill.: "Primitive temple," axonometric drawing by Le Corbusier, after the perspective of the *Stiftshütte* published by von Lichtenberg, *Haus, Dorf, Stadt* (note for p. 134), 19.

Added in 1924, after "while it would otherwise be chance, anomaly, arbitrariness" (*alors qu'autrement ce serait hasard, anomalie, arbitraire*): "Geometry is the language of man" (*La géométrie est le langage de l'homme*).

p. 136. "creating his universe" (*créant son univers*). 1923 ed.: "recreating his universe" (*recréant son univers*).

"The man of today" (*L'homme d'aujourd'hui*). 1923 ed.: "The modern man" (*L'homme moderne*).

"The man of yesterday" (*L'homme d'hier*). 1923 ed: "The less modern man" (*L'homme moins moderne*).

p. 137. Ill.: Facade of the Arsenal at Peiraeus; from Choisy, *Histoire de l'architecture* (note for p. 115), 1:389.

"The man of today" (*L'homme d'aujourd'hui*). 1923 ed.: "The modern man" (*L'homme moderne*).

"and that his instincts suffice; but these express themselves only through the artificial means learned in the schools. A lyric poet set loose with shackles round his neck, someone who knows things, but things that he has neither invented nor even mastered, who in the course of his education has lost that candid and essential energy of the child who keeps asking: 'Why?'" (*et que ses instincts suffisent; mais ceux-ci ne s'expriment qu'au moyen d'artifices acquis dans les écoles. Un lyrique déchaîné avec carcan au cou, quelqu'un qui sait des choses, mais des choses qu'il n'a ni inventées ni même contrôlées, qui a perdu au cours des enseignements reçus cette candide et capitale énergie de l'enfant questionnant inlassablement: "Pourquoi?"*). 1923 ed.: "A lyric poet set loose, a gentleman who doesn't know much and who by nature is not very curious" (*Un lyrique déchaîné, un monsieur qui ne sait pas grand'-chose et qui de nature est bien peu curieux*).

"it determines one of the fundamental impressions" (*il détermine donc l'une des impressions fondamentales*). 1923 ed.: "it fixes" (*il fixe*).

p. 138. Ill.: Achaemenid cupolas; from Marcel Dieulafoy, *L'art antique de la Perse, Achéménides, Parthes, Sassanides,* **pt. 4, "Les monuments voûtés de l'époque aché-ménide" (Paris: Vve A. Morel, 1885), 28: figs. 22, 23. See first reproduction of the section in the sketchbook A2 of 1915, pp. 113 and 114.**

Added in 1924, after "The facade of the Arsenal" (*La façade de l'Arsenal*): "in Peiraeus" (*du Pirée*).

Deleted in 1924, after "statics" (*statiques*): "and dynamics" (*et dynamiques*).

p. 139. Ill.: Notre-Dame de Paris, 1163–1345, probably a reproduction of a postcard with drawing of the regulating lines by Le Corbusier. See the version in perspective: L5(6)113, FLC.

p. 140. Ill.: The Capitol, Rome, 1538–1650; probably a postcard of an Alinari photograph with the regulating lines drawn by Le Corbusier.

"EXTRACT FROM BLONDEL'S OWN COMMENTS ON THE PORTE SAINT-DENIS": In Jacques-François Blondel, *Cours d'architecture enseigné dans l'Academie royale d'architecture* (Paris: Imprimerie de Lambert Roulland, 1675–83), 623, Blondel writes: "Furthermore, here are the general measurements of this work, whose width is perfectly equal to its height. This width divided into three parts produces one part for the opening of the large gate, and one part for the width of each of the supports" (*Au reste, voici les mesures générales de cet ouvrage, dont la largeur est parfaitement égale à la hauteur. Cette largeur divisée en trois parties donne une partie pour l'ouverture de la grande Porte, et une partie pour la largeur de chacune des piles*).

p. 141. Top ill.: Petit Trianon, Versailles, 1762–68, drawing of the regulating lines by Le Corbusier; original document L4(19)47, FLC.

Bottom ill.: Charles-Édouard Jeanneret, garden elevation of the Villa Schwob with regulating lines, La Chaux-de-Fonds, 1917; based on drawing 30075, FLC (without the regulating lines). Replaced the street elevation of the same location in the 1923 ed.

Pol Abraham notes in his review that Le Corbusier should have known "that, at the École des Beaux-Arts, there were scarcely any candidates for the Grand Prix who did not make some use of Egyptian triangles and geometric diagonals" (*qu'il ne fut guère, à l'École des Beaux-Arts, de candidat au Grand Prix qui ne jouât plus ou moins aux triangles égyptiens et à la diagonale rabattue*); Pol Abraham, "'Vers une architecture' par Le Corbusier-Saugnier," pt. 2, *L'Architecte* 1, no. 3 (1924): 18.

p. 142. Top ill.: Le Corbusier and Pierre Jeanneret, elevations of the Ozenfant House, Paris, 1922; drawing, 7850, FLC. Added in 1924.

Bottom ill.: Facade of the house. In the 1923 ed., this page was devoted to a garden elevation of the Villa Schwob, La Chaux-de-Fonds, 1917, and a photograph showing a detail of it.

p. 143. Ill.: Charles-Édouard Jeanneret, street facade of the Villa Schwob. The facade called "rear" faces in fact the rue du Jura on the north of the lot and was considered by many locals to be the front facade.

p. 144. Top ill.: Le Corbusier and Pierre Jeanneret, the La Roche and Jeanneret houses, Paris, 1923–24, main elevation with regulating lines; drawing, 15232, FLC. Added in 1924.

Bottom ill.: Photograph of the houses. Added in 1924.

p. 145. Ill.: The liner *Flandre*, built in 1914 for the Compagnie générale transatlantique and used on the lines to Mexico.

p. 146. Added in 1924, after "are not able to discern it" (*ne savent pas le discerner*): "yet" (*encore*).

p. 147. "coming to encumber a mental system that alone provides the elements of a style" (*venant encombrer un système de l'esprit qui seul fournit les éléments d'un style*). 1923 ed.: "on a structure that, in itself, constituted the 'styles'" (*sur une structure qui, à elle seule, constituait les "styles"*).

In 1924, the entire text beginning with: "The 'decorative arts' flourish!" (*Les "arts décoratifs" sévissent!*) and ending with "architecture's time has come" (*On peut croire que l'heure de l'architecture a sonné*) replaced 1923 ed.: "M. Guillaume Janneau, charging zealously forward in the *Renaissance* of April 1920, using language of kid-glove suavity, writes things that are enormous, considerable, imposing: 'It is a regeneration of French art that is being elaborated in painting by M. Guillaume Dulac, M. René Francillon; in decoration, by MM. Suë and André Mare, M. Ruhlmann, M. Paul Véra. They are uncovering the laws of a profoundly traditional style. They strive to recover the manifestly eternal geometric schemas with which the old masters strengthened their compositions. From the Greeks to Percier and Fontaine, from the Romans to Blondel, by way of Philibert Delorme, etc. They permit their severe pencil no improvisation. From what master thinker does M. Paul Véra seek counsel? From Pascal, from Descartes, and, in art, from the Grand Siècle'" (*M. Guillaume Janneau, dans la* Renaissance *d'avril 1920, parti sur son destrier, écrit en un langage ganté de daim, des choses énormes, considérables, imposantes: "C'est une régénération de l'art français qu'élaborent dans la peinture, M. Guillaume Dulac, M. René Francillon; dans la décoration, MM. Suë et André Mare, M. Ruhlmann, M. Paul Véra. Ils dégagent les lois d'un style profondément traditionnel. Ils s'ingénient à retrouver les schémas géométriques évidemment éternels dans lesquels les vieux maîtres affirmaient leurs compositions. Des Grecs à Percier et Fontaine, des Romains à Blondel, en passant par Philibert Delorme, etc. À leur crayon sévère, ils ne permettent aucune improvisation. À quel maître à penser, M. Paul Véra va-t-il demander conseil ? C'est à Pascal, c'est à Descartes, et, dans l'art, c'est au Grand Siècle"*).

p. 148. "mistakenly called to testify in favor of the decorative arts, have enlightened our judgment, and now we find ourselves in architecture, architecture that is everything, but that is not the decorative arts" (*appelés par erreur à témoigner en faveur des arts décoratifs ont éclairé notre jugement, et nous voici maintenant dans l'architecture, l'architecture qui est tout, mais qui n'est pas les arts décoratifs*). 1923 ed: "[the] regeneration of French art, only that in service to the frills that are now the fashion: linden and chamomile tea, the aisles at the Galeries Lafayette!" (*régénération de l'art français, rien que cela au service de fanfreluches à la mode du jour: tilleul et camomille, rayons des Galeries Lafayette!*).

Le Corbusier also removed a footnote here in which he had acknowledged the positive response of Guillaume Janneau to his *L'Esprit nouveau* articles.

Added in 1924: "boudoirs decorated with 'pumpkin' cushions in black and gold velvet are no longer anything but the insufferable witnesses to a dead spirit. These sanctums smothered in coke and soppy 'peasant' idiocies are offensive to us" (*les boudoirs garnis de coussins en potirons de velours, d'or et de noir, ne sont plus que les témoins insupportables d'un esprit mort. Ces sanctuaires étouffés de la coco ou par ailleurs les bêtises "gnangnan" des paysanneries nous offensent*).

III. **Paul Véra, tailpiece; frontispiece to "Les petits jardins," in André Véra, *Les jardins* (Paris: Emile-Paul Frères, 1919), 113. Véra was one of the founders of the Art Deco aesthetic and is clearly mocked in the passage excised from p. 147.**

Le Corbusier alludes to "coke," using the familiar French term *coco* (cocaine).

p. 149. III.: The liner *Aquitania*, compared to the Notre-Dame Cathedral, Saint-Jacques Tower, Arc de Triomphe, and Opéra Garnier (not to scale). The *Aquitania*, 275 meters long, was the last large ship created for the Cunard Lines before the war and entered service in 1914 in order to compete against the *Olympic* for the annual Blue Ribbon award for the fastest transatlantic crossing, thanks to its improved turbines. The "objects" of "modern life" mentioned in the text are for the most part reproduced in Le Corbusier, *L'art décoratif d'aujourd'hui* (Paris: G. Crès, 1925).

"windows meant to introduce light" (*conçues pour introduire la lumière*). 1923 ed.: "windows intended to introduce light" (*projetées pour introduire la lumière*).

p. 150. III.: The liner *Aquitania*; reproduction of a painting.

"would be just as efficient" (*seraient d'égale efficacité*). 1923 ed.: "would suffice" (*suffiraient*).

p. 151. III.: The liner *Lamoricière*, built in 1921 in Newcastle for the Compagnie générale transatlantique and sunk in 1942.

Added in 1924, after "hazelnuts!" (*noisettes!*): "The 'styles' are still with us!" (*Les "styles" demeurent!*).

"A house is a machine for living in" (*une maison est une machine à habiter*). 1923 ed.: "A house is a machine for residing in" (*Une maison est une machine à demeurer*). *Demeurer* carries the connotation of conservatism.

Bernard Palissy: French Renaissance ceramic designer whose production was saturated with sculptural motifs to the point of being sometimes useless. Here Corbu is deliberately distorting the known fact that Palissy's more elaborate works were virtuoso exercises that were never meant to be used as functional objects.

["Maple": reference to Maple & Company, a furniture manufacturer and retailer whose giant London warehouse (on Tottenham Court Road) was a major tourist site in the first two decades of the twentieth century and whose products were exported to all of Europe. "Twyford": British company (est. 1849) specializing in bathroom fixtures.]

p. 152. Top ill.: The deck of the *Aquitania*, designed by Leonard Peskett.

Bottom ill.: Interior of the same, designed by Charles Mewès and Arthur J. Davis, whose other eclectic designs — ranging from Tudor to Louis XIV — Le Corbusier didn't care to show.

p. 153. III.: The liner *France*. First and last French four-funnel ship, 218 meters long, launched in 1912. Nicknamed *Le Château de l'Atlantique* because of its lavish decoration.

p. 154. III.: Bow of the liner *Aquitania*.

Bottom ill.: Corridor of the same.

p. 155. Ill.: The liner *Lamoricière.* Apparently this image is a detail from the same source as the ill. on p. 73.

p. 156. Ill.: The liner *Empress of France* of the Canadian Pacific. Launched in Glasgow in 1913 as the *Alsatian* for the Allan Line, it was given a new name in 1919.

Added in 1924: "confused with respect for decor" (*confondu avec le respect du décor*).

p. 157. Ill.: The liner *Empress of Asia,* same as cover.

["Art is in its essence elevated": *L'art est d'essence hautaine.*]

p. 158. "governed by economy" (*régi par l'économie*). 1923 ed.: "governed by the law of economy" (*la loi d'économie*).

Added in 1924: the text beginning with "conditioned by the inevitability of physics" (*conditionné par la fatalité de la physique*) and ending with "our admiration" (*notre admiration*) and the phrase "and required by this century of great endeavors that has just taken a giant step forward" (*requises par ce siècle de grand effort qui vient de faire un pas de géant*).

p. 159. Ill.: Maurice Farman MF 11 "Shorthorn" reconnaissance and bombing aircraft, 1914. Widely used by the French *Armée de l'Air* during the war and also built in Italy, England, Russia, and Japan.

p. 162. Ill.: Farman F 60 Goliath aircraft, 1920, civilian version. See Farman brochure owned by Le Corbusier, A1(16)24, FLC. Henri Farman was a friend of Gabriel Voisin, who built his first aircraft. He set up a factory in Mourmelon and developed the production in partnership with his brother Maurice. See Jean Liron, *Les avions Farman* (Clichy: Éditions Larivière, 1984).

"Arts et métiers": Le Corbusier refers to the École nationale supérieure des arts et métiers, a civil engineering school first created in 1780, with branches in several French towns. The "Gad'zarts," as these engineers were nicknamed, were known for being technical virtuosi.

p. 163. Ill.: Cockpit of a Farman aircraft.

"stirring formal relationships" (*rapports émouvants*). 1923 ed: "proportional relationships" (*rapports proportionnés*).

p. 164. Ill.: SPAD 33 aircraft, 1921; photograph Marcel Rol. This six-seat *berline* (enclosed cabin) transportation airplane was built by Louis Blériot under the trademark SPAD (Société anonyme pour l'aviation et ses dérivés) and used by Compagnie de messageries aériennes. Second craft produced.

Added in 1924: note 1, insisting on the failure of postwar reconstruction in the north of France.

p. 165. Ill.: Caproni CA-60, "Capronissimo" tri-cellular seaplane, 1920. This mammoth aircraft had eight engines and was destroyed upon its maiden flight on Lake Maggiore on 4 March 1921. Le Corbusier had a copy of the article by J.-A. Lefranc, *breveté mécanicien d'avion* (licensed plane mechanic): J.-A. Lefranc, "L'hydravion géant Caproni," *La Nature,* no. 2454 (1921): 248–54.

p. 166. Ill.: Caproni CA-58 triplane, 1919. This aircraft was a development of the CA-48, the civilian version of the CA-40 bomber. Equipped with five engines, it carried thirty passengers in a two-story cabin.

p. 167. Ill.: Civilian version of the Farman Goliath, adapted from the 1918 bomber.

[p. 168. Ill.: The photo credit misspells the name *Baranger.*]

Ill.: Farman Moustique "moto-aviette" lightweight aircraft, 1919.

p. 169. Top ill.: SPAD XIII fighter, 1917. The main engineer of the SPAD was Louis Béchereau and not "Bechneau," as spelled by Le Corbusier. This was one of the most popular fighters of the entire war. Bottom ill.: Interior of a civilian Goliath.

p. 170. Ill.: Farman F 60 Goliath, military version, 1920.

"if it rains at night, you get drenched closing them" (s'il pleut le soir, pour les tirer, on reçoit l'averse). 1923 ed.: "you have to get drenched to close them" (pour les tirer, il faut recevoir l'averse).

Added in 1924: "The modern man and woman are bored at home; they go dancing" (L'homme et la femme modernes s'ennuient chez eux; ils vont au dancing).

p. 171. In the eighteenth century, the Faubourg Saint-Antoine, east of the place de la Bastille, was home to many luxury furniture ateliers. In the nineteenth century, however, it became widely associated with the production of furniture imitating historical styles.

Top ill.: Front view of a civilian Goliath.

Bottom ill.: Farman MF 11; from the cover of a Farman brochure owned by Le Corbusier, A1(16)25, FLC.

p. 173. Ill.: Civilian version of the Farman Goliath; enlarged section of ill. on p. 91.

p. 174. Ill.: Set of Beaux-Arts projects. When this plate was published in L'Esprit nouveau, no. 9 (1921): 986, Le Corbusier included the names of the six architects and four of the projects. The images are fragments of plates he cut out from Les salons d'architecture. Société des artistes français et Société nationale des beaux-arts 1913 (Paris: Ch. Massin, 1920). The detailed captions are: top left: Pierre Vorin, project for the organization of the La Baule beach, p. 115; top right: Gaston Castel, "Salle des séances d'un palais législatif," p. 36; center left: Paul Lajoie, Municipal casino in Annecy, p. 67; center right: Garriguenc and Gosselin, hotel close to an excursion area in the mountains, p. 85; bottom left: Alexandre Marcel, competition project for the Magasins modernes in Strasbourg, 1912, p. 43; bottom right: Jules Lavirotte, pavilion of the scales for the Société des courses de Compiègne (Horse-racing society of Compiègne), p. 65, very similar to the Saulot hunting lodge designed by Jeanneret for Perret in 1908. More radical projects featured in the book, such as Louis Bonnier's school at Grenelle in Paris, were omitted.

p. 175. Ill.: Civilian version of the Farman Goliath.

p. 176. Ill.: Handley Page O/400 heavy bomber, 1917. Developed for the British Royal Naval Air Service and used for night raids over Germany.

"of esteem" (d'estime). 1923 ed.: "of admiration" (d'admiration).

Added in 1924: note 1: "1921. Today it would be as high as 28 or 40,000 francs" (1921. Aujourd'hui nous en sommes bien à 28 ou 40.000 francs).

The laws written by Louis Loucheur (1872–1931) and Laurent Bonnevay (1870–1957) would have ensured state funding for low-cost housing but were not voted until 1928 and 1930, respectively.

p. 177. Ill.: Front brake of GL 95 x 140 Delage car, with six-cylinder motor; reproduction of a photographic print glued on paper, A1(07)499, FLC. The Delage firm operated from 1905 to 1954; Françoise Jolly, La grande aventure des Delage 3 litres (Pontoise: Edijac, 1988).

p. 179. Ill.: Front view of GL 95 x 140 Delage car. This chassis could be produced in four models: "sleeping," "standard," "sport," and "grand sport."

p. 180. Top ill.: Basilica at Paestum, circa 550–525 B.C.

Bottom ill.: British Humber (not "Humbert") 1907 car; reproduced from *La Vie automobile*.

p. 181. Top ill.: The Parthenon, Athens, fifth century B.C.; from Maxime Collignon, *Le Parthénon: L'histoire, l'architecture et la sculpture,* with photographs by Frédéric Boissonnas and W.-A. Mansell (Paris: Librairie Centrale d'art & d'architecture, 1910–12), pls. 2, 3.

Bottom ill.: Delage Grand-Sport, four-seat version of GL 95 x 140 model, 1921.

p. 182. Ill.: Hispano-Suiza coachwork, designed by Amédée Ozenfant and his younger brother, Jean, in Saint-Quentin, 1911.

[*Oedipus (Tyrannus):* play by Sophocles; *Phaedra:* play (1677) by Jean Racine; the *Prodigal Son:* parable in the Gospel of Luke (15:24) and subject of many paintings; *Paul and Virginia:* novel (1787) by Jacques-Henri Bernardin de Saint-Pierre; *Philemon and Baucis:* ancient myth about an elderly peasant couple who entertained Zeus and Hermes and who, upon their deaths, were transfigured into an oak and a linden tree springing from the same trunk (see, e.g., Ovid, *Metamorphoses* 8.618–724); *The Poor Fisherman:* oil painting by Pierre Puvis de Chavannes (1881; Paris, Musée d'Orsay); the *Marseillaise:* French national anthem; "[Quand] Madelon vient nous [servir] à boire": French soldiers' drinking song (1914), lyrics by Louis Bousquet, music by Camille Robert.]

p. 183. Ill.: Bignan-Sport, 1921. The Bignan firm operated from 1918 to 1931 in Courbevoie. The Bignan-Sport was produced jointly with Grégoire.

In the 1923 ed. the graph on aerodynamic evolution (moved to p. 190 in 1924) was featured on this page.

p. 184. Ill.: North side of the Parthenon; from *L'Acropole d'Athènes, le Parthénon,* intro. Gustave Fougères (Paris: Albert Morancé, 1910), upper-right detail of pl. 10. The same photograph appears in Collignon, *Le Parthénon* (note for p. 181), pl. 10.

"Bretons beds" are traditional beds enclosed behind sliding wood doors.

p. 185. Ill.: North side of the Parthenon; from *L'Acropole d'Athènes, le Parthénon* (note for p. 184), lower-right detail of pl. 10. The same photograph appears in Collignon, *Le Parthénon* (note for p. 181), pl. 10.

Added in 1924: "reads as categorical" (*s'y lit catégorique*).

p. 186. Ill.: Cockpit of the "Capronissimo" seaplane.

Caption: "sole instigation" (*seule instigation*). 1923 ed.: "sole indication" (*seule indication*).

p. 187. Ill.: Cockpit of the "Caproni exploration" airplane; from Paolo Azzolini, *I grandi artefici della nostra vittoria: Gianni Caproni* (Milan: Varietas, n.d.). Le Corbusier's copy is A1(16)26, FLC.

Added in 1924: "relationships that create the imponderable" (*les rapports qui créent l'impondérable*).

[p. 187: "Decoration is the necessary superfluity or quantum of the peasant" (*Le décor est le superflu nécessaire, quantum du paysan*). Cf. Voltaire, "The superfluous, a very necessary thing" (*Le superflu, chose très-nécessaire*); "Le Mondain," 1736, line 22.]

p. 188. Ill.: Bellanger 15 HP car body and interior, 1921. The firm produced cars in Neuilly from 1913 to 1925. Le Corbusier owned the brochure for the car: A1(7)379, FLC.

p. 189. Ill.: Voisin, Torpédo-Sport car, 1921. The firm produced cars from 1919 to 1939.

"an art of great dignity" (*un art très digne*). 1923 ed.: "an elevated art" (*un art hautain*).

p. 190. Bottom ill.: "Looking for a standard"; newspaper clippings assembled by Le Corbusier. Added in 1924. Le Corbusier uses throughout his writings the German spelling "standart," revealing his first exposure to this concept in pre-1914 Germany.

p. 191. Ill.: Western peristyle of the Parthenon; from *L'Acropole d'Athènes* (note for p. 184), pl. 68.

p. 193. Ill.: Hadrian's Villa, Tivoli, A.D. 120; from *Italie, 2e partie, Italie centrale et Rome* (Leipzig: Karl Baedeker, 1909), insert after p. 450, lower part cut out.

p. 195. "Victor-Emmanuel": Le Corbusier alludes to the monument built between 1884 and 1913 by Giuseppe Sacconi adjacent to Rome's Capitoline Hill, on Piazza Venezia, at the end of the Corso.

p. 196. Ill.: The Pyramid of Caius Cestius, 12 B.C., and Porta San Paolo, Rome, 3rd century A.D.; postcard or Alinari photograph.

p. 197. Top ill.: The Colosseum, Rome, A.D. 80; drawing published as postcard.

Bottom ill.: View from the north of the Arch of Constantine, Rome, fourth century A.D.; postcard. According to his notes, Le Corbusier seems to have lost it for a while: B2(15)87, FLC, p. 12.

p. 198. Ill.: Interior view of the Pantheon, Rome, A.D. 118–128; probably a postcard.

p. 199. Ill.: The Pantheon; reproduction of upper-right corner of postcard owned by Le Corbusier, L5(8)197, FLC.

p. 200. Top ill.: Platonic and other elementary solids; a detail from a didactic chart for schoolchildren, A2(5)53, FLC. This chart is reproduced in *Urbanisme,* with the caption, "This is printed on the back cover of France's elementary schools' class notebooks, this is geometry" (*Ceci est imprimé au dos des cahiers de classe des écoles primaires de France; c'est la géométrie*); Le Corbusier, *Urbanisme* (Paris: G. Crès, 1925), v.

Bottom ill.: Le Corbusier, drawing made in 1915 after parts of Pirro Ligorio's *Anteiqvae Vrbis Imago* engraving of Rome made in 1561. This montage is also published in Le Corbusier and Ozenfant, "Sur la plastique I" (note for p. 92). The original tracing was made during his research visit in 1915 at the Bibliothèque nationale de France in Paris for *La construction des villes*; tracing, B2(20)655, FLC.

["it renders": *ça rend.*]

p. 201. Ill.: Santa Maria in Cosmedin, Rome, built beginning in A.D. 772; Alinari photograph 26561, retouched by Le Corbusier in order to make the interior more structural and more abstract. See his graphic and verbal instructions on sketch sheet B2(15)87, FLC.

p. 202. Ill.: Santa Maria in Cosmedin; photograph retouched by Le Corbusier, who eliminated the Gothic baldachin and redrew the windows. See B2(15)87, FLC.

"Pertaining to the face of man" (*touchant au visage de l'homme*). 1923 ed.: "pertaining closely to man" (*touchant de près à l'homme*).

p. 203. Ill.: Pulpit of Santa Maria in Cosmedin; Alinari photograph 26562, retouched by Le Corbusier, who eliminated a series of columns and blackened the windows. See B2(15)87, FLC.

p. 204. Ill.: Basilica of Saint Peter, Rome, sixteenth century; Alinari photograph 26469. Inverted by Le Corbusier, who cropped away the left side of the original photo, with the sacristy by Carlo Marchionni (1702–86).

p. 205. Ill.: Apse of Basilica of Saint Peter; Anderson photograph 17593, right side cropped.

"fine bunch of fellows who had talent" (*un tas de bonshommes à talent*). In 1923, the same phrase appears but with *bonshommes* printed as two words (*bons hommes*).

p. 206. Ill.: Basilica of Saint Peter, rotated; detail of Anderson photograph 17595.

p. 207. Ill.: Basilica of Saint Peter; detail of Anderson photograph 17595.

p. 208. Top ill.: Plan with galleries of the Basilica of Saint Peter, redrawn by Le Corbusier.

Bottom ill.: Michelangelo, Porta Pia, Rome, 1561–65, detail; probably an Alinari photograph.

p. 209. Top ill.: Basilica of Saint Peter, perspective and plan of Michelangelo's scheme, compared to the Colosseum; drawing, 5425, FLC. Manuscript note relative to the plan: "the apses that were to the scale of the Colosseum" (*les absides qui étaient à l'échelle du Colysée*), and relative to the elevation: "he would have treated the interior like the Laurentian Library (provide photos)" (*l'intérieur il l'aurait traité comme la Laurentienne (donner clichés)*).

Bottom ill.: View of Saint Peter's Square, Rome, 1656–67; Anderson photograph 173, right side cropped away by Le Corbusier.

p. 210. Ill.: Apse window of Basilica of Saint Peter; Anderson photograph 17596.

p. 211. Ill.: "The Rome of Horrors." 1. Castel Sant'Angelo, Rome, A.D. 135–39, papal apartments; 2. Galleria Colonna, Rome, 1654–65; postcard, F2(12)67, FLC, and Alinari photograph 6318. 1. Guglielmo Calderini, Palazzo di Giustizia, Rome, 1884–1911; Alinari photograph 20177. 2. Ceiling of Palazzo Barberini, Rome, 1625–33. Combined with Dadaist collages, this assemblage is the likely source of Pietro Maria Bardi's *Tavolo degli orrori* (Table of horrors), the most polemical piece shown at the second exhibition of the Movimento Italiano per l'Architettura Razionale (Italian rational architecture movement), held in Rome during the spring of 1931.

p. 213. Ill.: Plan of Karlsruhe, Germany, ca. 1715; apparently from an exhibition panel.

p. 216. Ill.: Charles-Édouard Jeanneret, sketch of the Sulemaniye Mosque from the Beyazit tower, Istanbul, 1911. Also reproduced in Le Corbusier, *Almanach d'architecture moderne: Documents, théorie, pronostics, histoire, petites histoires, dates, propos standarts, organisation, industrialisation du bâtiment* (Paris: G. Crès, 1926).

p. 217. Top ill.: Charles-Édouard Jeanneret, plan of the Külliye of Mohammed I or Green Mosque, Bursa, Turkey, 1911; in Le Corbusier, *Voyage d'Orient: carnets,* 6 vols. (Milan: Electa; Paris: Fondation Le Corbusier, 1987), 4:19.

Bottom ill.: View of Hagia Sophia, Istanbul, 1911. Le Corbusier had envisioned adding a plan of the Invalides as a "counterexample"; B2(5)87, FLC, p. 15.

p. 218. Top ill.: Charles-Édouard Jeanneret, view of the Casa delle Nozze d'Argento (captioned by him "del Noce"), Pompeii, 1911. It was excavated in 1893, the year of the king's silver wedding anniversary.

Bottom ill.: Plan of the same house; in Le Corbusier, *Voyage d'Orient* (note for p. 147), 5:126, 127.

"a sensation of strength and witness to potent means" (*sensation de force et témoignage de moyens puissants*). 1923 ed.: "the sensation of a cathedral" (*sensation de cathédrale*).

p. 219. Ill.: Charles-Édouard Jeanneret, view and plan of the Oecus of the "Oriental garden" at Hadrian's Villa, 1911; in Le Corbusier, *Voyage d'Orient* (note for p. 147), 6:45, 44.

p. 220. Top ill.: Charles-Édouard Jeanneret, section and plan of three apses of the temple on the Golden Square of Hadrian's Villa, 1911; in Le Corbusier, *Voyage d'Orient* (note for p. 147), 6:83.

Bottom ill.: Room in a Pompeii house, 1911; in *Voyage d'Orient,* vol. 5, p. 121.

[p. 221. "ordonnance": *ordonnance*. On the decision to anglicize the French term in this translation, see "From the Translator."]

"an orthogonal perception" (*perception orthogonale*). 1923 ed.: "an orthogonal sensation" (*sensation orthogonale*).

p. 222. Top ill.: The Acropolis; from Choisy, *Histoire de l'architecture* (note for p. 115), same ill. as on p. 115 (source not acknowledged).

Bottom ill.: Plan of the Pompeii forum, 1911; in Le Corbusier, *Voyage d'Orient* (note for p. 217), 5:47.

p. 223. Ill.: Plan of the House of the Tragic Poet, Pompeii, 1911; from Le Corbusier, *Voyage d'Orient* (note for p. 217), 5:87.

p. 225. Top ill.: View of the Propylaea and of the Temple of Nike on the Acropolis, 1911; photograph by Charles-Édouard Jeanneret; in Le Corbusier, *Voyage d'Orient* (note for p. 217), 4:111.

Bottom ill.: View of the Propylaea, Athens, 1911; in Le Corbusier, *Voyage d'Orient* (note for p. 217), 4:125.

p. 226. Top and bottom ills.: Views of the Poekile at Hadrian's Villa, 1911; photographs by Charles-Édouard Jeanneret; in Le Corbusier, *Voyage d'Orient* (note for p. 217), 6:61, 34.

p. 227. Ill.: View of the Pompeii forum, 1911; photograph by Charles-Édouard Jeanneret; in Le Corbusier, *Voyage d'Orient* (note for p. 217), 5:103.

p. 228. Left ill.: Plan of Basilica of Saint Peter and Saint Peter's Square; from *Italie, 2e partie, Italie centrale et Rome* (Paris: Ollendorf, 1909): insert between pp. 272 and 273, right part cut out; personal library of Le Corbusier, 143, FLC.

Right ill.: Plan of Hagia Sophia, probably from *Baedeker.*

p. 229. Ill.: Charles-Édouard Jeanneret, perspective of Versailles, after an engraving by Gabriel Pérelle. An early version in pencil of 1915 is preserved: drawing, B2(20)256, FLC.

"a vision of the whole" (*une vision d'ensemble*). 1923 ed.: "a view of the whole" (*une vue d'ensemble*).

["a perfect 'knockout'": *le "knock-out" parfait.* Le Corbusier seems to have misunderstood the English phrase; the context suggests that he meant something like "a complete flop."]

p. 231. Ill.: The Parthenon; photograph by Frédéric Boissonnas; from Collignon, *Le Parthénon* (note for p. 181), pls. 2, 3.

[p. 232 and passim: "contour modulation": *la modénature.* See "From the Translator."]

p. 233. Added in 1924: "There are millions of faces built on these essential types, yet all are different: there is variation in the quality of the features and variation in their unifying relationships" (*Il y a des millions de visages construits sur ces types essentiels; pourtant tous sont différents: variation de qualité des traits et variation des rapports qui les unissent*).

p. 234. Top ill.: The Parthenon; source not identified.

Bottom ill.: The Propylaea; source not identified.

p. 235. Ill.: The Propylaea; source not identified.

p. 236. Ill.: The Propylaea; source not identified.

p. 237. Ill.: The Erechtheum, the Caryatids, seen from the back toward the south; the Propylaea; source not identified.

p. 238. Ill.: The Parthenon; photograph by Frédéric Boissonnas; from Collignon, *Le Parthénon* (note for p. 181), pl. 14.

p. 239. Ill.: The Parthenon; photograph by Frédéric Boissonnas; from Collignon, vol. II: *Le Parthénon* (note for p. 181), detail of pl. 68.

p. 240. Ill.: The Parthenon. Photograph by Frédéric Boissonnas; from Collignon, *Le Parthénon* (note for p. 181), 65.

p. 241. Ill.: The Parthenon; photograph by Frédéric Boissonnas; from Collignon, *Le Parthénon* (note for p. 181), pl. 19.

p. 242. Ill.: Entablature of the south wing of the Propylaea; identical view in *L'Acropole d'Athènes, l'enceinte, l'entrée, le bastion d'Athéna Niké, les Propylées,* intro. Charles Picard (Paris: Albert Morancé, n.d.), pl. 63.

p. 243. Ill.: The Parthenon; photograph by Frédéric Boissonnas; from Collignon, *Le Parthénon* (note for p. 181), pl. 71. Caption: The curve of the echinus is as rational as that of a large artillery shell. One could read here an anticipation of the metaphor of the shell (*obus*), used in 1932 for the Algiers plan.

p. 244. Ill.: Cast of the Parthenon at the École des Beaux-Arts, Paris; source not identified.

Caption: "quai Voltaire." A (self-conscious?) confusion by Le Corbusier between Quai Voltaire, the location of the Académie des Beaux-Arts, and Quai Malaquais, the actual location of the École des Beaux-Arts. The Grand Palais is here taken as the epitome of historicism.

p. 245. Ill.: The Parthenon; photograph by Frédéric Boissonnas; from Collignon, *Le Parthénon* (note for p. 181), pl. 53.

p. 246. Ill.: The Parthenon; photograph by Frédéric Boissonnas; from Collignon, *Le Parthénon* (note for p. 181), pl. 20.

p. 247. Ill.: The Parthenon; photograph by Frédéric Boissonnas; from Collignon, *Le Parthénon* (note for p. 181), pl. 20.

p. 248. III.: The Parthenon; photograph by Frédéric Boissonnas; from Collignon, *Le Parthénon* **(note for p. 181), pl. 72.**

p. 249. III.: The Parthenon; photograph by Frédéric Boissonnas; from Collignon, *Le Parthénon* **(note for p. 181), pl. 73.**

p. 250. III.: View of the Acropolis, 1911. Photograph by Charles-Édouard Jeanneret; in Le Corbusier, *Voyage d'Orient* **(note for p. 217), 4:98. Illustration added in 1924.**

p. 251. III.: The Parthenon; photograph by Frédéric Boissonnas; from Collignon, *Le Parthénon* **(note for p. 181), pl. 45.**

p. 253. III.: Citroën and Ford posters in a Paris street, circa 1921; photograph by Hostache. In 1924, it replaced the initial image of the Bellanger car (see p. 188).

LC tries to recruit Hostache as a stockholder of *L'Esprit nouveau:* Le Corbusier to Hostache, 22 July 1922, A1(19)222, FLC.

p. 254. "only through it are our conceptions viable" (*nos conceptions ne sont viables que par elles*). 1923 ed.: "and our thoughts" (*et nos pensées*). Exceptionally (perhaps inadvertently, as a result of oversight during textual revision between the 1923 and 1924 eds.), this sentence in the chapter heading proper diverges from the corresponding one in the opening argument. Argument: "The law of Economy necessarily governs our actions and our thoughts" (*La loi d'Économie gère impérativement nos actes et nos pensées*). Chapter heading proper: "The law of Economy necessarily governs our actions and only through it are our conceptions viable" (*La loi d'Économie gère impérativement nos actes et nos conceptions ne sont viables que par elle*).

Added in 1924: "Beautiful too from all the life that the artistic sense can bring to these strict and pure organs" (*Belle aussi de l'animation que le sens artiste peut apporter à ces stricts et purs organes*).

p. 255. Loucheur and Bonnevay (note for p. 176). The chamber is the Chambre des députés, with the Sénat one of the two constitutive bodies of the French parliament.

p. 256–57. III.: Domino housing, drawings by Le Corbusier, 19131, FLC; perspective, 19209, FLC.

Houses made of poured concrete, drawing by Le Corbusier, 1920. Also published in Boesiger and Storonov, *Le Corbusier et Pierre Jeanneret* **(note for p. 125), 29.**

p. 258. The "cold storage building at Tolbiac," situated on the Seine embankment, still stands but has since been transformed into artists' housing.

p. 259. Added in 1924: "Urban and suburban site plans will be vast and orthogonal and no longer horribly misshapen; they will allow for the use of mass-produced parts and the industrialization of the construction site. Perhaps we will finally stop building 'to measure'" (*Les lotissements urbains et suburbains seront vastes et orthogonaux et non plus désespérément biscornus; ils permettront l'emploi de l'élément de série et l'industrialisation du chantier. L'on cessera peut-être enfin de construire "sur mesures"*).

"that is an opulent object manifesting wealth" (*qui est l'objet opulent par quoi se manifeste la richesse*). 1923 ed.: "which is a definite index of riches" (*qui est l'indice décisif de la richesse*).

"from our hearts and minds" (*du coeur et de l'esprit*). 1923 ed.: "from people's hearts and minds" (*du coeur et de l'esprit des gens*).

"Site plans": Le Corbusier refers to the speculative land subdivisions (*lotissements*) with small low-cost cottages that developed around Paris after World War I. Their inadequacy would lead to numerous revolts of the *mal-lotis* (literally, the "ill-subdivided" but also meaning "mistreated heirs").

p. 260–61. Ill.: Perspective and plan of the Domino House, drawing by Le Corbusier, 1915. This view reveals Jeanneret's knowledge of Frank Lloyd Wright's Prairie Houses. Also published in Boesiger and Storonov, *Le Corbusier et Pierre Jeanneret* **(note for p. 125), 24. Image deleted in 1924 from p. 261: "Type of electrical power plant for a small city with workers' houses for the workers of the night shift"** (*type de centrale électrique de petite ville avec maisons ouvrières pour les ouvriers attachés au service de nuit*).

p. 261. Added in 1924: "It will be beautiful too from all the animation that an artistic sense can bring to its strict and pure organs" (*Elle sera belle aussi de l'animation qu'un sens artiste peut apporter à ses stricts et purs organes*).

p. 262. Ill.: Plan of the Domino housing development, 19205, FLC; elevation by Le Corbusier, close to 30292, FLC. Also published in Boesiger and Storonov, *Le Corbusier et Pierre Jeanneret* **(note for p. 125), 25.**

p. 263. Ill.: Le Corbusier, interior perspective of the Domino House, 1915. Also published in Boesiger and Storonov, *Lc Corbusier et Pierre Jeanneret* **(note for p. 125), 25.**

Added in 1924: "and wacky ideas" (*et des idées loufoques*).

p. 264. Top ill.: Perspective of the house of an artist, 30199, FLC.

Bottom ill.: Houses made of coarse concrete for the Jourdain Society, Troyes, 1919. Also published in Boesiger and Storonov, *Le Corbusier et Pierre Jeanneret* **(note for p. 125), 29.**

p. 265. Ill. Mass-production workers' housing, 1920, 7946, FLC.

For the caption "Architecture is a matter of plastique, not of Romanticism," see the note for p. 92.

p. 266. Ill.: Perspective rendering of interior of the mass-production Citrohan House, drawing, 20707, FLC.

[p. 267. Bottom ill.: The typographical error "1621" appears in the 1924 ed. but not the 1923 ed.]

Bottom ill.: *Citrohan* stands for "Citroën." Le Corbusier had initially imagined calling this project "Renault," as shown on the untitled note, A2(15)153, FLC. But the intense propaganda campaign of Citroën probably persuaded him to change his mind.

p. 268–69. Top. ill.: Perspective rendering of the Monol House, 1919, 19121, FLC. Bottom ill.: Perspective rendering of the Monol House, 19122, FLC.

"Entire schemes": Le Corbusier also mentions here the *lotissements* (see note for p. 193).

p. 270. Top ill.: Perspective rendering of the Seaside Villa, location unknown, 1916, 30280, FLC.

Bottom ill.: Plan, 30281, FLC.

Probably designed for the couturier Paul Poiret; see the commentary by Josep Quetglas in the DVD *Le Corbusier: Plans*, vol. 1, *1905–26* (Paris: Echelle 1 and Fondation Le Corbusier, 2005).

p. 271. Top ill.: View of the salon in the Seaside Villa, 14711, FLC. Bottom ill.: Interior of the Monol House.

p. 272–73. Top ill.: Mirror assemblage of two half-plans of the villa apartments, Paris, 1922, 19082, FLC.

Bottom ill. on p. 272: Partial perspective, 19069, FLC. Bottom ill. on p. 273: structural scheme. Declared to be "under construction in Paris" (*en construction à Paris*) in 1923 but not in 1924. Added in 1924 to the top caption on p. 273: "1922."

["villa apartments": a rendering of the oxymoron *immeubles villas*.]

p. 274. Ill.: Two interior views of the villa apartments from drawing 19097, FLC, cropped.

p. 275. Top ill.: Perspective rendering of the villa apartments, 19083, FLC.

Bottom ill.: View of the hall, 19071, FLC.

p. 276–77. Top and bottom ill.: Perspective rendering of "Honeycomb" clusters for a garden city, 1924. Also published in Boesiger and Storonov, *Le Corbusier et Pierre Jeanneret* (note for p. 125), 76. Bottom ill.: Perspective of a building in "Lotissement 'à alvéoles' pour cités-jardins," drawing, 30834, FLC. Also published in Boesiger and Storonov, *Le Corbusier et Pierre Jeanneret* (note for p. 125), 76.

Double page added in 1924.

p. 278. Aerial perspective of the "Modern Frugès quarter," Pessac, 1925; drawing, 19879, FLC.

Page added in 1924.

p. 279. Plan of the modern Frugès quarter, 1925. The original of the right part is filed as drawing, 19772, FLC.

p. 280–81. Mass-production housing for craftsmen, location unknown, 1924. Top ill.: Perspective. On p. 280: plans and on p. 281: interior perspective. All illustrations were published in Boesiger and Storonov, *Le Corbusier et Pierre Jeanneret* (note for p. 125), 54.

Double page added in 1924.

p. 282. Ill.: Plan and perspective of the Peugeot Lotissement project, Audincourt, 1923. Also published in Boesiger and Storonov, *Le Corbusier et Pierre Jeanneret* (note for p. 125), 72.

For the workers of the Peugeot car factories.

Page added in 1924.

p. 283. Axonometric view of a cell of the villa apartments, 1923. Also published in Boesiger and Storonov, *Le Corbusier et Pierre Jeanneret* (note for p. 125), 95.

"The U P Businesses of Czechoslovakia" (*les Établissements U. P. réunis de Tchécoslovaquie*): Spojené uměleckoprůmyslové závody v Brně (United decorative arts factories in Brno), a consortium established in 1920 that produced modern furnishings.

Page added in 1924.

p. 284. Plan of a villa, Bordeaux, 1925; drawing, FLC 31518.

Designed in fact for Dr. Mont-Refet, in Royan.

Page added in 1924.

p. 285. Axonometric view of a villa, Bordeaux, 1925; drawing, 31519, FLC.

Page added in 1924.

p. 286. General axonometric view of the Cité universitaire, Paris, 1925. Also published in Boesiger and Storonov, *Le Corbusier et Pierre Jeanneret* (note for p. 125), 73.

Page added in 1924.

p. 287. Section, plan, and partial axonometric view of the Cité universitaire, 1925. Also published in Boesiger and Storonov, *Le Corbusier et Pierre Jeanneret* (note for p. 125), 73.

Page added in 1924.

p. 288. Le Corbusier, Pierre Jeanneret, interior of the atelier of the Ozenfant House. Page added in 1924.

p. 289. The old and new Procurator's Offices were built in the sixteenth century on Piazza San Marco in Venice; the Place des Vosges was built from 1609 to 1612 in Paris; and the Place de la Carrière took its final, classical form in the middle of the eighteenth century in Nancy.

["Laugier": Marc-Antoine (abbé) Laugier, Jesuit priest and author who contributed in print to many contemporary cultural debates, most notably in his *Essai sur l'architecture* (1753) and *Observations sur l'architecture* (1765).]

p. 290. Ill.: Low-pressure ventilator; from the brochure *Société Rateau, ventilateurs à haute pression,* n.d., p. 20, A1(16)114, FLC.

p. 291. Ill.: Electric turbine in the Genevilliers power plant, then the largest of the Paris region.

p. 293. "The human beast": Le Corbusier refers to Émile Zola's novel *La bête humaine* (1890), centered on the figure of the hardworking locomotive engineer Emile Lantier.

p. 294. Ill.: Ernest R. Graham, for Anderson, Probst & Co., Equitable Building, New York, 1913–15, seen from the corner of Trinity Place and Rector Street. The steeple of Trinity Church appears at the bottom right.

p. 295. Ill.: Gustave Lindenthal, Hellgate Bridge over the East River, New York, 1918. The upper part of the arch is under construction.

"Intelligence selection": Le Corbusier expresses here his approval for the organization of the division of labor according to "natural" class hierarchies.

p. 296. Ill.: Wisconsin Special racing car, 1922. Designed and built with power from an airplane engine by Sigurd Olson "Sig" Haugdahl to set a world speed record, a feat achieved in Daytona Beach on 7 April 1922. Le Corbusier has brushed out the context of the photo.

p. 297. Ill.: View of the East River in New York in 1912, with the USS *Michigan* battleship. Replaces a photograph of a Voisin triplane of 1916 used in 1923.

p. 298. Ill.: German Demag crane. Based in Duisburg, Demag was the leading manufacturer of cranes in Europe since the late nineteenth century.

p. 299. Ill.: Coal harbor in the Ruhr.

p. 300. Ill.: Electric turbine wheel produced by Le Creusot.

["Ribot law for workers": reference to French legislation (1908), named after minister Alexandre Ribot (1842–1923), that facilitated the purchase of small plots of land for the construction of houses by individuals with limited financial means.]

p. 301. Ill.: Rateau ventilator. Not featured in the brochure *Société Rateau* (note for p. 290).

p. 302. Top ill.: Bugatti car engine.

Bottom ill.: American window sample.

p. 303. Top ill.: Louis Bréguet, flying wing aircraft; from Louis Bréguet, "L'avion de demain," in *L'Exportateur français* 6, no. 277 (1921): 625.

Bottom ill.: Factory built by the Limousin firm with Eugène Freyssinet.

p. 304. Ill.: Eugène Freyssinet, Orly dirigible hangars, 1921–23 (destroyed 1944).

The spectacular building replaces the picture used in 1923 of a structure made of laminated wood (*lamelles de bois collées à la caséine*) by the engineers Terner and Chopard. This modification could be interpreted as a response to Freyssinet, who had requested a meeting with Le Corbusier after reading the first ed.: Eugène Freyssinet to Le Corbusier, 22 November 1923, E2(2)425, FLC.

p. 305. Ill.: Eugène Freyssinet, Orly. Added in 1924.

Erich Mendelsohn reproduced this image in his *Rußland, Europa, Amerika, ein architektonischer Querschnitt* (Berlin: R. Mosse, 1929), 193.

p. 306. Ill.: Giacomo Mattè-Trucco, Fiat automobile factory at the Lingotto, Turin, 1917–22. Le Corbusier would visit it in 1934, driving a car on the test runway.

Page added in 1924.

p. 307. Briar pipe produced by the La Pipe cooperative firm, established at Saint-Claude, in the Jura, the world's capital of briar-pipe production. Founded in the late nineteenth century, it operated until 2000. An obvious *objet-type,* similar to the ones featured in the purist still lifes painted by Jeanneret in the 1920s. On p. 152, Le Corbusier sees in the *Aquitania* the "same aesthetic as that of your English pipe" (*même esthétique que celle de votre pipe anglaise*).

Selected Bibliography

Works written by Le Corbusier

Étude sur le mouvement d'art décoratif en Allemagne. La Chaux-de-Fonds: Haefeli, 1912.

Après le cubisme, with Amédée Ozenfant. Paris: Éditions des Commentaires, 1918.

Vers une architecture. Paris: G. Crès, 1923. Translated by Frederick Etchells as *Towards a New Architecture*. London: John Rodker, 1927.

L'art décoratif d'aujourd'hui. Paris: G. Crès, 1925. Translated by James I. Dunnett as *The Decorative Art of Today*. Cambridge: MIT Press, 1987.

La peinture moderne, with Amédée Ozenfant. Paris: G. Crès, 1925.

Urbanisme. Paris: G. Crès, 1925. Translated by Frederick Etchells as *The City of Tomorrow and Its Planning*. London: John Rodker, 1929.

Almanach d'architecture moderne. Paris: G. Crès, 1926.

Une maison, un palais. Paris: G. Crès, 1928.

Précisions sur un état présent de l'architecture et de l'urbanisme. Paris: G. Crès, 1930. Translated by Edith Schreiber Aujame as *Precisions on the Present State of Architecture and City Planning*. Cambridge: MIT Press, 1991.

Croisade; ou, Le crépuscule des académies. Paris: G. Crès, 1933.

Aircraft. London: The Studio, 1935.

La ville radieuse: Éléments d'une doctrine d'urbanisme pour l'équipement de la civilisation machiniste. Boulogne: Éditions de l'Architecture d'aujourd'hui, 1935. Translated by Pamela Knight, Eleanor Levieux, and Derek Coltman as *The Radiant City: Elements of a Doctrine of Urbanism to Be Used as the Basis of Our Machine-Age Civilization*. New York: Orion, 1967.

Quand les cathédrales étaient blanches: Voyage au pays des timides. Paris: Plon, 1937. Translated by Francis Edwin Hyslop as *When the Cathedrals Were White: A Journey to the Country of Timid People*. New York: Reynal & Hitchcock, 1947.

Des canons, des munitions? Merci! Des logis... s.v.p. Boulogne: Éditions de l'Architecture d'aujourd'hui, 1938.

Destin de Paris. Paris: F. Sorlot, 1941.

Sur les quatre routes. Paris: Gallimard, 1941. Translated by Dorothy Todd as *The Four Routes*. London: D. Dobson, 1947.

La maison des hommes, with François de Pierrefeu. Paris: Plon, 1942. Translated by Clive Entwistle and Gordon Holt as *The Home of Man*. London: Architectural Press, 1948.

Les maisons "murondin." Paris: E. Chiron, 1942.

La charte d'Athènes. Paris: Plon, 1943. Translated by Anthony Eardley as *The Athens Charter.* New York: Grossman, 1973.

Entretien avec les étudiants des écoles d'architecture. Paris: Denoël, 1943.

Les trois établissements humains. Paris: Denoël, 1945. Translated by Eulie Chowdhury as *The Three Human Establishments.* Chandigarh: Punjab Government, Department of Town and Country Planning, 1979.

Manière de penser l'urbanisme. Boulogne: Éditions de l'Architecture d'aujourd'hui, 1946. Translated by Eleanor Levieux as *Looking at City Planning.* New York: Grossman, 1971.

UN Headquarters. New York: Reinhold, 1947.

Le modulor: Essai sur une mesure harmonique à l'échelle humaine applicable universellement à l'architecture et à la mécanique. Boulogne: Éditions de l'Architecture d'aujourd'hui, 1950. Translated by Peter de Francia and Anna Bostock as *The Modulor: A Harmonious Measure to the Human Scale Universally Applicable to Architecture and Mechanics.* London: Faber & Faber, 1954.

Poésie sur Alger. Paris: Falaize, 1950.

Une petite maison, 1923. Zurich: Éditions Girsberger, 1954.

Modulor 2, 1955: La parole est aux usagers; suite de "Le modulor," "1948." Boulogne: Éditions de l'Architecture d'aujourd'hui, 1955. Translated by Peter de Francia and Anna Bostock as *Modulor 2, 1955: Let the User Speak Next; Continuation of "The Modulor," 1948.* London: Faber & Faber, 1958.

Poème de l'angle droit. Paris: Tériade Éditeur, 1955.

Les plans de Paris. Paris: Éditions de Minuit, 1956.

Le poème électronique Le Corbusier. Paris: Éditions de Minuit, 1958.

L'atelier de la recherche patiente. Paris: Vincent & Fréal, 1960. Translated by James Palmes as *Creation Is a Patient Search.* New York: Praeger, 1960.

Mise au point. Paris: Éditions Forces Vives, 1966. Translated by Ivan Žaknić as *The Final Testament of Père Corbu: A Translation and Interpretation of* Mise au point. New Haven: Yale Univ. Press, 1997.

Le voyage d'Orient. Paris: Éditions Forces Vives, 1966. Translated by Ivan Žaknić as *Journey to the East.* Cambridge: MIT Press, 1987.

Architectural works, posthumous publications of Le Corbusier's manuscripts and correspondence, and facsimile editions of sketchbooks, in chronological order

Oeuvre complète. Edited by Willi Boesiger and Max Bill. 8 vols. Zurich: Éditions Girsberger, 1957–70.

Le Corbusier Sketchbooks. Edited by Françoise de Franclieu. 4 vols. Cambridge: MIT Press, 1981–82.

The Le Corbusier Archive. Edited by H. Allen Brooks. 32 vols. New York: Garland; Paris: Fondation Le Corbusier, 1982–84.

Voyage d'Orient: Carnets. Edited by Giuliano Gresleri. 6 vols. Milan: Electa Architecture; Paris: Fondation Le Corbusier, 1987.

La construction des villes: Genèse et devenir d'un ouvrage écrit de 1910 à 1915 et laissé inachevé. Edited by Marc E. Albert Emery. Lausanne: L'Âge d'Homme,

1992.

Les voyages d'Allemagne: Carnets. Edited by Giuliano Gresleri. 5 vols. Milan: Electa
 Architecture, 1994.

Album La Roche. Introduction by Stanislaus von Moos. Paris: Gallimard, 1996.

Le Corbusier: Choix de lettres. Edited by Jean Jenger. Basel: Birkhäuser, 2002.

Lettres à ses maîtres, vol. 1, *Lettres à Auguste Perret.* Edited by Marie-Jeanne
 Dumont. Paris: Éditions du Linteau, 2002.

Schnoor, Christoph. "La construction des villes, Charles-Edouard Jeannerets erstes
 Städtebauliches Traktat von 1910/1911." Ph.D. diss., Technische Universität, Berlin,
 2003.

Le Corbusier: Plans. 16 DVDs in 4 vols. Paris: Echelle 1 and Fondation Le Corbusier,
 2005.

Lettres à ses maîtres, vol. 2, *Lettres à Charles L'Eplattenier.* Edited by Marie-Jeanne
 Dumont. Paris: Éditions du Linteau, 2006.

Selected books on Le Corbusier's work, in chronological order

Gauthier, Maximilien. *Le Corbusier; ou, L'architecture au service de l'homme.* Paris:
 Denoël, 1944.

Choay, Françoise. *Le Corbusier.* New York: G. Braziller, 1960.

Besset, Maurice. *Who Was Le Corbusier?* Translated by Robin Kemball. Geneva: Éditions d'Art Albert Skira, 1968.

Moos, Stanislaus von. *Le Corbusier: Elemente einer Synthese.* Frauenfeld: Huber,
 1968. Translated by Beatrice Mock, Joseph Stein, and Maureen Oberil as *Le
 Corbusier: Elements of a Synthesis.* Cambridge: MIT Press, 1979.

Petit, Jean. *Le Corbusier lui-même.* Geneva: Éditions Rousseau, 1970.

Jencks, Charles. *Le Corbusier and the Tragic View of Architecture.* Cambridge:
 Harvard Univ. Press, 1973.

Olmo, Carlo, and Roberto Gabetti. *Le Corbusier e "L'Esprit nouveau."* Turin: G.
 Einaudi, 1975.

Turner, Paul. *The Education of Le Corbusier.* New York: Garland, 1977.

Walden, Russell, ed. *The Open Hand: Essays on Le Corbusier.* Cambridge: MIT Press,
 1977.

Tentori, Francesco. *Vita e opere di Le Corbusier.* Roma: Laterza, 1979.

Gresleri, Giuliano. *Le Corbusier, viaggio in oriente.* Venice: Marsilio, 1984.

Brady, Darlene. *Le Corbusier: An Annotated Bibliography.* New York: Garland, 1985.

Monnier, Gérard. *Le Corbusier.* Lyon: La Manufacture, 1986.

Benton, Tim, ed. *Le Corbusier: Architect of the Century.* Exh. cat. London: Arts
 Council of Great Britain, 1987.

———. *The Villas of Le Corbusier, 1920–1930.* New Haven: Yale Univ. Press, 1987.

Bosman, Jos, ed. *Le Corbusier und die Schweiz: Dokumente einer schwierigen
 Beziehung.* Zurich: Institut für Geschichte und Theorie der Architektur,
 Eidgenössische Technische Hochschule Zürich, 1987.

Cohen, Jean-Louis. *Le Corbusier et la mystique de l'URSS: Théories et projets pour
 Moscou, 1928–1936.* Liège: Pierre Mardaga Éditeur, 1987. Translated by Kenneth
 Hylton as *Le Corbusier and the Mystique of the USSR: Theories and Projects for*

Moscow, 1928–1936. Princeton: Princeton Univ. Press, 1992.

Gans, Deborah. *The Le Corbusier Guide.* Princeton: Princeton Architectural Press, 1987.

Lucan, Jacques, ed. *Le Corbusier: Une encyclopédie.* Paris: Centre Georges Pompidou, 1987.

Moos, Stanislaus von, ed. *L'Esprit Nouveau: Le Corbusier et l'industrie 1920–1925.* Exh. cat. Strasbourg: Musées de la ville, 1987.

Pauly, Daniele, ed. *Le Corbusier et la Méditerranée.* Exh. cat. Marseille: Parenthèses, 1987.

Ragot, Gilles, and Mathilde Dion. *Le Corbusier en France: Réalisations et projets.* Paris: Electa Moniteur, 1987.

Baker, Geoffrey H. *Le Corbusier, the Creative Search: The Formative Years of Charles-Edouard Jeanneret.* New York: Van Nostrand Reinhold, 1996.

Vogt, Adolf Max. *Le Corbusier, der edle Wilde: Zur Archäologie der Moderne.* Wiesbaden: Vieweg, 1996. Translated by Radka Donnell as *Le Corbusier, the Noble Savage: Toward an Archaeology of Modernism.* Cambridge: MIT Press, 1998.

Brooks, H. Allen, ed. *Le Corbusier's Formative Years: Charles-Edouard Jeanneret at La Chaux-de-Fonds.* Chicago: Univ. of Chicago Press, 1997.

Eliel, Carol S., ed. *L'Esprit nouveau: Purism in Paris, 1918–1925.* Exh. cat. Los Angeles: Los Angeles County Museum of Art, 2000.

Jencks, Charles. *Le Corbusier and the Continual Revolution in Architecture.* New York: Monacelli, 2000.

Frampton, Kenneth. *Le Corbusier: Architect and Visionary.* London: Thames & Hudson, 2001.

Bacon, Mardges. *Le Corbusier in America: Travels in the Land of the Timid.* Cambridge: MIT Press, 2001.

Tzonis, Alexander. *Le Corbusier: The Poetics of Machine and Metaphor.* London: Thames & Hudson, 2001.

Moos, Stanislaus von, and Arthur Rüegg, eds. *Le Corbusier before Le Corbusier: Applied Arts, Architecture, Painting, Photography, 1907–1922.* Exh. cat. New Haven: Yale Univ. Press, 2002.

Cohen, Jean-Louis. *Le Corbusier, 1887–1965: The Lyricism of Architecture in the Machine Age.* Cologne: Taschen, 2004.

de Smet, Catherine. *Le Corbusier, Architect of Books.* Translated by Deke Dusinberre. Baden: Lars Müller, 2005.

Cohen, Jean-Louis. *Le Corbusier, la planète comme chantier.* Paris: Textuel, 2006.

Illustration Credits

All photographs of illustrations from Le Corbusier, *Vers une architecture,* 2nd ed. (Paris, G. Crès, 1924), are courtesy the Getty Research Institute, Research Library, 84-B10997. © 2007 Fondation Le Corbusier. The following sources have granted permission to reproduce the other illustrations in this volume:

p. 2   Fondation Le Corbusier, B2(15)17

p. 7   Archives nationales, Cité de l'architecture et du patrimoine/Archives d'architecture du XXème siècle, Fonds Auguste Perret

p. 9   Fondation Le Corbusier, B2(15)'/7, p. 4

p. 12   Fondation Le Corbusier, L5(6)113

p. 15   Fondation Le Corbusier, A1(16)24, p. 1

p. 16   Fondation Le Corbusier, B2(15)71, p. 2

p. 18   Fondation Le Corbusier, L4(19)123

p. 19   Fondation Le Corbusier, B2(15)87, p. 12

p. 21   Photo: Research Library, Getty Research Institute, 86-B41

p. 23   Fondation Le Corbusier, B2(15)157, p.1

p. 27   Fondation Le Corbusier, B2(15)67

p. 28   Fondation Le Corbusier, B2(15)165, p. 11

p. 31   Fondation Le Corbusier, B2(15)87, p. 17

p. 32   Photo: Alinari/Art Resource, New York

p. 33   Fondation Le Corbusier, B2(15)87, p. 15

p. 34   Fondation Le Corbusier, B2(15)87, p. 14

p. 35   Fondation Le Corbusier, B2(15)87, p. 13

p. 36   Photo: Alinari/Art Resource, New York

p. 38   Fondation Le Corbusier, A1(16)114, p. 20

p. 39   Fondation Le Corbusier, B2(15)155

p. 44   Photo: Naïma and Jean-Pierre Jornod

p. 46   Hans and Lily Hildebrandt Papers, 1899–1979. Research Library, Getty Research Institute, 850676 (box 41, folder 38)

p. 51   Photo: Research Library, Getty Research Institute, 84-B21644

p. 53   Photo: Research Library, Getty Research Institute, 88-B24000

p. 59   Fondation Le Corbusier, B2(15)205

Index

Toward an Architecture
Le Corbusier
Introduction by Jean-Louis Cohen
Translation by John Goodman

Jean-Louis Cohen was trained as an architect and received a doctorate in history at the École des hautes études en sciences sociales. Since 1993, he has held the Sheldon H. Solow Chair in the History of Architecture at New York University's Institute of Fine Arts. From 1998 to 2003, he led the project for the Cité de l'Architecture, a cultural center that opened in 2007 in Paris. Cohen's research activity focuses on twentieth-century architecture and planning in Germany and Russia, as well as on colonialism in North Africa. He has written extensively on Le Corbusier's work.

John Goodman is a translator and art historian. He has rendered some thirty books from French into English, notably work by Denis Diderot, Hubert Damisch, and Georges Didi-Huberman. Goodman has published widely on the visual culture of eighteenth-century Europe and is currently preparing a synthetic study of neoclassicism for Thames and Hudson's World of Art series.

Other Translations Published in Texts & Documents
A Series of the Getty Research Institute Publications Program

Johann Joachim Winckelmann, *History of the Art of Antiquity* (1764)
Introduction by Alex Potts
ISBN 978-0-89236-668-2 (paper)

Jacob Burckhardt, *Italian Renaissance Painting according to Genres*
(1885–93)
Introduction by Maurizio Ghelardi
ISBN 978-0-89236-736-8 (paper)

Gottfried Semper, *Style in the Technical and Tectonic Arts; or, Practical
Aesthetics* (1860–63)
Introduction by Harry Francis Mallgrave
ISBN 978-0-89236-597-5 (hardcover)

Julien-David Le Roy, *The Ruins of the Most Beautiful Monuments of Greece*
(1770)
Introduction by Robin Middleton
ISBN 978-0-89236-669-9 (paper)

Giovanni Battista Piranesi, *Observations on the Letter of Monsieur Mariette;
with Opinions on Architecture, and a Preface to a New Treatise on the
Introduction and Progress of the Fine Arts in Europe in Ancient Times*
(1765)
Introduction by John Wilton-Ely
ISBN 978-0-89236-636-1 (paper)

Carl Gustav Carus, *Nine Letters on Landscape Painting, Written in the Years
1815–1824; with a Letter from Goethe by Way of Introduction* (1831)
Introduction by Oskar Bätschmann
ISBN 978-0-89236-674-3 (paper)

Karel Teige, *Modern Architecture in Czechoslovakia and Other Writings*
(1923–30)
Introduction by Jean-Louis Cohen
ISBN 978-0-89236-596-8 (paper)

Jean-Nicolas-Louis Durand, *Précis of the Lectures on Architecture* (1802–5)
with *Graphic Portion of the Lectures on Architecture* (1821)
Introduction by Antoine Picon
ISBN 978-0-89236-580-7 (paper)

Walter Curt Behrendt, *The Victory of the New Building Style* (1927)
Introduction by Detlef Mertins
ISBN 978-0-89236-563-0 (paper)

Alois Riegl, *The Group Portraiture of Holland* (1902)
Introduction by Wolfgang Kemp
ISBN 978-0-89236-548-7 (paper)

Aby Warburg, *The Renewal of Pagan Antiquity: Contributions to the
Cultural History of the European Renaissance* (1932)
Introduction by Kurt W. Forster
ISBN 978-0-89236-537-1 (hardcover)

Adolf Behne, *The Modern Functional Building* (1926)
Introduction by Rosemarie Haag Bletter
ISBN 978-0-89236-363-3 (hardcover), ISBN 978-0-89236-364-3 (paper)

Hendrik Petrus Berlage: Thoughts on Style, 1886–1909
Introduction by Iain Boyd Whyte
ISBN 978-0-89236-333-9 (hardcover), ISBN 978-0-89236-334-6 (paper)

Sigfried Giedion, *Building in France, Building in Iron, Building in
Ferroconcrete* (1928)
Introduction by Sokratis Georgiadis
ISBN 978-0-89236-319-3 (hardcover), ISBN 978-0-89236-320-9 (paper)

Hermann Muthesius, *Style-Architecture and Building-Art: Transformations
of Architecture in the Nineteenth Century and Its Present Condition* (1902)
Introduction by Stanford Anderson
ISBN 978-0-89236-282-0 (hardcover), ISBN 978-0-89236-283-7 (paper)

Friedrich Gilly: Essays on Architecture, 1796–1799
Introduction by Fritz Neumeyer
ISBN 978-0-89236-280-6 (hardcover), ISBN 978-0-89236-281-3 (paper)

Robert Vischer, Conrad Fiedler, Heinrich Wölfflin, Adolf Göller, Adolf
Hildebrand, and August Schmarsow, *Empathy, Form, and Space: Problems
in German Aesthetics, 1873–1893*
Introduction by Harry Francis Mallgrave and Eleftherios Ikonomou
ISBN 978-0-89236-260-8 (hardcover), ISBN 978-0-89236-259-2 (paper)

Claude Perrault, *Ordonnance for the Five Kinds of Columns after the
Method of the Ancients* (1683)
Introduction by Alberto Pérez-Gómez
ISBN 978-0-89236-232-5 (hardcover), ISBN 978-0-89236-233-2 (paper)

Heinrich Hübsch, Rudolf Wiegmann, Carl Albert Rosenthal, Johann
Heinrich Wolff, and Carl Gottlieb Wilhelm Bötticher, *In What Style Should
We Build? The German Debate on Architectural Style* (1828–47)
Introduction by Wolfgang Herrmann
ISBN 978-0-89236-199-1 (hardcover), ISBN 978-0-89236-198-4 (paper)

Nicolas Le Camus de Mézières, *The Genius of Architecture; or, The Analogy
of That Art with Our Sensations* (1780)
Introduction by Robin Middleton
ISBN 978-0-89236-234-9 (hardcover), ISBN 978-0-89236-235-6 (paper)

Otto Wagner, *Modern Architecture: A Guidebook for His Students to This
Field of Art* (1902)
Introduction by Harry Francis Mallgrave
ISBN 978-0-89236-938-4 (hardcover), ISBN 978-0-89236-939-9 (paper)

Designed by Chris Rowat Design, Chris Rowat and Daiva Villa
Production coordinated by Anita Keys
Type composed by Chris Rowat Design with assistance from Archetype, Toronto,
in Sabon, News Gothic, DeVinne, Block Gothic, and Akzidenz Grotesk
Printed in China through Asia Pacific Offset, Inc., on Cougar Opaque Vellum